Social Psychiatry across Cultures

Studies from North America, Asia, Europe, and Africa

TOPICS IN SOCIAL PSYCHIATRY

Series Editor: Ellen L. Bassuk, M.D.

The Better Homes Foundation
Newton Centre, Massachussetts
and Harvard Medical School
Boston, Massachusetts

ANATOMY OF PSYCHIATRIC ADMINISTRATION
The Organization in Health and Disease
Milton Greenblatt, M.D., in collaboration with Paul Rodenhauser, M.D.

HOMELESSNESS
A National Perspective
Edited by Marjorie J. Robertson, Ph.D., and Milton Greenblatt, M.D.

PUERTO RICAN WOMEN AND CHILDREN
Issues in Health, Growth, and Development
Edited by Gontran Lamberty, Dr. P.H., and Cynthia Garcia Coll, Ph.D.

RESPONDING TO THE HOMELESS
Policy and Practice
Russell K. Schutt, Ph.D., and Gerald R. Garrett, Ph.D.

SOCIAL PSYCHIATRY ACROSS CULTURES
Studies from North America, Asia, Europe, and Africa
Edited by Rumi Kato Price, Ph.D., M.P.E., Brent Mack Shea, Ph.D.,
and Harsha N. Mookherjee, Ph.D.

A Continuation Order Plan is available for this series. A continuation order will bring delivery of each new volume immediately upon publication. Volumes are billed only upon actual shipment. For further information please contact the publisher.

Social Psychiatry across Cultures

Studies from North America, Asia, Europe, and Africa

Edited by

Rumi Kato Price, Ph.D., M.P.E

Washington University School of Medicine
St. Louis, Missouri

Brent Mack Shea, Ph.D.

Sweet Briar College
Sweet Briar, Virginia

and

Harsha N. Mookherjee, Ph.D.

Tennessee Technological University
Cookeville, Tennessee

PLENUM PRESS • NEW YORK AND LONDON

Library of Congress Cataloging-in-Publication Data

On file

ISBN 0-306-44971-4

October 30, 1997

© 1995 Plenum Press, New York
A Division of Plenum Publishing Corporation
233 Spring Street, New York, N. Y. 10013

10 9 8 7 6 5 4 3 2 1

Contributors

MARTIN BÚTORA, Center for Social Analysis, Bratislava, Lubinská 6, 811 03, Bratislava, Slovakia

DAVID J. HILDITCH, Department of Psychiatry, Washington University School of Medicine, St. Louis, Missouri 63110

JANE HOLSCHUH, School of Social Work, University of Wisconsin, Madison, Wisconsin 53705

CHARLES E. HOLZER III, University of Texas Medical Branch, Galveston, Texas 77550

SUE KEIR HOPPE, Department of Psychiatry, University of Texas Health Science Center at San Antonio, San Antonio, Texas 78284

DAVID R. JOHNSON, Department of Sociology, University of Nebraska—Lincoln, Lincoln, Nebraska 68588–0324

ROBERT L. LEON, Department of Psychiatry, University of Texas Health Science Center at San Antonio, San Antonio, Texas 78284

SAMITA MANNA, Department of Sociology, Kalyani University, Kalyani 741235, Nadia, West Bengal, India

HARRY W. MARTIN, Department of Psychiatry, University of Texas Health Science Center at San Antonio, San Antonio, Texas 78284

Peter C. Meyer, University Hospital, Culmannstr. 8 CH-8091 Zürich, Switzerland

Harsha N. Mookherjee, Department of Sociology and Philosophy, Tennessee Technological University, Cookeville, Tennessee 38505

Keith S. Murray, Department of Psychiatry, Washington University School of Medicine, St. Louis, Missouri 63110

A. I. Odebiyi, Department of Sociology and Anthropology, Obafemi Awolo University, Ile-Ife, Nigeria

R. O. Ogedengbe, Department of Sociology and Anthropology, Obafemi Awolo University, Ile-Ife, Nigeria

Suzanne T. Ortega, Department of Sociology, University of Nebraska—Lincoln, Lincoln, Nebraska 68588–0324

Rumi Kato Price, Department of Psychiatry, Washington University School of Medicine, St. Louis, Missouri 63110

Maria Eugenia Rangel, Instituto de Salud Mental de Nuevo Leon, Monterrey, Nuevo Leon, Mexico

Jerry Savells, Department of Sociology, Wright State University, Dayton, Ohio 45435

Steven P. Segal, Mental Health and Social Welfare Research Group, School of Social Research, University of California, Berkeley, California 94720

Brent Mack Shea, Department of Sociology and Anthropology, Sweet Briar College, Sweet Briar, Virginia 24595

Jeffrey W. Swanson, Department of Psychiatry, Duke University Medical Center, Durham, North Carolina 27710

Kiyoshi Wada, Division of Drug Dependence and Psychotropic Drug Clinical Research, National Institute on Mental Health, 1-7-3 Kohnodai, Ichikawashi, Chiba, Japan

Charles J. Wooding, Postbox 16202, 25000 BE Den Haag, The Netherlands

Foreword

The World Health Organization's concept of health as "the condition of psychophysical and social well-being" must be translated into operational terms. The objective is to place the human person within the social system, given that mental health, mental illness, and suffering are individual, despite the fact that their causes are to be sought in the society and environment that surround and interact with the individual.

One dimension that must be emphasized in this field is the continuum that exists between social environment and cerebral development. This continuum consists of the physical and biological features of the two interacting systems: on one hand, the brain managed and controlled by the genetic program, and, on the other hand, the environment, be it natural or social. A simple dichotomy of individual and environment is no longer a sufficient concept in understanding the etiology of mental health and illness.

Needless to say, socioepidemiological research in psychiatry and transcultural psychiatry is useful in reaching these ends. However, at the root of mental illness, one can always find the same causal elements: informational chaos, inadequate dietary intake, substance abuse, trauma, conditioning, and so on, which make the interactive systems dysfunctional. Subsequent organic and psychotic disorders occur to the detriment of both the individual and society. Current biological psychiatry is inadequately equipped in treating mental illness.

The present limits of psychiatry stress the need for further conceptual parameters that may enable researchers to integrate the neurophysiological aspect into the psychological and social aspects, in order to restrain the iatrogenic action of pharmacological therapy. In our opinion, the concept of "prevention of mental illness" should always be associated with the concept of social psychiatry. To this end, a holistic science is required that takes into account that the individual develops within society, hence it is society—first of all through its most basic expression, the family—that determines his or her development, and as a result, the condition either of well-being or illness.

Thus, we are led to consider that the "science of prevention" should be designed more as a subfield of sociology than of psychiatry, insofar as the latter, by its very definition, is devoted to treatable diseases. The one who treats the disease should be not charged with preventing it.

Therefore, sociology ought no longer to confine its research to "trial-and-error" methodology, which is typical of specialized research in medicine. Rather it should design multidisciplinary, integrated research programs to deepen the knowledge of physiological dynamics, including the pathological ones, in order to formulate and implement social actions suitable to the real prevention of mental illness. The mission of psychiatry then is left to the study and treatment of pathologies. It seems obvious that the best "therapy" is and always will be prevention.

The Research Committee on Mental Health and Illness is directed by these concepts and pursues integration of the multifactorality of mental illness, which will contribute to socially preventing such etiological elements as alienation, distress, individual and social conflicts, and discomfort. We believe that the present state of the evolution of scientific knowledge offers the means to integrate the dynamics of individual–environment–societal relationships within a global perspective. Our endeavors therefore must be applied in this direction to optimally consider social needs that can no longer wait to be addressed.

MICHELE S. TRIMARCHI
Centuro Studi per l'Evoluzione Umana
Rome, Italy

Preface

The flowering of social psychiatry requires a certain readiness among intellectuals, as well as the demand for such an area of inquiry in a society. When problems confront the very survival of the society, as in civil war, famine, and epidemics of fatal infectious diseases, social psychiatry and mental health research do not assume high priorities in minds of intellectuals. Although we still find such conditions of despair in many parts of the world, where natural disaster and human conflict have led to the total destruction of the community, we also see signs of an increasing demand and readiness for the development of social psychiatry in some developing countries.

English-language literature on social psychiatry that investigates cultural specificity of an aspect of mental health or illness in non-Western societies is typically written by one of three types of researchers: Medical anthropologists describe indigenous concepts and their relevance to mental health; Western epidemiologists extend the Western psychiatric paradigm to non-Western societies to confirm the universality of their findings; only when a hypothesis fails to hold in a specific culture will theory be modified. The third category of researcher encompasses a growing number of native researchers trained in Western research paradigms who then apply Western concepts to their native cultures.

We rarely find indigenous researchers, applying their indigenous concepts, reaching an English-language publisher. Far from attempting such an ambitious agenda, this volume nevertheless can be seen as a start at making available to the English-speaking audience research in social psychiatry written by indigenous researchers, with indigenous concepts, and ultimately for their indigenous cultures. Traditional Chinese herbal medicine or Brazil's endangered rain forest plants are finding their way into the U.S. National Institutes of Health for scrutiny. Similarly, we may, one of these days, find indigenous concepts of mental health and illness that provide useful means for prevention and intervention of mental illness in our own society.

The idea of publishing a volume of research papers in social psychiatry from around the world originated during the planning phase of research sessions organized by the Research Committee on Mental Health and Illness for the 1990 World Congress of Sociology in Madrid. Throughout the planning of the Congress sessions, efforts were made to ensure the geographical diversity of participants and the diversity of research topics, because we feel one of our missions is to increase networks of research collaboration across many societies.

As papers were collected after the conference, sharp qualitative differences were observed between those presented by Western researchers and those by indigenous researchers addressing indigenous problems (although all authors had some training in Western institutions). Nevertheless, common themes were also apparent, such as the friction between traditional and new "cultures," whether the paper described problems in one society or groups within one society. The volume editors selectively chose papers according to two criteria: the quality of the paper, and papers written by researchers in societies currently underrepresented in social psychiatry. Peer reviews were conducted to assure that only quality work would be selected.

Methodological paradigms were diverse, ranging from a socio-anthropological study of aborigines to secondary analyses of a large general-population epidemiological study. Currently, the appearance of exploratory studies and case studies is unusual in most journals of social psychiatry, given that journals impose a restrictive methodological style. Thus we intentionally avoided using methodological sophistication as a prime priority for paper selection.

Eleven original contributions were eventually selected over a two-year period. The authors of these papers encompass eight countries: the United States, Mexico, Switzerland, the Czech Republic, the Netherlands, India, Japan, and Nigeria. One chaper written by a U.S. author concerns a culture that differs from mainstream America. Another chapter written by a Dutch clinician considers the African Surinamese culture in the Netherlands, which, despite enforced emigration from West Africa to South America, life in a Dutch colony, and subsequent emigration to the Netherlands, has retained a traditional world view.

Although the volume's coverage is not representative of all regions of the world, it is an unusual attempt to represent many different cultures.

Each chapter has gone through extensive editing involving a minimum of several revisions. All contributing chapters were submitted in English. Editing proved a daunting task as the need for uniform presentation was balanced against differences in language, underlying logic and reasoning style, methodology, and discursive format. The volume editors are particularly thankful to the production editor, Keith S. Murray, and the editorial assistant, David J. Hilditch. Without their dedicated and persistent efforts, our collection may not have become readily accessible to lay English-speaking readers. Their contributions, however, went beyond editorial assistance. They were informative contributors for the chapter reviews and the ideas integrating diverse papers such as these, which are expressed in the Introduction and Conclusion.

Admittedly, the introjection of Western logic in editing chapters was necessary at times to avoid confusion to English-speaking readers. Since two of the volume editors are bilingual and bicultural, we believe that the underlying integrity of the papers was preserved through the editing process. We were sensitive to the potential damage that the transliteration process could do. Final drafts were circulated to the chapter authors for proofreading, and any final questions about editorial choices were addressed before the page proofs became available. Even with these precautions, however, we admit that some elements of cultural specificity may have been lost through editing. The volume editors are solely responsible for such shortcomings.

The Series Editor, Ellen Bassuk, provided perhaps the most critical yet constructive review of the volume when it was half completed. Her suggestions led to the reorganization of contributed chapters and the refinement of our themes. We also thank Plenum Editor Mariclaire Cloutier for her generous and understanding cooperation through the long process of bringing this volume to print.

A National Research Service Award to the senior editor (R.K.P.) from the National Institute of Mental Health through the Training Program in Psychiatry Epidemiology and Biostatistics (MH17104) enabled the travel, paper collection, and editing required for this volume. The Program Director, Lee N. Robins, who is both an epidemiologist and sociologist, provided a rare role model at the time of critical transition. A subsequent Research Scientist Development Award from the National Institute on Drug Abuse (DA00221) made the pursuit of cross-cultural research on substance abuse and mental health possible. Completion of this volume became an integral part of the senior editor's overall research programs.

Support was provided to the second editor (B.M.S.) from Sweet Briar Faculty Fellowship funds. General faculty funds from Tennessee Technological University were provided to the third editor (H.N.M.), who initiated volume production in 1989. Portions of the travel funds for the 1990 World Congress of Sociology also were subsidized for the senior editor from the National Science Foundation to the American Sociological Association.

We also thank the International Sociological Association for providing both the opportunity to start this project and a modest amount of general support funds. The ISA has been instrumental in aiding researchers from developing countries who experience financial and other difficulties in attending conferences and maintaining involvement in professional associations. Support provided to the authors of the contributed chapters is noted in each chapter.

Contents

10. Family Composition, Birth Order, and Gender of Mexican Children in Psychological Treatment...................... 161

Harry W. Martin, Maria Eugenia Rangel, Sue Keir Hoppe, and Robert L. Leon

11. Protective Factors for Drug Abuse: A Prospectus for a Japanese-U.S. Epidemiologic Study............................... 169

Rumi Kato Price, Kiyoshi Wada, and Keith S. Murray

Introduction

Culture, Stratification, and Social Psychiatry

RUMI KATO PRICE, BRENT MACK SHEA,
KEITH S. MURRAY, AND DAVID J. HILDITCH

The study of mental health and illness encompasses many disciplines, including psychiatry, psychology, social work, public health, nursing, anthropology, and sociology. Researchers in social psychiatry study diverse topics: the spread and distribution of psychiatric and substance use disorders in different populations; social and cultural factors in mental disease etiology; the organization, financing, and delivery of mental health care services; the social and cultural aspects of psychiatric

RUMI KATO PRICE, KEITH S. MURRAY, and DAVID J. HILDITCH • Department of Psychiatry, Washington University School of Medicine, St. Louis, Missouri, 63110. BRENT MACK SHEA • Department of Anthropology and Sociology, Sweet Briar College, Sweet Briar, Virginia, 24595.

Social Psychiatry across Cultures: Studies from North America, Asia, Europe, and Africa, edited by Rumi Kato Price, Brent Mack Shea, and Harsha N. Mookherjee. Plenum Press, New York, 1995.

1

and mental health practices; and people's attitudes, beliefs, and social representations regarding mental health, illness, substance abuse, disability, and mental health care providers and organizations. Social psychiatry thus is commonly conceived of as a subfield within the broad field of mental health and illness, with concepts, theories, and methods derived primarily from the social and behavioral sciences.

Social psychiatry has played a critical role in the evolution of medicine in several ways. First, the underlying assumption of social psychiatry is that the origin of human ills often lies in social conditions. This assumption is a widely held view in Western societies. However, only a few other branches of medicine (e.g., social and behavioral medicine) focus attention on social and cultural causes of disease. Social psychiatry in this sense complements other subfields of psychiatry, such as psychopathology, biological psychiatry, and clinical psychiatry (Henderson, 1988). Researchers in social psychiatry fulfill a necessary function in medicine by enabling it to maintain the scope of its research topics as that of human diseases, and not merely of biological pathologies existing in human bodies.

A second critical position that social psychiatry holds in medicine is through its contributions to the methods and knowledge in the health sciences. Not only can social psychiatric principles be used in training social workers and psychiatrists to implement social interventions (Gallagher, 1987; Henderson, 1988), but dissemination of findings derived from methodologically sound studies can assist in shaping and changing public perception of mental illness. A role for social psychiatry, Leighton (1986) states, "could be that of educating mental health professionals, the public, the media and policy makers so that they would have a more empirical view of cultural processes in relation to mental health and mental illness" (p. 223).

The primary aim of this volume is to introduce works in social psychiatry that describe unique cultural elements of a society, and their association with mental health and illness. Chapters addressing this aim were written by authors who were born into or have lived in the cultures they describe. In the discussion following, we trace social psychiatry's development, largely in North America and Western Europe. We describe some consequences of the history of social psychiatry on emerging research in non-Western societies. We contend that works about and by people in non-Western societies are not well disseminated, an effect and ongoing cause of Western ethnocentrism in social psychiatry.

The second aim of this volume is to contrast these descriptive, culturally focused works with highly quantitative research pieces written by Western researchers. Social psychiatry has not developed in a linear fashion. Across traditional disciplinary boundaries, parallel and even competing developments have been a feature of social psychiatric research. We therefore introduce two central concepts used throughout this volume, "culture" and "stratification," which comprise core expressions of two intellectual camps typically associated with traditional research disciplines: anthropology on the one hand, and epidemiology and sociology on the other.

A further aim of this volume is to contribute to future cross-cultural research. We also have chosen chapters that incorporate aspects of the intellectual heritage of the anthropologic and epidemiologic–sociologic camps. To assist in understanding how authors integrated some aspects from both traditions, we present both historic and contemporary debate about cross-cultural research, contrasting the views of epidemiologists and anthropologists. Our discussion will be carried forward in the Conclusion, where we state our opinions on what is needed to accomplish culturally sensitive cross-culture research in the future. The last portion of this introductory section further describes the organization of the volume.

HISTORICAL BACKGROUND

Sociological inquiry into the etiology of mental health and illness began more than a century ago. Early attempts to understand geographic differences in rates of suicide (Durkheim, 1897/1951), provide a convenient reference point. Specific to the field of psychiatry, Kraepelin's (1904) studies of psychosis in Java may be considered as the beginning of comparative psychiatry (Jablensky, 1989). It is, nevertheless, common practice to trace the beginning of social psychiatry as we now define it to the late 1930s, when researchers began documenting significant relationships between mental illness and social environments, such as social class and residential mobility (Faris & Dunham, 1939; Malzberg, 1940).

Following World War II, the first-generation landmark studies were carried out in the United States (Hollingshead & Redlich, 1958; Leighton, Harding, Macklin, Macmillan, & Leighton, 1963; Srole, Langner, Michael, Opler, & Rennie, 1962). These studies departed significantly from most pre-World War II studies. Rather than using aggregate data, these studies directly collected information from individuals to arrive at the associations between social and cultural variables and mental health outcomes. Association thus was considered valid at the individual level. Sociocultural and epidemiologic studies also were conducted during this period in most regions of the world, including Asia (Lin, 1959), Europe (Chomabert de Lauwe, 1959), and Africa (Lambo, 1965).

Beginning in the late 1960s and continuing into the early 1980s, social psychiatry gradually shifted its focus and approaches. In the United States, psychiatry as a whole witnessed the emergence of the neo-Kraepelinian paradigm and a biological focus that emphasized categorical approaches to mental illness (Klerman, 1990). Social and behavioral scientists, on the other hand, shifted their interests from mental illness to mental health problems. Concurrently, microenvironmental variables such as social support and life events began to dominate the attention of researchers (Brown & Harris, 1978; Thoits, 1982), although the effects of macrosociological variables on mental illness, particularly social class, continued to be debated (Kohn, 1974; Rushing & Ortega, 1979).

The period from the late 1970s through the 1980s also marked the flowering of psychiatric epidemiology (Robins, 1978), which utilizes survey research to estimate the incidence and prevalance of psychiatric disorders, and to identify their risk factors. Significant new developments in this period included the use of more precise and uniform case definitions with standardized psychiatric assessment, and the increased application of epidemiologic analysis methods. Large scale, second-generation community mental health surveys were conducted in North America (Eaton & Kessler, 1985; Orn, Newman, & Bland, 1988), Europe (Jablensky, 1986), and other parts of the world (Lee, Rhee, & Kwack, 1986). At the same time, follow-up studies of the first-generation epidemiological studies found not only that the incidence and correlates of mental health and illness changed over time, but also that cultural differences were factors in these changes (Sartorius, Neilsen, & Strömgren, 1989).

The influence of anthropology in psychiatry and mental health research has been more subtle than that of sociology and epidemiology. Although well-known anthropologists such as Kroeber and Malinowski kept an interest in psychiatry, it was not until the 1950s that anthropology and psychiatry (then dominated by psychoanalysts) came together in what was called at the time the "Culture and Personality" school (Kleinman, 1987).

Still, social psychiatry moved forward without substantial input from anthropology. It wasn't until the late 1970s that cultural anthropologists became more vocal in their critique of social psychiatry. This activity came largely as a response to a series of cross-cultural studies initiated by the World Health Organization (WHO, 1973), and subsequent initiatives by the U.S. National Institute of Mental Health to develop standardized diagnostic instruments (Kleinman & Good, 1985; Robins & Helzer, 1988).

Anthropologists were highly critical of the application of Western psychiatric classification and standardized assessment to cross-cultural research because of doubts that construct validity could be assumed across cultures (Littlewood, 1990). Even within the context of U.S. research, culturally sensitive research was called for (Fabrega, 1989; Rogler, 1992) in an attempt to overcome the blind application of new diagnostic systems such as *The Diagnostic and Statistical Manual of Mental Disorders* (DSM-III) (APA, 1980). The conceptual underpinning of anthropologists' criticism on social psychiatry is discussed later in more detail.

SOCIAL PSYCHIATRY IN NON-WESTERN SOCIETIES

The course social psychiatry has taken in non-Western societies has differed in significant ways from that in Western developed societies. A difference relevant to this volume is that Western mental health research has tended to ignore cultural aspects of mental health problems and indigenous mental health practices in non-Western societies. As noted, this point has been criticized by anthropologists (Fabrega, 1989).

The tendency may have been a result of a slow dissemination of information. Scant attention has been given to findings from research conducted in non-Western societies. Although sociocultural and epidemiological studies carried out by researchers in Pacific Rim countries have been published in well-circulated journals (Helzer & Canino, 1991; Mak & Gow, 1991), research efforts in Central Asia, the Middle East, Eastern Europe, and Africa are much less known.

Developing countries lack a strong tradition in the social and behavioral sciences. Theoretical approaches developed in the past few decades typically reflected the problems found in Western countries. Therefore, mental health research in developing countries lacks culturally specific theories that can be uniquely applied to mental health problems and practices in those societies.

Furthermore, developing countries frequently do not rate psychiatric disorders and mental health problems as high priorities, given competition from overwhelming domestic problems such as civil war, famine, and poverty. Unfortunately, developing nations by definition are undergoing rapid social change, where past experience in Western societies (Hagnell, Lanke, Rorsman, & Öjesjö, 1982) leads to predictions of increases in psychiatric and mental health problems. A lack of commitment and resources for research, prevention efforts, and service delivery will exacerbate the effects of rapid social change in these countries.

Western social psychiatry has by and large attempted to respond only to the first issue, namely the criticism of Western ethnocentrism. We will elaborate this criticism fully in this chapter. Issues concerning dissemination, indigenous theories, and resource scarcity will be touched upon in the introduction to Part III and more fully discussed in the Conclusion.

CULTURE AND STRATIFICATION

The foregoing brief historical account indicates that social psychiatry is not really a unified subfield of mental health and illness. Parallel developments were occurring in psychiatry, sociology, epidemiology, and anthropology, sometimes without communication among the fields. Open discourse, when it occurred, tended to be of a confrontational nature. On the other hand, major breakthroughs in the field of mental health and illness, such as in the post-World War II series of community studies, were achieved in part because of close collaboration among researchers from different disciplines. Such collaboration is a necessary condition for a large-scale study, because no concepts developed in one field are sufficient to describe the variety of etiological factors, as well as phenomenology, of mental health and illness.

As noted, culture and stratification are concepts primary to the themes of this volume. They represent two of the most central concepts in social psychiatry. While applied in a variety of social and behavioral disciplines, the definitions of culture and stratification vary quite considerably across disciplines. Each discipline weighs the relative importance of the concepts differently: anthropology concentrates more on culture, and sociology and epidemiology concentrate on stratification.

In epidemiology and sociology, a culture is most commonly defined in terms of a geopolitical sense, such as a nation. Culture can be equated with a nation if a nation refers to a boundary of distinctive cultural features and the possible ethnic differences within a nation are less prominent than those between two nations (Mari, Sen, & Cheng, 1989). Culture also can be used as an ethnic concept within a nation in a pluralistic society (Murphy, 1982).

One would quickly recognize an inherent tautology in attempting to define culture in terms of some existing social entities. A nation as a culture, for example, exists only if the nation has a set of *culturally* distinctive features. Another ambiguity in the epidemiological definition is that, if one begins to apply this logic to different layers of commonly used categories of epidemiology, all categories sooner or later would be considered cultures: nation, race, ethnic group, family, and gender.

The term "culture" may not need a fixed denotation or connotation. It then becomes a semantic tool for describing distinctive aspects of our surroundings and experiences that affect us and are affected by our behaviors. There are no a priori reasons why the application of the word "culture" cannot be made more flexible than to mean a fixed entity. Indeed, Kleinman (1987), a leading advocate of cultural psychiatry, regards culture as the intersection of meaning and experience, which is far from defining it as a fixed entity.

Some of the less orthodox conceptions of culture, such as gender as culture, are more typically considered in sociology and epidemiology as operationalizations of stratification, the specific dimensions of social structure. Interestingly enough, anthropologists such as Radcliffe-Brown (1940) and Lévi-Strauss (1953) fundamentally influenced the development of structuralism in sociology. A central notion was that sociology was the discipline of describing and understanding the causes and consequences of social structure, "the patterns discernible in social life, the regularities observed, the configurations detected" (Blau, 1975).

Moving from abstraction to empirical investigation, those variables typically thought of affecting individuals' beliefs and behaviors naturally became central variables of stratification studies in sociology.

The development of risk factor analysis in epidemiology did not take such a deductive approach. In the beginning, seen as a humanistic approach to psychiatry, social psychiatry was vulnerable to charges that it lacked scientific foundations and that its ideas were speculative (Leighton, 1986). Psychiatric epidemiology, acting as a research arm for social psychiatry, was able to replace speculation with data. For example, the relationship of socioeconomic status, one of the most commonly used variables of stratification, and mental illness has long been speculated about. Yet it was only with psychiatric epidemiology that the causal mechanism began to unravel. Though psychiatric epidemiology moved to a more sophisticated multivariate causal analysis paradigm, stratification variables are still considered as major determinants of mental health and illness. Even if researchers are interested in the microlevel stress process, typical stratification variables are included as demographic controls or background variables.

In this volume, for the sake of organization, culture is used in the most traditional sense; that is, we use society as the boundary of a culture. We chose five chapters in which a set of traditional meanings, values, and experiences (culture in an anthropological sense), by their presence, alteration, or disappearance, affect peoples' lives and mental health and illness in the face of social change and instability.

The idea of stratification is used in this volume in the same sense as that used in structuralism in sociology. Three chapters were chosen to represent the kind of quantitative studies often associated with psychiatric epidemiology and sociology in Western societies, particularly in the United States. One should note, however, that groups and subgroups described by combing variables found significant in multivariate analysis can be considered, at an abstract level, as cultural entities within which people share similar meanings and experiences. Culture and stratification thus diverge and converge.

CULTURAL SPECIFICITY AND UNIVERSALITY

In the literature of cross-cultural psychiatry, the two intellectual camps represented by the epidemiological and anthropological approach have also been polemically contrasted in the "old versus new" social psychiatry debate (Kleinman, 1987; Leff, 1990; Littlewood, 1990). Theorists who gravitated toward emphasizing the universal nature of psychiatric categories, focusing on biological terms, attempted to make sense of obvious cultural differences through such metatheoretical distinctions as form and content, and disease and illness. Theorists who favored the cultural anthropology approach tended to emphasize the influence of cultural variables all the way down, as it were, to the roots of psychiatry, and to mental health and illness.

Epidemiologic View

Coined by cultural anthropologists as the *old* social psychiatry, the epidemiological approach to cross-cultural psychiatry is wedded to the medical model and to Western psychiatric nosologies. This approach views cultural differences in psychiatric disorders as reflecting differences in content, but not differences in form. Researchers in this camp are more optimistic about the chances of developing a truly comparative social psychiatry following the path of biological medicine.

Such a view is clearly expressed by leading figures of the WHO advancements in cross-cultural psychiatry. Comparative psychiatry, Jablensky (1989) says, "is to the study of the nature of mental disorder what comparative anatomy once was to the construction of a scientific taxonomy of the living organisms" (p. 455). He went on to say, "Psychiatry has yet to resolve the question whether the psychopathological symptoms and syndromes represent a universal code of abnormal mental life" (p. 455).

The World Health Organization's (WHO) cross-cultural schizophrenia study (WHO, 1973) and subsequent outcome study (Sartorius et al., 1986) exemplify this approach. These impressively large-scale studies led to some conclusions that support cross-cultural universality of psychiatric disorder: overall prevalence of mental disorders seems to be similar across cultures; the functional psychoses appear with similar frequencies in all cultures; and the proportion of people with mental disturbances to those who are receiving general health care is similar across cultural setting (Sartorius, 1988). Differences found across cultures and other stratifications include the age-specific prevalence of organic brain disorders between developed and developing countries; the clinical picture of those in contact with general health care; psychosocial problems related to alcohol and drug abuse across societies; and the course and outcome of mental disorders across sociocultural settings (Sartorius, 1988).

Much of the current effort is being spent in establishing and refining a common language that will ensure a useful degree of comparability between studies. Such uniformity of research tools is seen as a central methodological issue, because psychiatry lacks physical or biochemical indices (Wing, 1985). The development of the *Composite International*

Diagnostic Interview (WHO, 1994) is one of the most extensive efforts to date, jointly sponsored by WHO and the former U.S. Alcohol, Drug Abuse, and Mental Health Administration (ADAMHA). The instrument was designed to assess mental disorders and provide diagnoses according to the definitions and criteria of the *International Classification of Diseases, 10th Revision* (ICD-10), (WHO, 1993) and the revised third edition of the American Psychiatric Association's *Diagnostic and Statistical Manual of Mental Disorders, Third Edition, Revised* (DSM-III-R) (APA, 1987). The CIDI training centers are now spread over the world to cover eight languages (English, German, Kannada, French, Dutch, Chinese, Spanish, and Portuguese) and has already been translated into many other languages. This development is expected to lead to the next generation of large-scale cross-cultural studies, which researchers hope will overcome some of the methodological shortcomings in previous studies.

Anthropologic View

Cultural anthropologists who advocate the *new* social psychiatry movement, on the other hand, emphasize the importance of understanding. They claim that researchers need to see the disorder and symptoms as part of a culturally specific system of beliefs and practices. From this viewpoint, it is believed that the disorder cannot be teased out without understanding this system, although biological factors are not to be discarded. The emphasis is given to *explaining from within* and the importance of careful description. Cultural anthropologists argue that more context-sensitive methodologies and theories are needed in social psychiatry.

Kleinman (1987) presents several arguments why psychiatric epidemiology is focused on finding similarities across societies. He points out that reliance on biological models leads to interpreting results in a manner consistent with biological etiology and to deemphasizing the cultural dimensions of mental disorder.

Perhaps more important is his argument that the epidemiologic approach commits a categorical fallacy, which is an application of a nosological category of a particular cultural group to another, different culture. A South Asian psychiatrist who applied "semen loss syndrome," an indigenous Ayurvedic disease category, to North Americans would face certain ridicule (Obeyesekere, 1985). Whether or not the psychiatrist applied the same nosological rigor currently prescribed by Western psychiatry, with careful operationalization and instrumentation involving translation and back-translation, is beside the point. Kleinman challenges that this example of categorical fallacy is no different from the kind of categorical fallacy commonly committed by Western psychiatry and psychiatric epidemiology.

Another important point he makes is that translation in cross-cultural research is not a mere technical problem, but the very essence of ethnographic research from an anthropological viewpoint. Flaherty and colleagues (1988) pointed out several areas of problems achieving equivalence through translation: content (content of question needs to have relevance for the culture); semantic (words must have the same meaning); technical (applicability to nonliterate culture); criterion (measuring whether responses to similar items relate to the same normative concept); and conceptual (responses to relate to a theoretical construct within the culture) equivalence.

Achieving cross-cultural validity in all these criteria of equivalences may not be feasible from the current approach of translation and back-translation. Alternatively, the cultural psychiatry approach suggests that developing a culturally specific instrument that is conceptually equivalent to, but not a translation of, an existing instrument (Manson & Shore, 1981) may be found to yield more valid results.

Some sociologists too have been highly critical of the increasing standardization in psychiatric epidemiology methods within and across cultures. The opponents have questioned, for example, the appropriateness of psychiatric diagnoses as analysis measurements (Mirowsky & Ross, 1989), and have proposed to use dimensional measures. Their criticisms extend beyond the issues of measurements (Klerman, 1989). These sociologists deny the use of psychiatric disorder as the central concept of psychiatric epidemiology, echoing sociology's long antipsychiatric tradition represented by the labeling approach (Szasz, 1974).

Converging Trends

Although polemic arguments have their defenders, most researchers occupy a middle ground between the two extremes. They are willing to accept that some psychiatric categories can be cross-culturally valid but that we cannot simply assume that Western categorical schemes, such as DSM-III, embody those valid categories. Rather than simply assuming that Western psychiatry is cross-culturally valid, they argue that we ought to test Western schemes and instruments, correcting them when necessary, and move toward grounding cross-cultural research in the local ethnographic context (Kleinman, 1987).

Recognition appears to be growing that Western psychiatric categories are indeed culturally influenced, leading to a desire to make those categories less biased and to create new categories in specific cultural contexts (Fabrega, 1992; Rogler, 1989). There is also the acknowledgement that some common biological features cut across social contexts.

Thus, there appears to be a general trend toward rigorous cross-cultural research that can employ illness categories found to be cross-culturally valid. Unfortunately, we do not yet seem to have in hand the models and categories and common protocols necessary to carry out empirical research that is truly sensitive in cultural terms. Genuine ethnographic-type cultural studies are needed. Such studies will require collaboration between Western European and indigenous research workers. However, a dilemma appears in that detailed exploratory work needs to be done *before* cross-cultural psychiatric research can be attempted, while research protocols themselves need to be cross-culturally sensitive (Leff, 1990). Only by slow increments of knowledge and sensitization would we appear likely to reach a satisfactory level of cultural sensitivity in cross-cultural psychiatric research.

ABOUT THE VOLUME

The chapters included in this volume were selected by the Research Committee on Mental Health and Illness of International Sociological Association. The thought of compiling studies across several societies was articulated in 1991 after the Association's World Congress the previous year. The authors of the 11 contributed chapters represent eight nationalities from North America, Europe, Africa, and Asia. Seven chapters have authors from the countries of Nigeria, India, the former Czechoslovakia, Switzerland, The Netherlands, Mexico, and Japan. The remaining four chapters were authored or coauthored by researchers working in the United States.

The contributed chapters in this volume are divided into three parts. Part I, "Studies Across Cultures," includes chapters in which a set of traditional meanings, values, and experiences, or their disappearance, affects people's lives and mental health and illness in the face of social change and instability. No attempt is made to claim that these five chapters as a whole constitute cross-cultural work in the sense used in current epidemiologic literature (Helzer & Canino, 1992). Social psychiatry, nevertheless, is necessarily cross-cultural, insofar as society is a mesh of cultural entities. Comparison with Western societies is implicit (Chapters 1 and 2), or drawn between mainstream America and the coexistent Amish life-style (Chapter 4). In the study of alcoholism in the former Czechoslovakia (Chapter 3), alcoholism is described with respect to the consequence of the communist regime's social control. At the same time, differences in the Czech and Slovak drinking cultures are described (they became two separate republics after the 1989 velvet revolution).

The studies included in Part I are mostly descriptive. In contrast, the three studies chosen for Part II are more deductive and use an epidemiological framework. These chapters apply some major structural variables, such as ethnicity and socioeconomic status (Chapter 6), as determinants of psychiatric disorder, although more microenvironmental variables such as social support (Chapters 7 and 8) are also used.

Scientific reductionism masks cultural contexts. However, a major payoff from the structural approach is its ability to explicitly test hypotheses. Causal relationships between structural variables and outcome variables of mental health are elaborated by the introduction of mediating variables such as gender (Chapter 7) and community size (Chapter 8). By use of such an approach, these studies inch closer to the descriptive and anthropological studies included in Part I—fortified by an analytic rigor.

Section III, "Cultural Specificity and Universality," includes chapters that are distinctive in the light of anthropological versus epidemiologic views of cross-cultural research. The notion of cultural specificity and universality is elaborated on in the introduction for Part III. The three chapters attempt to integrate some elements of research orientation from both camps. The first chapter (Chapter 9) introduces an Afro-Surinamese disease classification system developed by a Dutch clinician who claims that a consideration for disease concepts retained by the indigenous sufferers is necessary to cure them. In the next chapter (Chapter 10), a group of U.S. and Mexican researchers started out with hypotheses developed by Mexican researchers. However, they apply the Western idea of gender to an understanding of the effect of birth order on children's psychiatric problems.

In the last chapter (Chapter 11), a prospectus for cross-cultural epidemiologic study is proposed by two drug abuse epidemiologists, one a bicultural epidemiologist and sociologist and the other a Japanese psychiatrist. They apply hypotheses derived from well-established findings of Western epidemiologic research. In addition, they incorporate culturally specific expressions of underlying syndromes as major modifiers of the course of drug abuse in the two countries. In the Conclusion, we attempt to make some suggestions for future cross-cultural research in mental health and illness especially in non-Western societies.

REFERENCES

American Psychiatric Association. (1980). *Diagnostic and statistical manual of mental disorders* (3rd ed.). Washington DC: American Psychiatric Association.
American Psychiatric Association. (1987). *Diagnostic and statistical manual of mental disorders* (3rd ed., rev.). Washington DC: American Psychiatric Association.
Blau, P. M. (1975). Introduction: Parallels and contrasts in structural inquiries. In P. M. Blau (Ed.), *Approaches to the study of social structure* (pp. 1–20). New York: Free Press.
Brown, G. W., & Harris, T. (1978). *Social origins of depression.* London, Tavistock.
Chomabert de Lauwe, M. J. (1959). *Psychopathologie sociale de l'enfant inadapté.* Paris: Centre National de la Recherche Scientifique.
Durkheim, E. (1951). *Suicide.* New York: Free Press. (Original work published 1897)
Eaton, W. W., & Kessler, L. G. (1985). *Epidemiologic field methods in psychiatry: The NIMH epidemiologic catchment area program.* Orlando, FL: Academic Press.
Fabrega, H. (1989). An ethnomedical perspective of Anglo-American psychiatry. *American Journal of Psychiatry, 146,* 588–596.
Fabrega, H. (1992). Commentary. Diagnostic interminable: Toward a culturally sensitive DSM-IV. *Journal of Nervous and Mental Disease, 180,* 5–7.
Faris, R. E., & Dunham, H. W. (1939). *Mental disorders in urban areas.* Chicago: University of Chicago Press.
Flaherty, J. A., Gavira, F. M., Pathak, D., Mitchell, T., Wintrob, R., Richmanm, J. A., & Birz, S. (1988). Developing instruments for cross cultural psychiatric research. *Journal of Nervous and Mental Disease, 176,* 257–263.
Gallagher, B. J., III. (1987). *The sociology of mental illness.* Englewood Cliffs, NJ: Prentice-Hall.
Hagnell, O., Lanke, J., Rorsman, B., & Öjesjö, L. (1982). Are we entering an age of melancholy? Depressive illness in a prospective epidemiological study over 25 years: The Lundby study, Sweden. *Psychological Medicine, 12,* 279–289.
Helzer, J. E., & Canino, G. (Eds.) (1992). *Alcoholism in North America, Europe and Asia.* New York: Oxford University Press.
Henderson, A. S. (1988). *An introduction to social psychiatry.* New York: Oxford University Press.
Hollingshead, A. B., & Redlich, F. C. (1958). *Social class and mental illness.* New York: Wiley.
Jablensky, A. (1986). Epidemiologic surveys of mental health of geographically defined populations in Europe. In M. M. Weissman, J. K. Myers, & C. E. Ross (Eds.), *Community surveys of psychiatric disorders.* New Brunswick: Rutgers University Press.
Jablensky, A. (1989). An overview of the World Health Organization Multi-centre Studies of Schizophrenia. In P. Williams, G. Wilkinson, & K. Rawnsley (Eds.), *The scope of epidemiological psychiatry: Essays in honour of Michael Shepherd* (pp. 455–471). London: Routledge.

Kleinman, A. (1987). Anthropology and psychiatry: The role of culture in cross-cultural research on illness. *British Journal of Psychiatry, 151,* 447–454.

Kleinman, A., & Good, B. (1985). Introduction: Culture and depression. In A. Kleinman & B. Good (Eds.), *Culture and depression: Studies in the anthropology and cross-cultural psychiatry of affect and disorder.* Berkeley: University of California Press.

Klerman, G. L. (1989). Psychiatric diagnostic categories: Issues of validity and measurement. *Journal of Health and Social Behavior, 30,* 27–34.

Klerman, G. L. (1990). Paradigm shifts in the USA psychiatric epidemiology since World War II. *Social Psychiatry and Psychiatric Epidemiology, 25,* 27–32.

Kohn, M. L. (1974). Social class and schizophrenia: A critical review and reformation. In P. Roman & H. Trice (Eds.), *Explorations in psychiatric sociology.* Philadelphia: F. A. Davis.

Kraepelin, E. (1904). Comparative psychology. In S. R. Hirsh & M. Shepherd (Eds.), *Themes and variations in European psychiatry.* Bristol: Wright.

Lambo, T. A. (1965). Developing countries and industrialization. In World Federation for Mental Health (Ed.), *Industrialization and mental health* (pp. 104–114). Geneva: World Federation for Mental Health.

Lee, C. K., Rhee, H., & Kwack, Y. S. (1986). *Alcoholism, anxiety, and depression in Korea.* Paper presented at the annual meeting of the American Psychiatric Association, Washington, DC.

Leff, J. (1990). The "new cross cultural psychiatry": A case of the baby and the bathwater. *British Journal of Psychiatry, 156,* 305–307.

Leighton, A. H. (1986). Psychiatric epidemiology and social psychiatry. *American Journal of Social Psychiatry, 4,* 221–226.

Leighton, D. C., Harding, J. S., Macklin, D. B., Macmillan, A. M., & Leighton, A. H. (1963). *The character of danger: The Stirling County study of psychiatric disorder and sociocultural environments* (Vol. 3). New York: Basic Books.

Lévi-Strauss, C. (1953). Social structure. In A. L. Kroeber, et al. (Eds.), *Anthropology today.* Chicago: University of Chicago Press.

Lin, T. (1959). Effects of urbanization on mental health. *International Social Science Journal, 11,* 24–33.

Littlewood, R. (1990). From categories to contexts: A decade of the "new cross-cultural psychiatry." *British Journal of Psychiatry, 156,* 308–327.

Mak, K., & Gow, L. (1991). The living conditions of psychiatric patients discharged from half-way house in Hong Kong. *International Journal of Psychiatry, 37,* 107–112.

Malzberg, B. (1940). *Social and biological aspects of mental disease.* Utica, NY: State Hospital Press.

Manson, S. M., & Shore, J. H. (1981). Psychiatric epidemiologic research among American Indians and Alaska natives: Some methodologic issues. *Journal of White Cloud Indian Reservoir Development Centers, 2,* 48–56.

Mari, J., Sen, B., & Cheng, T. A. (1989). Case definition and case identification in cross-cultural perspective. In P. Williams, G. Wilkinson, & K. Rawnsley (Eds.), *The Scope of Epidemiological Psychiatry: Essays in Honour of Michael Shepherd* (pp. 489–506). London: Routledge.

Mirowsky, J., & Ross, C. E. (1989). Psychiatric diagnosis as reified measurement. *Journal of Health and Social Behavior, 30,* 11–25.

Murphy, M. B. M. (1982). *Comparative psychiatry: The international and intercultural distribution of mental illness.* Berlin: Springer-Verlag.

Obeyesekere, G. (1985). Depression, Buddhism, and the work of culture in Sri Lanka. In A. Kleinman & B. Good (Eds.), *Culture and depression: Studies in the anthropology and cross-cultural psychiatry of affect and disorder* (pp. 134–152). Berkeley: University of California Press.

Orn, H., Newman, S. C., & Bland, R. C. (1988). Design and field methods of the Edmonton survey of psychiatric disorders. *Acta Psychiatrica Scandinavica, 77* (Suppl. 338), 17–23.

Radcliffe-Brown, A. R. (1940). On social structure. *Journal of the Royal Anthropological Society of Great Britain and Ireland, 70,* 1–12.

Robins, L. N. (1978). Psychiatric epidemiology. *Archives of General Psychiatry, 35,* 697–702.

Robins, L. N., & Helzer, J. C. (1988). New diagnostic instruments. In A. S. Henderson (Ed.), *Handbook of social psychiatry* (pp. 3–14). Amsterdam, The Netherlands: Elsevier.

Rogler, L. H. (1989). The meaning of culturally sensitive research in mental health. *American Journal of Psychiatry, 146,* 296–303.

Rogler, L. H. (1992). The role of culture in mental health diagnosis: The need for programmatic research. *The Journal of Nervous and Mental Disease, 180,* 745–747.

Rushing, W. A., & Ortega, S. T. (1979). Socio-economic status and mental disorder: New evidence and a sociomedical formulation. *American Journal of Sociology, 84,* 1175–1200.

Srole, L., Langner, T. S., Michael, S. T., Opler, M. K., & Rennie, T. A. C. (1962). *Mental health in the metropolis: The midtown Manhattan study.* New York: McGraw-Hill.

Sartorius, N. (1988). Future directions: A global view. In A. S. Henderson & G. D. Burrows (Eds.), *Handbook of social psychiatry.* Amsterdam: Elsevier.

Sartorius, N., Jablensky, A., Korten, A., Ernberg, G., Anker, M., Cooper, J. E., & Day, R. (1986). Early manifestations and first-contact incidence of schizophrenia in different cultures. *Psychol. Med., 16,* 909–928.

Sartorius, N., Nielsen, J. A., & Strömgren, E. (Eds.). (1989). Changes in frequency of mental disorder over time: Results of repeated surveys of mental disorders in the general population. *Acta Psychiatrica Scandinavica, 79* (Suppl. 348), 1–189.

Szasz, T. S. (1974). *The myth of mental illness* (rev. ed.). New York: Harper & Row.

Thoits, P. A. (1982). Conceptual, methodological, and theoretical problems in studying social support as a buffer against life stress. *Journal of Health and Social Behavior, 23,* 145–159.

Wing, J. K. (1985). Case identification and risk prediction in psychiatric epidemiology: Methodological issues. In E. K. Yeh, H. Rin, C. C. Yeh, & H. G. Hwu (Eds.), *Prevalence of mental disorders, Proceedings of International Symposia on Psychiatry Epidemiology, April 26–28, Taipei, Taiwan, Republic of China* (pp. 31–51). Republic of China: Department of Health.

World Health Organization. (1973). *International pilot study of schizophrenia.* Geneva, Switzerland: WHO.

World Health Organization. (1993). *The ICD-10 classification of mental and behavioral disorders: Diagnostic criteria for research.* Geneva, Switzerland: World Health Organization.

World Health Organization. (1994). *Composite international diagnostic interview 1.1.* Geneva, Switzerland: World Health Organization.

I

Studies across Cultures

Cultural anthropologists begin with the premise that a life is inseparable from its cultural context. Mental health and illness from this viewpoint are seen to a substantial degree to result from the social and
cultural conditions in which a person lives. A culture's role in mental
health, however, is not limited to that of external provider of stimuli,
to which the individual simply reacts. One's culture in large part determines how mental illness is defined, manifested, and effectively treated.
As noted in the Introduction, the term "culture" is applied here in its
broad, traditional sense of a discrete society. However, this definition
does not imply that cultures exist in isolation, or that cultures cannot
coexist within the same geographical area. In fact, an underlying theme
of this volume is the role culture plays in altering perceptions and the
prevalence of mental illness.

The five chapters in Part I each deal with mental health and illness
as informed by a particular culture. The studies described represent a
variety of topics, reflecting the historical influence of the disciplines of
sociology, anthropology, and epidemiology, on the current state of
social psychiatry.

Odebiyi's and Ogedengbe's chapter, "Mentally Disturbed Patients
in Nigeria: Problems and Prospects of Proper Rehabilitation," applies
the interactionist's perspectcive of stigma to examine the degree of
acceptance or rejection of the mentally ill in the Nigerian population.
Specifically, their study intended to investigate belief systems and attitudes about mental illness, and to assess the Nigerian government's
role in assisting or hindering the mentally ill.

The findings revealed unfavorable societal reactions to the mentally ill that were consistent with traditional beliefs about the causes and course of mental illness. These unfavorable perceptions appeared among the significant others of patients, who were most often their parents, among a sample that had no direct contact with the mentally ill, and among Western-oriented psychiatric professionals. Strong doubts about the curability of mental illness were voiced or inferred among all three groups, evidenced by a belief that former patients would not be able to work except at simple unskilled tasks. Spousal desertion was frequent, and the former mentally ill were not wanted as potential partners. The authors also describe how widespread perceptions of the familial disgrace associated with mental illness may have contributed to family members asserting a belief in the curability of mental illness.

A second phase of the study analyzed data obtained from rehabilitative facilities for the mentally ill. The legislative records concerning mental health policy and funding of services were also examined. The negative perceptions about mental illness seen among sample subjects also appeared in the society at large. For example, national laws continue to prohibit the former mentally ill from holding public office. The lack of an effective policy on provision of treatment and a severe shortage of psychiatric care facilities and psychiatric professionals exacerbates the plight of the mentally ill in Nigeria, whose numbers are growing.

In Chapter 2, "Alcoholism in the Czech and Slovak Republics in the Last 30 Years: An Uneasy Legacy for the Reformers," Martin Bútora approaches society's role differently by discussing how governmental policy contributed to changes in alcohol consumption. This chapter describes alcohol consumption and alcoholism in Czechoslovakia over the past 50 years, concentrating on the postwar period. Alcohol statistics compiled under the communist regime after 1948 were generally unavailable to Czechoslovakians until the November 1989 revolution.

Bútora states that official policy on the risks of alcohol consumption was somewhat contradictory over time. While alcoholism was initially described as a "bourgeois vestige," public policies toward it settled into a pattern of suppression of information. According to the author, information regarding both the consequences of substance abuse and the extent of the problem in the society were intentionally made unavailable. Drunk driving laws and limited treatment availability only slightly mitigated what in effect became a status quo of plentiful supplies of alcohol during periods when other goods were scarce. The author asserts that alcohol was used as a tool for social control, and was also adapted into a currency substitute by the populace.

These policies developed within an existing cultural framework. Drinking was a quite socialized, even ritualized behavior in Czechoslovakia. The Czech and Slovak republics, distinct societies with their own histories and languages, had been politically united since 1918, except for the period of German occupation during World War II between 1939 and 1944. Historical differences in alcohol consumption patterns in the two republics evolved in the postwar period as the populace also responded to changing tastes seen elsewhere in Europe.

Per capita alcohol consumption during the last 30 years under communism increased two-and-a-half times. Beer and spirits consumption were among the highest in the world between 1980 and 1985. Almost 2% of the population was registered in outpatient alcohol clinics in 1985, this despite the government downplaying of alcoholism at the time. Over one-third of all hospitalized psychiatric patients were treated for alcoholic diagnoses. Bútora notes an accompanying downward trend in general health indicators in the population during this time.

The author also speculates about new trends in alcohol consumption and alcoholism he expects to accompany the separation of the political unity of the Czech and Slovak republics and their transition to a market economy. Bútora predicts new subpopulations of alcoholics will emerge and that the number of untreated alcoholics will increase as a result of this transition. On the positive side, he also speculates that healthier drinking patterns and self-help organizations will emerge that will help lessen the impact of insufficient treatment programs.

Mookherjee and Manna approach the subject of culture and mental health from a different, more anthropological perspective in Chapter 3, "Psychoemotional Responses to the Existing Social Systems in the Tribal Populations in India." They provide descriptions of three groups of relatively isolated *autochthonese,* or isolated descendants of early settlers in India who have maintained individual cultures through myriad waves of immigration and political change.

Each of these groups, the Kadars, Chenchus, and Lodhas, has a distinctive identification and psychosocioemotional attachment to the features of their environment, such as animals, plants, and astronomic objects. Their characteristic world views have endured to the present day, which no doubt presents them with their culture's most relentless challenge. The authors describe the groups with respect to their economic life, use of technology, and the social systems that are embedded in their cultural patterns.

Special attention is given to the history and the contemporary life of the Lodha who live in West Bengal. It is argued that social systems that are expressed in the networks of social relationships, marriage customs and obligations, and ceremonial relationships have enabled the Lodhas to strive for and maintain slow acculturation in the midst of radical social changes in India. An example of this process is a limited assimilation of elements of Hinduism by all the groups.

However, the tribes' long-standing geographic isolation is inexorably coming to an end as outside contact, even migration, increases, and their environment changes. The authors also suggest that in the face of social change, members of these traditional Indian cultures respond to acculturative pressures by reemphasizing their traditional rituals. Such a response can be interpreted as one indication of the cultures' relative robustness, with social and cultural networks remaining strong enough to buffer the individual from the effects of social change or, even more, provide a renewed sense of cohesion.

Extending beyond the authors' observations, increased rituals in a time of rapid social change may be part of the mechanism for acculturation. Facing the appearance of new technology, members of these traditional Indian cultures could easily interpret elements of change and accompanying disorder as signs of evil influences; for example, the effects of sorcery. New elements symbolizing the arrival of new technology (the evidence of sorcery) can be incorporated into existing rituals. Thus ritualized resistance may be seen as a form of coping that can lead to assimilation of extracultural information. Such phenomena may occur across cultures, as seen in American Indian ghost dance rituals that developed during the nineteenth century of Euro-American's westward expansion.

Managing social change and developing effective coping strategies also is a main feature of Chapter 4, "The Amish Life-Style in an Era of Rapid Social Change" by Jerry Savells. There are over 100,000 Amish living in 20 states of the United States, a Canadian province, and one country in Latin America; proving the point made earlier that disparate cultures can occupy the same geography without overt ghettoization. The Amish have persistently resisted the acculturation process, despite the fact that they have been part of these societies for almost three centuries.

A stratified random sample of the local Amish population in six states was selected to conduct structured questionnaire interviews, in addition to pursuing a more traditional anthropological observational method. A group of conservative Mennonites, a religious group similar to the Amish in several ways but generally less restrictive of change, also were interviewed. Seeman's five criteria for powerlessness, meaninglessness, normlessness, social isolation, and self-estrangement were used to investigate alienation among the Amish in this sample. Comparisons were made between the norms and values internalized by the Old Order Amish and those usually embraced within the predominant American culture.

Savells asserts that the Amish do not comprehend the concept of powerlessness because they believe that all power exists in God's hands. They believe that the American culture's search for secular explanations for meaning are thus doomed to failure. The Amish do not feel alone because of strong family ties and community links with other Amish families. Isolation from the world is voluntary and not accompanied by a sense of loss.

Acculturation nevertheless is occurring in the majority of Old Order Amish communities. However, social change has been consistently scrutinized and accepted selectively. Results of this change are monitored so that unwanted negative effects can be minimized. Such apparently idiosyncratic compromises as not permitting telephones within the home but allowing them to be installed outside near the front porch thus reflect a careful balancing of the exigencies of modern life and traditional values.

A lengthy open-ended interview also was conducted with a board certified psychotherapist, who grew up in an Old Order Amish family, to identify unique stressors that affect Amish daily life and their coping strategies. This interview detailed how strong social support in the Amish life-style tended to reduce stress among members. But he also stated that maladies popularly associated with the stresses of mainstream life-styles, such as depression, ulcers, and migraine headaches do occur. He also described how such a strong and rigid support system itself can be a source of stress to the Amish, accompanied as it is by the possibility of ostracism and the strain of attempting to achieve a perfect life. The protective structure of a culture thus may have its costs.

Chapter 5, "Reciprocity and Support Networks of Sheltered-Care Residents" examines the role of supported housing in the development of mutually supportive relationships among sheltered care residents. It provides a glimpse of societal perception and treatment toward the mentally ill in the United States, a society in which for decades the deinstitutionalization movement has pushed psychiatric patients from hospitals out into the community, where alternative forms of care did not develop systematically. The sheltered-care environment therefore can be seen as a synthetic culture in an anthropological sense.

The authors, Segal and Holschuh, followed up members of a 1973 sample of sheltered-care residents between 1983 and 1985, using structured interviews. Three-fourths of this sample had schizophrenic disorders. The influences of psychopathology, institutionalism, age, gender, health status, and baseline social network characteristics were measured.

Segal and Holschuh found that supported housing, in general, and specific types of supported housing environments, were important in the development of mutually supportive emotional relationships. The results indicated that, given the proper amount of time, supported housing provides a proper incubator for the development of such relationships. Further, multiple experiences with such housing broadened the opportunity to develop supportive relationships.

The character of the environment also was found to be important. Conditions of high expectation were less conducive to reciprocal relationship building than more supportive environments. These results further reinforce earlier findings regarding the positive effects of supported housing. The results are inconsistent with the notion of the *revolving door*. The study may shed light on understanding essential components for successful transition to recovery, operating in a vacuum of the systematic community mental health policy for the severely mentally ill.

Each chapter in Part I deals with broad issues of the effects of social change on an individual's mental health. A brief synthesis of the experience described both in India and among the Amish is that where traditional social structures can be maintained, a culture can mitigate the effects of that change for its members. The ability of the Amish to manage change by carefully selecting it in forms considered appropriate to the culture is an unusual organizational trait. Bútora, in expecting a worsening of alcoholism rates in the Czech and Slovak republics, also suggests that even what an outsider may interpret as positive social change can have a deleterious effect on some members of a society.

Social change in the developing world is often interpreted as occurring as though it were a wholesale assimilation of traditional society into an emerging world culture that is pragmatic, consumer-based, and secular. A critical loss of cultural diversity undoubtedly accompanies the expansion of Western-oriented society. However, the enduring strength and complexity of many traditional cultural features challenge expectations that treatment of mental illness will increasingly become a matter of applying Western diagnostic and treatment techniques across the globe.

The world view of each of the cultures considered in Part I can also be seen to determine how mental illness is defined. Mental illness is culturally conceptualized as the effect of malevolent external forces as described in Nigeria, or as possession by evil spirits as with the Chenchus of India. Western treatment methods and the acceptance of recovery may prove problematic in such a cultural context.

Odebiyi and Ogedengbe found that Western-trained psychiatric professionals in Nigeria maintained elements of traditional beliefs about mental illness leading to permanent disability. Societal norms are resilient even where Western methods of treatment are nominally available to patients. A person's own belief system about the prospect of his or her recovery from mental illness is affected by such social norms. If a patient does not believe she is cured, can she be considered cured? Perhaps the future lies not in the exclusive acceptance of Western psychiatry, but in the selective adoption of what is workable for a society. As described by Mookherjee and Manna, the Chenchus accept Western-style care, but augment it with traditional treatment methods.

Odebiyi and Ogedengbe describe a context where the mentally ill, by ostracism, are prevented from resuming their place in Nigerian society. In some ways, their description resonates with the results of the sheltered-care environment in the United States. Segal and Holschuh found that what amounts to an artificial environment, removed from yet placed within a culture, assisted the mentally ill not only in being supported but in providing support, a key indication of successful transition. While community mental health policies in the United States have been under scrutiny for some time, Segal and Holschuch's results provide a hope for a workable solution for the mentally ill in the community.

The ability of a nation to provide all the requisites in prevention and treatment delivery appropriate to multiple cultures is of course doubtful. Mookherjee and Manna note that the three cultures they describe exist among more than 500 distinct cultural groups in India. Bútora discusses the inability of a nation to respond to issues of mental health and illness. By suppressing information and controlling supplies, the government of Czechoslovakia is believed to be responsible for the increased prevalence of alcoholism among its citizens. Denial of the problem inevitably restricted treatment availability. This point is quite different from that noted for Nigeria, where a state of severely limited resources and pressing needs in other areas of public life restrict funds and services available for psychiatric treatment.

As stated in the Introduction, critical social problems in other areas tend to take precedence over concern about psychiatric disorders in developing countries. A related argument can be made that in developing countries where the most basic mental health care is difficult to obtain, the energies of mental health professionals and researchers inevitably will be devoted to public policy issues and away from other areas of work. The chapters in this section thus depict some of the limitations that exist in the field. The ideal of informed, culturally specific, sophisticated research into the role cultures play in mental health and illness unfortunately gives way to the limitations of what is currently possible. The dilemma social psychiatry faces in developing countries will be treated separately at the end of this volume.

1

Mentally Disturbed Patients in Nigeria

Problems and Prospects of Proper Rehabilitation

A. I. ODEBIYI AND R. O. OGEDENGBE

The problems of mentally disturbed patients in Nigeria can be approached from various dimensions. Most relevant to this chapter is the social reaction to mental illness, which in itself is a function of various factors. These factors include the people's belief system as it pertains to the causes and prognosis of mental illness; their attitudes toward mental illness and the mentally disturbed; and the role of the government vis-à-vis these problems.

A. I. ODEBIYI and R. O. OGEDENGBE • Department of Sociology and Anthropology, Obafemi Awolo University, Ile-Ife, Nigeria.

Social Psychiatry across Cultures: Studies from North America, Asia, Europe, and Africa, edited by Rumi Kato Price, Brent Mack Shea, and Harsha N. Mookherjee. Plenum Press, New York, 1995.

Research findings on societal attitudes toward the mentally ill and former mentally disturbed patients in both developed and developing parts of the world have revealed negative attitudes in general. For instance, Nunnally (1961), in his attitudinal study in New York, discovered that public attitudes were generally negative and that the public was uninformed, rather than misinformed, about mental illness. One interesting aspect of Nunnally's finding is that possession of accurate information about mental illness correlated positively with age and education while attitudes toward the mentally ill did not.

In Miller and Dawson's (1965) study of families who readmitted patients to mental hospitals, 71% indicated that having a mental patient in the house was hard on them. Of these, 52% indicated that they were afraid or uncertain regarding the patient's social behavior, 33% felt embarrassed or concerned about the effect of the patient's interpersonal behavior, and 15% complained about the patient's excessive dependency; that is, patients required "too much care in the home." According to the authors, these responses refer to a cluster of feelings—rejection, exhaustion, depletion of resources, and so forth—in families who were returning the patient to the hospital.

Orley (1970) found in his study in Nairobi that mental illness excludes a man from inheritance or from becoming a chief, even if he is cured, because his brain is believed to be spoiled and, in most cases, his judgment is never trusted. Similarly, Ugwuegbu (1982) in his attitudinal survey in Nigeria discovered that irrespective of ethnic group and sex of subjects, a greater percentage of his respondents saw mental illness as different from other types of diseases. They considered the mentally ill as dangerous and agreed that mental illness is punishment for bad deeds.

These negative attitudes possibly reflect people's conception of the causes and prognoses of mental illness. For in most developing countries, and especially in Nigeria, mental illness is conceptualized to be caused by the "forces" in the environment rather than the "forces" within the victim. These environmental forces include machinations by wicked or envious relatives or neighbors; retribution for wicked deeds and the mystical forces of spirits. In addition, mental illness is conceptualized to be a dreadful disease with considerable stigma attached to it.

The present study extends from all the aforementioned studies to examine the degree of rejection of current or former patients by different socioeconomic categories in the Nigerian society. More importantly, it attempts to compare the perception and attitudes of those who have had some form of contact with current or former patients with those without prior contacts. For instance, would Western orthodox psychiatrists (who have had professional relationships with the mentally disturbed) maintain more favorable attitudes toward the mentally ill? Would they be prepared to employ the formerly mentally disturbed? How would the significant others of former patients perceive the mentally ill? Would they employ or marry a former patient? How would those who have had no previous contacts perceive the mentally ill? Would they be more hostile toward them than those who have had some forms of contact with them? Are government functionaries concerned in any way with the mentally ill or former patients? Are there adequate treatment and rehabilitative facilities for the mentally ill or former patients? What are the legislative attitudes toward these groups of people in Nigeria? These are the questions addressed in this chapter.

THEORETICAL FRAMEWORK

The theoretical approach for this work is the interactionist perspective, especially as it relates to people's conception of and reaction to mental illness and the mentally ill. Specifically, the theory of "stigma" as propounded by Goffman (1963) is adopted. He refers to stigma as an attribute that is deeply discrediting. According to him, in all of the various instances of stigma, the same sociological features are found: individuals who might have been received easily in ordinary social interactions possess a trait that can obtrude itself upon attention and turn those they meet away from them, breaking the claim that their other attributes have on others. They are stigmatized, being seen as possessing an undesired differentness from what the "normals" had anticipated.

Goffman discussed further how feelings of shame and an expectation of discrimination or inferior treatment from others are evident in stigmatization. On the issue of "mixed contacts," moments when the stigmatized and the normals are in the same social situation, whether in a conversation-like encounter or in the mere copresence of an unfocused gathering, both normals and the stigmatized can purposefully arrange to avoid direct contact.

METHODOLOGY

The data were derived from two independent but related studies and archival research. For both studies, data were collected by means of self-administered questionnaires from respondents selected using a systematic random sampling technique.

In the first study, the significant others (here defined as those significant in the patients' lives) of former mentally disturbed patients who were discharged from two therapeutic centers in Abeokuta, a town in the southwestern part of Nigeria, were given self-administered questionnaires to assess their perception of the prognosis of mental illness. The treatment centers are the Aro Village, a community-based treatment center, and Aro Neuro-Psychiatric Hospital, which is an inpatient oriented treatment center. The significant others of the former patients of the two centers included their spouses, parents, coworkers, friends, and employers. In addition, Western orthodox psychiatrists who are practicing at Aro Neuro-Psychiatric Hospital were given self-administered questionnaires to ascertain their perceptions of those who are mentally ill and former patients. The significant others of former patients and the Western orthodox psychiatrists belonged to the group of respondents in contact with the mentally ill, even though with the Western orthodox psychiatrists the contact is mainly a professional one.

To obtain the sample of the significant others, the records of patients at the two aforementioned treatment centers were used to compile the list and the contact addresses of discharged patients who came from Abeokuta and its environs between July 1983 and August 1985.

A total of 162 patients who came from Abeokuta and its environs were discharged within the above stipulated time period. A random sampling technique was used to select 81, 50% of the total discharged patients. From this, 50 former patients were available for interview. Among unavailable former patients, some had left fictitious addresses at the hospital, which made outreach efforts impossible; some had moved; and some could not be reached because of a poor house-numbering system.

From the records of Aro Neuro-Psychiatric Hospital, 285 patients who came from Abeokuta and its environs were discharged within the 2-year time period. The same random sampling technique was used to select 95 names, a third of the total. Sixty subjects were locatable, and 50 cooperated.

Altogether, 100 names of former patients were obtained from the two treatment centers. A significant other was interviewed for each former patient. To choose these significant others, an accidental sampling technique was used. These significant others included those found in the company of the former patients who either brought the patients for follow-up, lived with the former patient, or were identified by the former patient as important to him or her. Interviews were conducted using a self-administered questionnaire.

Because of their limited numbers, all the western orthodox psychiatrists practicing at Aro Neuro-Psychiatric Hospital were given self-administered questionnaires.

In the second study, selected members of the society who have had no contact with the mentally ill were chosen from Ile-Ife, a university town in the southwestern part of Nigeria. These respondents also were given self-administered questionnaires to elicit information on their perceptions of the mentally ill or those who had once been mentally disturbed. To obtain the sample of this noncontact group at Ile-Ife, a multistage sampling technique was used. The town was divided into 18 zones, from which 3 zones were randomly selected. Each selected zone was divided into blocks, defined as pieces of land bounded by identifiable streets. Seventeen blocks were identified for zone A, 18 blocks for zone B, and 7 blocks for zone C, with an estimated ratio of 2:2:1 obtained. Thus, two blocks were randomly selected in A and B while one block was randomly selected in C. The households in the selected blocks were listed, and using a systematic sampling technique of one in every 4, a manageable sample size was obtained. The head of household was chosen as the reliable source of information.

Self-administered questionnaires were used to collect data. The questions that were raised covered the following areas: (1) The sociodemographic characteristics of respondents; (2) respondents' attitudes toward the current or former mentally ill patients; and (3) respondents' perceptions of the prognosis of mental illness.

Concerning governmental activities with respect to the mentally ill, information was gathered through library research of materials indicating legislative attitudes toward mental illness and the former mentally disturbed in Nigeria. This search was supplemented with information collected by mail questionnaires sent to government-owned psychiatric hospitals and government ministries regarding facilities available for the mentally ill in Nigeria.

RESULTS AND DISCUSSION

The contact group for this study comprised 100 significant others of former mentally disturbed patients and 12 Western orthodox psychiatrists. Association with the patients, therefore, was based on affinity or blood ties on the one hand and professional contact on the other. Seventy-four respondents from Ile-Ife (literates and nonliterates) represented the noncontact group.

Table 1 presents information on the sociodemographic characteristics of the two groups of respondents. Among the contact group of significant others of discharged mentally disturbed patients, women outnumbered men (67% were women and 33% were men). However, there were no women among the Western orthodox psychiatrists interviewed for the study. This fact could result from culturally maintained gender roles of men and women, for not only are certain professions seen as male enclaves, but certain areas of medicine are also seen as male domains (Odebiyi, 1989).

The preponderance of females among the significant others of discharged patients could be attributed to women's mothering roles, because it was later discovered that the majority of these female significant others are mothers of the former patients (67.2% of the females). The high proportion of female significant others also confirms that women are the health providers for their families. This finding could again be attributed to the fact that patients were deserted by their spouses after the diagnosis of the mental problem, and such patients had to move in with their parents after discharge. In fact, this observation was confirmed by the former patients themselves (Ogedengbe, 1986).

Women also out-numbered male respondents in the noncontact group. With the exception of the Western orthodox psychiatrists, the majority of respondents in both contact and noncontact groups were of low educational background and a large proportion fell under the unskilled occupational grouping during the time of the survey.

Respondents' Perception of the Prognosis of Mental Illness

The respondents were asked to state if mental illness is curable (Table 2). Of those having contact with the mentally ill, 71.4% indicated that mental illness is curable, while only 5.4% of those without any contact indicated that mental illness is curable (χ^2 76.3 df 1 $P < 0.05$).

Table 1
Sociodemographic Characteristics of Respondents (Those Who Have Had Some Form of Contact with the Mentally Ill and Those without Contact)

Social classification	Contact group				Noncontact group	
	Significant others of former patients		Western orthodox psychiatrist			
	No.	%	No.	%	No.	%
Sex						
Male	33	33.0	12	100.0	30	40.5
Female	67	67.0	—	—	44	59.5
Total	100	100.0	12	100.0	74	100.0
Age						
21–30	15	15.0	3	25.0	14	19.0
31–40	33	33.0	7	58.3	14	19.0
41–50	23	23.0	2	16.7	24	32.4
51 and above	29	29.0	—	—	22	29.6
Total	100	10.0	12	100.0	74	100.0
Religion						
Christian	70	7.0	11	91.7	38	51.4
Muslim	21	21.0	1	8.3	22	29.7
Traditional religion	4	4.0	—	—	14	18.0
Other	5	5.0	—	—	—	—
Total	100	100.0	12	100.0	74	100.0
Education[a]						
Nonliterate	42	42.0	—	—	42	56.8
Primary	22	22.0	—	—	20	27.0
Modern school	10	10.0	—	—	8	10.8
Secondary	15	15.0	—	—	3	4.0
Arabic	2	2.0	—	—	1	1.4
University education	4	4.0	12	100.0	—	—
Other	5	5.0	—	—	—	—
Total	100	100.0	12	100.0	74	100.0
Occupation						
Professional	4	4.0	12	100.0	—	—
White collar	7	7.0	—	—	10	13.5
Skilled	21	21.0	—	—	22	29.7
Unskilled	68	68.0	—	—	38	51.4
Unemployed	—	—	—	—	4	5.4
Total	100	100.0	12	100.0	74	100.0

[a]The Nigerian educational system is different from that of other countries.
Primary: This refers to the elementary school for children between 6 and 12 years old.
Modern School: This has been phased out in recent times, but it was organized for those who failed to get admission into junior high school.
Secondary School: This is comprised of junior and senior high school.
Arabic education: This is the formal Islamic/Koranic education sometimes utilized by Muslims in Nigeria as an alternative to the Western educational system.

Table 2
Prognosis of Mental Illness as Perceived by Respondents

Mental illness curable	Contact group (N = 112)	Noncontact group (N = 74)
Yes	80	4
No	32	70
Total	112	74

X^2 76.3 df 1 $P<0.05$

Those having contact gave various reasons as to why they felt mental illness was curable. Among the significant others of discharged patients, the most frequently cited reason was that they had been assured by the patient's psychiatrist. They stated that the psychiatrist had explained to them that if patients take their medication regularly and keep hospital appointments, they will have no further problems. However, it must be noted that a large percentage of the contact group, which perceived mental illness as curable, were mainly the former patients' parents. This could be explained in terms of the societal perception of mental illness as stigmatizing. Hence it is logical that parents of patients (who are thus connected by blood) would tend to perceive mental illness as being curable. They would not want their families to be labeled as possible "carriers," especially since family histories are investigated before a marriage to ensure that families do not have cases of stigmatizing illnesses, such as insanity or epilepsy (Fadipe, 1970).

However, the majority of professional psychiatrists stated that mental illness can only be controlled (58.3%). According to these psychiatrists, if patients keep hospital appointments and take their medication as prescribed, it is possible to keep the symptoms of mental illness under control. Those who indicated that mental illness is curable among this professional group quickly added that it depends on the types of disorder. They indicated that neurotic conditions and reactive depression are curable if the causes are controlled.

The respondents were also asked to state the type of job that they think the former mentally disturbed patient was capable of doing. It was surprising to discover that a great majority of both significant others (92.0%) and those who had no contact with the mentally ill (91.8%) indicated that such individuals should be given unskilled, less mentally demanding occupations. They specifically mentioned petty trading and farming as appropriate work. The most frequently cited reason by those who had contacts with the former patients is that since the brain was already affected, a relapse could occur if the former patient undertook any strenuous job. In fact, 71% of the significant others living with discharged patients indicated that they had decided to relieve former patients of part of their former roles for this very reason.

It can be deduced from these attitudes about appropriate work and changes in household roles that the significant others' perception of mental illness as being curable was not supported by their perception of the former patients' capabilities. This implies that the former patient was no longer perceived as being able to function normally by both the majority of the contact and noncontact groups.

Respondents' Attitudes toward the Mentally Ill

The noncontact group of respondents were asked to state whether or not they would employ people who had formerly been mental patients if they were employers. Of the 74 respondents, 86.5% indicated that they would not want to employ such individuals if they were employers. Reasons given included the possibility that such former patients could become aggressive at any time and could inflict injuries on other workers, that their presence would cause insecurity and fear among other workers, and that they could be less productive since their brains had been affected.

When the same employment question was given to the contact group, all the Western orthodox psychiatrists stated that they could employ former patients. However, the psychiatrists said that the former patients would be under close supervision, and that they would be given work suitable to their mental ability.

The significant others, as already noted, felt that former patients could cope only with less demanding jobs that would not be mentally stressful, so as to prevent a relapse. Thus, it may be inferred from the contact group responses that if they were employers, they too would discriminate against former patients in hiring or supervision.

With regard to intimate relationships, members of the noncontact group were asked to state if they would marry a former mentally disturbed patient. As would be expected from the earlier findings, all of them stated that they would never marry a former patient because he or she could break down at any time. In fact, to buttress this, it was discovered in the second study that the majority of former patients, as earlier indicated, were living with their parents because their spouses (especially husbands) had deserted them.

Furthermore, when the psychiatrists were asked to state if they would marry a former mental patient, the two who gave a positive response indicated that they would do so only if the person suffered from reactive depression. Thus, even these professionals abhorred any form of intimate relationship with former patients.

What then are the chances of readjustment for former mentally disturbed patients in Nigeria? They appear slim, since this and other studies have found that former mental patients face rejection and discrimination in the society on discharge from treatment. They are deserted by spouses, rejected by employers, and rejected by former customers.

Consequently, discharged patients take up jobs that barely enable them to earn a living. In fact, to buttress this fact, the responses of the former mental patients who were interviewed in the second study showed that the majority of those who were formerly skilled workers before the illness were now petty traders. According to them, most of their former customers deserted them as a result of their former illness. There is no doubt that the mentally disturbed and former mental patients face a lot of problems in society.

CURRENT PUBLIC POLICY ON MENTAL ILLNESS

What are the legislative attitudes toward these stigmatized individuals? What is the role of the federal, state, and local governments in dealing with these problems? The law and policy on psychiatric matters as contained in legislative enactments can be grouped into three categories (Sowemimo, 1985):

1. Those laws relating to the identification, committal, treatment, and rehabilitation of the mentally ill, as well as the regulation of the practice of medicine in general and psychiatric medicine in particular;
2. Those legislations dealing with the civil disabilities and criminal liability of the mentally ill;

3. Those laws dealing with the regulation and control of the dissemination of harmful psychoactive substances, including punitive and deterrent provisions to enforce the law and to eliminate drug-induced psychiatric maladies.

Since this discussion is concerned with the problems and prospects of the mentally ill in Nigeria, the first two items will be examined in the context of the main thesis of the chapter. The existing legislation on mentally disturbed persons has been adopted to prevent injury to society and provide treatment to the mentally ill. However, there is a large gap between intent and practice in Nigeria.

The situation is depressing when one considers that the needs of the mentally ill are not being met as stipulated by legislation. The Western orthodox psychiatric facilities, including personnel, are grossly inadequate to meet the needs of the population (Ogedengbe, 1990).

In the present study, mailed questionnaires were sent to all psychiatric hospitals in Nigeria to inquire about the patient-to-personnel ratio and the bed complement of these psychiatric hospitals and units. First, a lopsided distribution of Western orthodox mental health care services was discovered. While some states have as many as four psychiatric units and one psychiatric hospital, some states do not have any. The states that have neither hospitals nor clinics include Borno State, with a population of 5 million in 1984; Gongola State, with a population of 1 million; Katsina State (newly created, with population estimates not available); and Sokoto State, with a population of 7 million.

The information collected on mental health care manpower in Nigeria reveals that, at present, there are 60 psychiatrists and 1,628 registered psychiatric nurses in the entire country. Aro Neuro-Psychiatric Hospital, the largest psychiatric hospital in Nigeria, with a bed complement of 526, has an average of one clinical psychologist to 175 patients and one psychiatric social worker to 263 patients. It is unfortunate that at a time when authors, agencies, and the developed world are stressing community-based mental health care (Boroffka & Olatawura, 1976; Ogedengbe, 1986; WHO, 1976), the single community-based mental health care center in Nigeria is only half-functioning because of a lack of funds (Jegede, 1982).

Moreover, legislative attitudes toward the former mentally disturbed patients in Nigeria is not rehabilitative. For instance, according to Ajibola (1985), the law restricts the right of a person with a history of psychiatric illness from seeking or holding elective office, even if he or she has recovered. However, a person convicted of a crime more than 10 years earlier is allowed to run for and hold public office. With this legislative bias at the governmental level, how can one expect or require a private employer to employ a former mentally disturbed patient if he or she is found to be qualified for the job? Since nobody can insure against illness (Ajibola, 1985), it is dehumanizing and unjustifiable to prevent the full rehabilitation of former mentally disturbed persons by permanently banning them from particular types of jobs.

THE NEED FOR A MENTAL HEALTH CARE POLICY IN NIGERIA

The need for a mental health care policy becomes more pressing given the fact that rates of mental illness are increasing in Nigeria (Ogedengbe, 1990), a trend likely to continue given the present socioeconomic conditions in the country. The legislative attitude toward mental illness is not rehabilitative. Also, mental health issues continue to be lumped with general national health care policy, which has not specifically addressed or solved the pressing mental health problems. Although various Nigerian government agencies have shown interest in the improvement of the state of health of the general population, as evident in the National Development Plans in which health programs featured prominently, mental health care services have not been given much consideration.

This lack of consideration is evident in the poor state of mental health care facilities discussed earlier. More importantly, while mental health is now incorporated into the Primary Health Care Program in Nigeria, it has yet to be put into practice (Ogedengbe, 1990). The Primary Health Care concept was designed to bring health care to the majority of people in rural areas at an affordable price. Since about 80% of the Nigerian population lives in these rural areas, there is an urgent need to put into practice the mental health component of the Primary Health Care scheme.

From the foregoing discussion, an appropriate mental health care policy would include the following features. First, community-based mental health care centers should be established in Nigeria, with at least one per local government area. Members of society should be mobilized to be actively involved in the treatment process.

Second, legislation for rehabilitative services for current and former patients should be enacted. This legislation should make provisions to:

1. Ameliorate the civil disabilities of persons with a history of mental illness but who have been cured;
2. Give social welfare support for the mentally ill;
3. Establish fully equipped and staffed facilities in each local government area.
4. Enforce sections 300 and 339 of the criminal code, which state that it is an offense for anybody having charge of an insane person to omit to provide necessities of life for them. This will help make the relatives of the mentally ill more responsible and caring.

Thus, in order to improve the conditions both of mental patients and those in remission in Nigeria, there is a need for a viable mental health policy. Furthermore, there is a need for public education programs through the mass media, so that the public will be better informed about mental illness. Such programs would help promote a more positive attitude toward mental illness and its sufferers.

ACKNOWLEDGMENTS. We would like to commend the cooperation of government ministries of health in Borno, Oyo, and Osun States of Nigeria for their prompt attention to the mail questionnaires used for this study. Similarly, we would like to thank the consultants and staff at the government-owned psychiatric hospitals/units, particularly the Chief Records Officer of the Aro Neuro-Psychiatric Hospital in Abeokuta.

REFERENCES

Ajibola, B. (1985). Legislative perspective on law and psychiatry. *Proceedings of the National Conference on Law and Psychiatry* (pp. 122–150). Aro Neuro-Psychiatric Hospital, Abeokuta, Ogun State, Nigeria.
Boroffka, A., & Olatawura, M. O. (1976). Community psychiatry in Nigeria: The current status. *International Journal of Social Psychiatry, 23,* 1154–1158.
Fadipe, N. A. (1970). *The sociology of the Yoruba.* Ibadan, Nigeria: Ibadan University Press.
Goffman, E. (1963). *"Stigma": Notes on the management of spoiled identity.* New York: Prentice-Hall.
Jegede, R. O. (1982). Aro village system in perspective. In O. A. Erinosho and N. W. Bell (Eds.), *Mental health in Africa: Tropical medicine series.* Ibadan, Nigeria: Ibadan University Press.
Miller, D., & Dawson, W. (1965). *Worlds that fail: Part II. Disbanded worlds: A study of returns to the mental hospital* (Monograph, No. 7). California Mental Health Research.
Nunnally, J. C. Jr. (1961). *Popular conceptions of mental health, their development and change.* New York: Holt, Rinehart & Winston.

Odebiyi, A. I. (1989). *Gender differences in medicine: Male physicians' view.* Unpublished manuscript.

Ogedengbe, R. O. (1986). *Post hospital adjustments of former mentally disturbed patients: A case study of discharged patients from two psychiatric centers in Abeokuta, Nigeria.* An unpublished master's thesis, Obafemi Awolowo University, Ile-Ife.

Ogedengbe, R. O. (1990). The state of western orthodox mental health care services in Nigeria: Need for a formal recognition of the traditional psychiatric healing services. Unpublished manuscript.

Orley, J. H. (1970). *Culture and mental illness.* Nairobi: East African Publishing House.

Sowemimo, S. (1985). Address on legislative perspective. *Proceedings of the National Conference on Law and Psychiatry* (pp. 118–121). Aro Neuro-Psychiatric Hospital, Abeokuta, Ogun State, Nigeria.

Ugwuegbu, D. C. (1982). Defensive attribution and attitude to mental illness. In O. A. Erinosho & N. W. Bell (Eds.), *Mental health in Africa.* Ibadan, Nigeria: Ibadan University Press.

World Health Organization. (1976). *African Traditional Medicine* (Afro Technical Report Series, No. 1). Brazzaville, Congo: WHO Regional Office for Africa.

2

Alcoholism in the Czech and Slovak Republics in the Last 30 Years

An Uneasy Legacy for the Reformers

Martin Bútora

INTRODUCTION: DENIAL OF THE PROBLEM

As in other European countries, alcohol consumption in the Czech and Slovak Republics is a common aspect of everyday life. But alcohol not only has a soothing and relaxing effect, it also causes suffering and many problems. This self-evident fact was not fully recognized in the past because the Czechoslovak communist regime either denied the existence of alcohol-related problems or underplayed their significance.

Martin Bútora • Center for Social Analysis, Bratislava, Lubinská 6, 811 03, Bratislava, Slovakia.

Social Psychiatry across Cultures: Studies from North America, Asia, Europe, and Africa, edited by Rumi Kato Price, Brent Mack Shea, and Harsha N. Mookherjee. Plenum Press, New York, 1995.

During the 1950s, alcoholism was considered as one of the "bourgeois vestiges" that were to be wiped out when the communist construction was completed. When this illusion failed, an officially proclaimed struggle was waged against alcoholism as an antisocial phenomenon, and some alcohol-related problems were ritually recognized. However, widespread prevention and treatment efforts failed to materialize due, in part, to an absence of systematic data collection and pertinent research.

A few measures, such as the strict control of drunk driving and advanced treatment for alcoholics were successful, albeit the latter was not generally available. A general prevention-oriented strategy of curbing alcohol consumption, however, was not implemented. Supplies of and easy access to alcohol beverages, which provided substantial income for the state, instead worsened the magnitude of alcohol problems.

Typically, the regime's denial was reflected in the way alcoholism was treated in the press, which presented portraits of habitual drunkards, bizarre stories of intoxicated individuals, and the criminalization of alcoholism. All of this made people think it could never happen to them (Bútora, 1980, 1989; Skala, 1988).

ASSESSING THE MAGNITUDE
OF ALCOHOL PROBLEMS

Alcohol in an Economy of Shortage

In the decades of the Czechoslovak economy of shortage, alcoholic beverages enjoyed a privileged position. Unlike other goods, alcohol was always in ample supply. It frequently happened that at 5 o'clock in the afternoon the grocery store was out of bread and milk, but the shelves were full of spirits and wine. As for beer, whose consumption in Czechoslovakia has been consistently one of the highest in the world (Armyr, Elmer, & Herz, 1984), its price remained practically unchanged over the 30-year period from 1955 to 1985, in contrast to increased prices in other countries. This price-setting policy undoubtedly had its social and political undertones.

Inexpensive and omnipresent beer was part of a social contract between the regime and the population. It can be said that beer became one of the material assets that the regime used to reward the adapted mass of the apolitical population for their silence. Moreover, alcohol became a universal means of payment. It was used as a bribe to gain access to goods or services that were in short supply. Drinking in the workplace was commonplace despite repeated formal bans.

Public Attitudes

Traditionally lenient public attitudes about drinking alcohol contribute to widespread alcohol use and abuse. In the Slovak and Czech cultures, alcohol is a socially acceptable drug. Drinking is often considered an expected behavior, and abstaining from it could entail some negative consequences.

In a representative study by Kubicka (1985) of a sample of more than 1,000 men aged 22 to 33 living in Prague, a majority of respondents considered drinking five large beers (a large beer is 0.5 L) at one sitting as acceptable behavior. Forty-one percent of young men considered it normal for a person to drink six to eight large beers per night. According to other studies, warning about the detrimental effects of drinking did not influence the behavior of children and youngsters in Bratislava, Banska, Bystrica, and Prague (Bútora, 1989; Kunda & Cellarova, 1982). These studies showed that social pressure from peer groups and from a society with ingrained drinking habits and permissive attitudes toward drinking have a more powerful impact on drinking behaviors than unimaginative school education or a fear of the health and social consequences of drinking (Turcek, 1971).

The population of the Czech and Slovak Republics has not, on the whole, come to perceive alcoholism as a phenomenon so negative that it would present a social challenge. This contrasts with environmental pollution, about which public awareness has been much more acute. This lack of recognition partly resulted from the communist regime's policy, which continued until its demise of not disclosing alarming information about alcoholism. Prior to the nonviolent November 1989 revolution, health care workers and scholars had been worried about a general decline in the health status of the population, due in part to alcoholism. However, alcohol consumption statistics were currently unknown to most citizens.

Alcohol Consumption Patterns

As illustrated in Table 1, per capita alcohol consumption in Czechoslovakia more than doubled over the 30-year period (1955–1985) considered, increasing from 4.3 to 9.4 L. Per capita consumption was 9.3 in 1990. During the 1980s, alcohol consumption in Czechoslovakia consistently ranked between 12th and 14th place in the world.

As seen in Table 2, beer consumption is especially high in the Czech Republic, with the highest average consumption in the world between 1980 and 1985. A similar trend was observed in Slovakia for the consumption of spirits during this period as noted in Table 3.

Slovakia's 1980–1985 average spirits consumption (13.0 L per capita) ranked second in the world (Walsh & Grant, 1985). While alcohol consumption decreased slightly after 1985, within one year after the 1989 Velvet Revolution, consumption in both countries still was higher than most nations in the world. In 1990, alcohol consumption again increased, with per capita beer consumption in the Czech Republic reaching 155.2 L, and spirits consumption in Slovakia reaching 14.2 L. The increasing trend continued into the early 1990s.

As elsewhere in the world, new drinking styles in Czechoslovakia were added to old drinking habits (Armyr, Elmer, & Herz, 1984). For example, Slovaks consumed 11.6 L of beer per capita in 1936, compared to 64.8 L consumed per capita that year in the Czech part of the old Czechoslovakia. By 1970, however, Slovakia had become a typical beer drinking country, with about 10 times as much beer consumed per capita as in 1936. Beer became an inseparable part of the life-style of many social groups and classes. As already noted, beer prices were controlled during this period, which may have contributed to its in-

Table 1
Per Capita Consumption of Alcoholic Beverages in Czechoslovakia in 1936–1990 (in Liters of 100% Ethanol)

Year	Czechoslovakia	Czech Republic	Slovak Republic
1936	3.4	—	2.4
1949	3.9	4.2	3.3
1955	4.3	4.5	3.8
1960	5.4	5.7	4.5
1965	6.7	6.5	7.0
1970	8.2	7.8	9.0
1975	9.0	8.3	10.2
1980	9.6	9.0	10.7
1985	9.4	9.0	10.2
1988	8.5	8.1	9.5
1989	8.7	8.2	9.6
1990	9.3	8.9	10.4

Source: *Statistical Yearbooks of Czechoslovakia*

Table 2
Per Capita Consumption of Beer in Czechoslovakia in 1936–1990 (in Liters)

Year	Czechoslovakia	Czech Republic	Slovak Republic
1936	51.8	64.8	11.6
1955	79.1	89.2	55.0
1960	100.1	109.0	77.4
1965	130.0	140.7	106.1
1970	139.9	154.1	109.3
1975	143.4	157.3	113.9
1980	137.8	148.5	115.5
1985	130.8	146.9	98.5
1988	131.7	149.7	96.3
1989	131.8	151.0	94.0
1990	135.1	155.2	95.6

Source: *Statistical Yearbooks of Czechoslovakia.*

creased popularity. In the early 1980s, the largest new beer drinking establishment in east-central Europe outside Germany, nicknamed Mammoth, opened in Bratislava, the capital of Slovakia, with a seating capacity of 1,900. In the subsequent period of 1985–1990, 97 L of beer was consumed per capita.

At the same time, hard liquor drinking did not diminish, but instead grew extensively and contributed substantially to the overall increase of 100% in total alcohol consumption recorded in the whole of Czechoslovakia. For the last 30 years, per capita wine consumption

Table 3
Per Capita Consumption of Spirits (Beverages with 40% Alcohol Content) in 1936–1990 in Czechoslovakia (in Liters)

Year	Czechoslovakia	Czech Republic	Slovak Republic
1936	2.4	2.2	2.8
1955	3.9	3.6	4.8
1960	2.4	2.0	3.4
1965	2.7	2.0	4.3
1970	5.9	4.2	9.5
1975	7.2	5.0	12.2
1980	8.8	6.8	13.0
1985	8.8	6.4	13.2
1988	8.3	6.2	12.4
1989	8.4	6.3	12.7
1990	9.5	7.2	14.2

Source: *Statistical Yearbooks of Czechoslovakia.*

in Slovakia has been about 2 to 3 L higher than in the Czech Republic. An average consumption of wine was 15.3 L between 1985 and 1990. Today's Slovakia displays a number of different consumer cultures and drinking habits, with spirits in the lead, followed by beer and wine.

Although alcohol consumption decreased during the second half of the 1980s, a high proportion of income was still spent on alcohol. In 1987, Czechoslovakian residents over age 15 spent an average of 85% of a month's income per year on alcoholic beverages. An average of one month's income in 1987 went to the purchase of alcohol among Slovakians aged over 15 years. In 1985, alcohol expenditures made up more than one-fifth of all food expenditures in Czechoslovakia as a whole and one-fourth of food expenditures in Slovakia.

In the whole Czechoslovakia, people spent 17 times more money on alcoholic beverages than they did buying books. In Slovakia the population spent 26 times more money on alcohol than books. Also in 1985, retail sales of all household goods in Czechoslovakia was only 92% of the total amount spent on alcohol. Further, all expenditures on transportation and sports, which include car, motorcycle, bicycle sales, hunting anf fishing supplies, and gasoline sales, represented less than 80% of expenditures made on alcohol. Finally, expenditures on all cultural and entertainment goods in Czechoslovakia represented only 68% of those for alcohol in 1985. In Slovakia, even greater differences were observed (Bútora, 1989).

THE AFFLICTED POPULATION

Drinking patterns obviously have not been distributed evenly in the population. Typically, a relatively small proportion of people account for a substantial share of alcohol consumption in any given country (Skog, 1985). Estimates for Czechoslovakia in 1984 indicated that 7% of the population over 15 years of age (i.e., more than 814,000 people) could be described as heavy drinkers. This group accounted for 38% of the total alcohol consumption. These individuals consumed an average of 68.4 L of pure alcohol a year, compared with an average of 8.4 L for the remaining 93% of the population. Converted to a daily dose, heavy drinkers thus consumed about 10 large 12-proof beers per day (or six large beers and four 5 cL shots per day), compared to two small 12-proof beers (or 2 dL of wine or one 5 cL shot of spirits) in the rest of the population. Obviously, this residual 93% of the population includes total abstainers as well as very moderate drinkers and occasional drinkers, so that the amount of drinking varies considerably between subgroups (Bútora, 1989).

One of the classic alcoholism indicators is death caused by liver cirrhosis. The mortality rate from cirrhosis increased 470% over the 40-year period of 1950–1990 in the whole Czechoslovakia, from 5.4 to 24.7 deaths per 100,000 population. In Slovakia, the increase was 1,060%, from 3.0 to 31.8 per 100,000. In the first half of the 1980s, Czechoslovakia ranked among the 15 countries with the highest liver cirrhosis mortality in the world.

How many people are affected by alcoholism? Almost 250,000 people, representing over 1.5% of the population of Czechoslovakia, were registered at outpatient alcohol clinics in 1985. More than one-third of hospitalized psychiatric patients were treated for alcohol-related diagnoses (Skoda, 1987). Approximately 35,000 people per year were treated for alcoholism in the specialized inpatient alcohol treatment centers. If we consider the fact that one person's immoderate alcohol consumption adversely affects an average of two or three people around the alcoholic, at least 1 million people of the total population of 15 million were directly or indirectly affected by alcoholism in Czechoslovakia in 1985.

Who are the clients of outpatient alcohol clinics, detoxification detention centers, and of specialized inpatient treatment centers? Detailed systematic data at the national level are not available. However, a limited amount of information available from treatment centers provides some indications of trends.

The average age of alcoholics undergoing treatment ranged between 31 and 40 years for men and from 41 to 50 years for women. As in other countries, the fact that people began drinking at increasingly younger ages could also be obsreved. As observed elsewhere, the mean life expectancy of alcoholics in Czechoslovakia is 52 to 54 years. Research data also indicate a higher rate of disability among alcoholics (Skala, 1982, 1988).

The number of women treated is on the rise. The male to female ratio in 1985 was 13:1 for the whole of Czechoslovakia, and 12:1 in Slovakia. Regional differences also are observed, most pronounced being the difference seen in the capitals, with ratios of 10:1 in Prague and 7:1 in Bratislava. Women in capital cities are more likely to be treated for alcoholism than are women living elsewhere.

During the 1970s, the groups most highly represented were blue-collar workers and less educated people. This trend was even more conspicuous for people who were treated in the detention centers. Our studies of clients at the outpatient clinic for alcoholism in Bratislava from 1975 to 1977 revealed that more than one quarter of patients performing unskilled manual work were overqualified for their jobs. They had a higher educational background or higher skill levels (Bútora, 1979, 1980). Waste of human resources (skills and education) also was evident in other research (Vozehova & Vozeh, 1981).

One hundred individuals were selected for each year in our study of 1,000 randomly selected persons treated in detention centers in Bratislava in the decade between 1974 and 1983. Blue-collar workers represented a disproportionately high proportion in this sample. While blue-collar workers comprised 27% of the economically active population of Bratislava, they accounted for 85% of the economically active alcoholics in our sample. The trend was most pronounced in agriculture, construction, and public and other services (Bútora, 1988).

In the 1980s, several therapeutic facilities in Czechoslovakia started to provide treatment to more individuals with higher education (college and university graduates) or with higher skill levels. The number of members of higher social classes in treatment also increased.

In the 1980s, the first epidemiological surveys on problem drinkers in the country were conducted. The study of problem drinking in the Western Slovak region (Missik & Ivanka, 1983) conducted on a sample of 4,026 respondents using the modified Michigan Alcohol Screening Test (MAST) technique detected problem drinking in as much as 27.6% in the productive age population, with 39% among men and 13% among women in these ages. Similar results (27.7%) were obtained in our study of 850 respondents conducted in 1984 in Bratislava. The number of problem drinkers was higher among people with elementary education, trade school dropouts, and blue-collar workers. It was also higher among divorced and single individuals. We also found that problem drinkers have a higher morbidity and accident rate than the rest of the population (Bútora, 1984). In his survey of the whole of Slovakia, Missik (1987) found even higher proportions of problem drinking in the population, up to 32.5%.

Health services are not adequate. In 1985, the national health statistics office registered only 58 full-time medical staff in the whole of Czechoslovakia available for the almost 250,000 individuals treated by outpatient alcohol clinics. This figure is somewhat mitigated by the fact that physicians and therapists working in this field served almost exclusively as part-timers and were therefore not included in the count. Nevertheless, it was alarming to find that one full-time psychologist served nearly 10,000 patients (Bútora & Butorova, 1988).

Counseling services as a step preceding treatment has been notably absent. The number of sociotherapeutic groups for recovered alcoholics was rather low, about 60 in the whole of Czechoslovakia throughout the 1980s. Volunteer organizations, church and charity associations, and independent self-help groups were few in number in the 1980s and are only now coming into existence (Bútora, 1990).

As suggested, alcohol-related problems and disabilities were accompanied by deterioration in the overall health status of the population over the last 20 years. While Czechoslovakia ranked 13th in the world for mean life expectancy at birth in the early 1960s, it had dropped to 41st by the first half of the 1980s. Unfortunately, there was a marked lack of social response toward this worsening quality of life. No efficient alcohol policy or preventive strategies were developed comparable to those in other countries (Grant, 1983; Mäkelä, Room, Single, Sulkunen, & Walsh, 1981; Moser, 1980; Single, Morgan, & De Lint, 1981).

PROSPECTS AND CONCLUSIONS

In the last 30 years, almost all alcohol-related problems and disabilities increased substantially throughout Czechoslovakia. The impact of alcoholism has been most devastating in Slovakia, where the alcoholic subculture is more deeply rooted, and average consumption and prevalence of alcoholism are higher than in the area of the Czech Republic. There has not been adequate social response to this alcoholization of society. Alcohol-related problems represent an additional, yet not sufficiently recognized burden in the arduous period of transition after the fall of the communist regime.

What trends can be expected in the coming years? First, transition to a market economy and overall changes in the political system will create new social tensions and will probably lead to the emergence of new, diverse subpopulations of alcoholics. Such subpopulations could include people who lost their jobs and members of ethnic groups such as Gypsies, but also middle-class abusers and overburdened managers. New drinking habits will emerge, including not only ostentatious and status-oriented consumption, but also health-aware, moderate drinking styles.

Businesses competing in the market will tend to rid themselves first of their weakest links, undisciplined workers such as immoderate alcohol abusers. The time for indulging these people in the workforce is over. However, some companies will develop employee assistance programs for problem drinkers to avoid the additional investment needed for training new staff.

The practice of unpaid treatment for alcoholics probably will be challenged in response to criticism of the custodial state, as well as cuts in the social and welfare budgets. A deep financial crisis in the health care system would probably leave more people with alcohol-related problems untreated. It is expected that self-help groups and clubs for recovered alcoholics will become increasingly important, as will charity and church organizations focusing on alcohol problems.

The Czech and Slovak societies must come to grips with new types of activities designed to alleviate expected negative consequences of rapid social change and the persistent challenges presented by alcohol-related problems. Sociologists can play various roles here, whether as researchers, writers, program officers, active participants in socio-therapy, or supporters of self-help initiatives. They can thus continue in a remarkable tradition of domestic social thinking; leading Czech and Slovak thinkers in the past showed a high sensitivity to the problems of alcoholism. This applies in particular to prominent Slovak leaders who created temperance and moderation organizations in the mid-19th century to counteract increases in alcoholism in Slovakia (Duka-Zolyomi, 1976–1982).

This sensitivity to the problems of alcoholism also was evident in the first presidents of Czechoslovakia, T. G. Masaryk and E. Benes, both of whom were sociologists, studied the issue, and wrote a number of books about it (Benes, 1915; Masaryk, 1906, 1912). In this sense, Masaryk's favorite saying, "The future belongs to sober people," remains a challenge. More sober life-styles could improve the chances for Czechs and Slovaks to cope with the tough competition they are going to face over the coming decade.

REFERENCES

Armyr, G., Elmer, A., & Herz, U. (1984). *Alcohol in the world of the 80s*. Stockholm: Sober Forlags AB.
Beneš, E. (1915). *Problem alkoholove vyroby a abstinence*. [Problem of alcohol production and abstinence]. Prague: Českoslovanský abstinentri svaz.

Bútora, M. (1979, 1980). K sociologickym dimenziam alkoholizmu a jeho terapie I–IV [On sociological dimensions of alcoholism and its therapy I–IV]. *Csekoslovenska Psychiatrie, 4,* 243–249; *1,* 47–54; *2,* 115–122; *4,* 256–263.

Bútora, M. (1984). Alkoholicka subkultura vo svetle epidemiologickeho vyskumu [Alcoholic subculture in epidemiological research]. *Zdravotna Vychova, 3,* 128–137.

Bútora, M. (1988). Sociologicke dimenzie alkoholizmu [Sociological dimensions of alcoholism]. In S. Kunda (Ed.), *Klinika alkoholizmu* (pp. 171–188). Martin: Osveta.

Bútora, M. (1989). *Mne sa to nemoze stat: Sociologicke kapitoly z alkoholizmu* [It cannot happen to me: Sociological chapters on alcoholism]. Martin: Osveta.

Bútora, M. (1991). *Prekrocit svuj stin. Kluby abstinujicich a svepomocne skupiny v peci o zdravi* [To overstep one's shadow. Clubs of recovered alcoholics and other self-help groups in health care]. Prague: Avicenum.

Bútora, M., & Butorova, Z. (1988). Rozsirenost konzumu a abuzu alkoholu a dostupnost niektorych zdravotnickych sluzieb v CSSR [The spread of alcohol consumption and of alcohol abuse and the availability of some alcohol abuse health services in the CSSR]. *Protialkoholicky Obzor, 2,* 109–122.

Duka-Zolyomi, N. (1976–1982). Problem alkoholu a alkoholizmu v slovenskej literature I–XXX [Problems of alcohol and alcoholism in Slovak literature I–XXX]. *Protialkoholicky Obzor.*

Grant, M. (1985). *Alcohol policies.* Copenhagen: WHO Regional Office for Europe.

Kubička, L. (1985). Konzum alkoholu a jeho kontext u prazskych mladych muzu [Alcohol consumption and its context in young males in Prague]. *Zapisy z Apolinare, 5–6,* 111–128.

Kunda, S., & Cellarova, A. (1983). Nazory ucnovskej mladeze na alkoholicke napoje: Longitudinalna studia [Opinions of apprentice youth on alcoholic beverages: A longitudinal study]. *Protialkoholicky Obzor, 4,* 217–228.

Mäkelä, K. Room, R., Single, E., Sulkunen, P., & Walsh, B. (1981). *Society and the state. 1. Comparative study of alcohol control.* Toronto, Canada: Addiction Research Foundation.

Masaryk, T. G. (1912). *Ethika a alkoholism* [Ethics and alcoholism]. Prague: Knihovna Stredy.

Miššík, T. (1987). Skring problemoveho alkoholizmu na Slovensku [Screening of the "problem alcoholism" in Slovakia]. *Protialkoholicky Obzor, 5,* 271–280.

Miššík, T., & Ivanka, L. (1983). Skrining problemoveho pitia v Zapadoslovenskom kraji [Screening of problem drinking in Western Slovakia]. *Protialkoholicky Obzor, 3,* 135–143.

Moser, J. (1980). *Prevention of alcohol-related problems: An international review of prevention measures, policies and programmes.* Geneva, Switzerland: WHO Offset Publications.

Single, E., Morgan, P., & De Lint, J. (1981). *Alcohol, society and the state: Vol. 2. The social history of control policy in seven countries.* Toronto, Canada: Addiction Research Foundation.

Skala, J. (1982). Alkohol a invalidita [Alcohol and disability]. In L. Kubicka & J. Skala (Eds.), *Sbornik studii o abuzu alkoholy a jinych havykovich latek* [Studies on alcohol and other drugs] (pp. 127–149). Prague: Vyzkumny ustav psychiatricky.

Skala, J. (1988). *Az na dno!? Fakta o alkoholu a jinych navykovytch latkach* [Down to the bottom!? Facts on alcohol and other drugs]. Prague: Avicenum.

Skoda, C. (1987). Vyvoj incidence hospitalizace pro zavisdlost na alkoholu a jinych navykovych latkach v CSR a SSR v obdobi 1963–1985 [Alcoholism and other drug addictions-related hospitalization in the CSR and the SSR in 1963–1985]. *Protialkoholicky Obzor, 4,* 193–202.

Turček, M. (1971). Verejna mienka a alkoholizmus [Public opinion and alcoholism]. *Protialkoholicky Obzor, 1,* 25–27.

Vozehova, S., & Vozeh, F. (1981). Problematika alkoholismu z pohledu protialkoholni zachytne stanice I–II [Alcoholism issues as seen from detention centers I–II]. *Protialkoholicky Obzor, 3*, 139–145; *4*, 193–197.
Walsh, B., & Grant, M. (1985). *Public health implications of alcohol production and trade.* Geneva: World Health Organization.

3

Psychoemotional Responses to the Existing Social Systems in Tribal Populations in India

HARSHA N. MOOKHERJEE AND SAMITA MANNA

Due to India's recent massive urban growth, its tribal populations are being increasingly uprooted from their rural economies and traditional homes and villages to be relocated in urban slums and industrial areas, and confronted there with wholly uncertain new ways of living. High unemployment, violence and various types of crime, traffic congestion and accidents, and the lack of educational facilities in the urban areas

HARSHA N. MOOKHERJEE • Department of Sociology and Philosophy, Tennessee Technological University, Cookeville, Tennessee, 38505. SAMITA MANNA • Department of Sociology, Kalyani University, Kalyani 741235, Nadia, West Bengal, India.

Social Psychiatry across Cultures: Studies from North America, Asia, Europe, and Africa, edited by Rumi Kato Price, Brent Mack Shea, and Harsha N. Mookherjee. Plenum Press, New York, 1995.

make it extremely difficult for new migrant tribal populations to care for their children and disabled and older family members. These difficulties create a great sense of frustration and helplessness among the migrants, which, in turn, often leads to the increased use of alcohol and other drugs. But, despite the momentary "benefits," the use of alcohol and other drugs necessarily fails to allay the stresses and strains and continued dissatisfactions the individuals experienced initially. Withal, some tribal populations somehow manage to remain flexible enough to contend satisfactorily with their available resources, and, with their own rural-based technologies and traditions, manage to successfully combat and absorb the immediate shocks to their cultures which disruption and relocation bring about.

The tribal groups to which we now refer are considered autochthones, or early settlers in India, and are labeled "Scheduled Tribes" by the Government of India. Based on our field work, this chapter will illustrate the traditional resources to which selected tribal groups turn in response to the stresses and strains brought about by massive cultural dislocation. As with people everywhere, the tribal populations in India have, it seems to us, quite logically sought relief from these new assaults on their established modes of life by turning to what they have historically considered reliable sources of relief: their centuries-old beliefs and ritualistic practices. Only now, instead of being quick to adopt more modern "therapies" for the distress their modern-day circumstances have brought them, these so-called primitives are found to have rather markedly increased the passion with which they observe their traditional religiomagical ways.

PROFILES OF SELECTED TRIBES IN INDIA

It is generally accepted that the ancestors of these autochthones or scheduled tribes, were ancient settlers in India, dating back at least to 80,000 B.C. It is believed that these people may have moved about from time to time, and thus led a life characterized by acculturation and assimilation. Thus today we find their cultures characterized by a mosaic of cultural phenomena. There are still more than 500 distinctive tribal groups living in India. Slowly, they are accommodating themselves to their changed social and physical environments.

There are three principal tribal zones in India: (1) the North and North-East Indian Zone; (2) the Central Indian Zone, and (3) the South

Indian Zone. In addition, some oceanic tribes live in the Andaman and Nicobar islands, leading more isolated and archaic lives. Here and there are also to be found examples of distinctive economic patterns suggesting the existence of tribes with even more primitive backgrounds and slower processes of cultural transformation. On the basis of their food-gathering economies, these tribal populations can be divided into the following categories:

1. Groups with hunting–gathering economies represented by the Jarwas and Onges in the Andaman and Nicobar islands, the Chenchus of Andhra Pradesh, the Kadars of Kerala in South India, and the Lodhas of West Bengal in East India.

2. Pastoral groups represented by the Todas of the Nilgiri Hills in South India, the Gujjars of Himachal Pradesh, and the Bhots of Almora in North India.

3. The slash-and-burn cultivators represented by such tribal groups in South and Central India as the Savaras, the Juangs, and the Gonds, and, in North-East India by the Kukis and Garos.

4. Settled agriculturists who, with harnessed animal power, subsist with plow cultivation and gardening in the plains and in terraced fields nearer the slopes. The most pronounced tribal groups in this category are the Gonds of Central India, the Bhils of West India, and the Oraons and Santals of East India.

5. Those isolated cottage industrialists found among certain tribal populations in India, such as the basket-making Mahalis, the rope-making Birhors, the iron-ore mining Agarias or Asuras, the weaving Kukis and Nagas.

Many of these and other tribal groups have migrated to urban and industrial areas. These tribal populations have distinctive economies, social systems, and cultures that they have been forced to adjust to their changing social and physical circumstances. The emotional and physical shocks these individuals and groups experience due to abrupt and culturally radical shifts in their ways of life are principally absorbed by their social and cultural networks. Their unique cultural histories have given each group a colorful "supernatural world" to which they can turn for support in the face of often wrenching lifestyle changes.

When seeing their problems as being largely due to the evil influences of witchcraft and sorcery and the wrath of malevolent spirits and angry divinities, the members of these tribes also turn for relief to a host of social arrangements, marriage customs and obligations, and ceremonial relationships.

RESPONSES TO SOCIAL CHANGE
AMONG SELECTED TRIBES

We have selected three hunting–gathering tribes, the Kadars of Kerala, the Chenchus of Andhra Pradesh, and the Lodhas of West Bengal, to describe some of these tribes' psychoemotional responses to social change, including, most recently, the special strains they have experienced from cultural, economic, and geographic dislocation.

The Kadars

The Kadars are a food-gathering tribe in Southern India. They live mainly in the interior forests and on the hills of the Cochin district in the State of Kerala. They are also found in the States of Tamilnadu and Karnataka. The Kadars are short-statured people with dark skin, black curly hair, and scant body hair, and with typically protruding flat noses and thick lips. They often exchange their staples such as honey, jungle roots, and tubers for rice, chilies, clothes, iron knives, pottery, and salt.

The Kadars believe strongly in the existence of tree spirits, and in invisible nature spirits. However, the influence of the Hindu religion has recently brought many significant changes in the Kadars' traditional life. In some villages, one will find little temples with pictures and idols of Hindu gods. In addition to asking the blessings of spirits, demons, and deities, the Kadars also invoke ancestral spirits for their favor in all ceremonies, rituals, social undertakings, and during generally difficult times. With prayers, a flame is always displayed on festive and ceremonial occasions, such displays being considered necessary to invoke the supportive blessings of deities and the spirits of ancestors. The headman of a village functions as a priest, and is called upon to drive out various demons and malignant spirits (Bhowmik, 1971; Ehrenfels, 1955; Tampy, 1959; Thurston, 1909).

The Chenchus

The Chenchus, a seminomadic tribe, are regarded as a representative group of the former jungle tribes of South India. They are mostly found in the State of Andhra Pradesh, but are also present in the States of Karnataka, Tamilnadu, and Orissa. The Chenchus are presently concentrated mainly in Andhra Pradesh in the districts of Mahaboobnagar and Nalgonda. In the most current population estimates, they number approximately 32,720 persons, just slightly more than 1% of the total population of scheduled tribes (3,176,000) in Andhra Pradesh (*Census of India*, 1981). Physically, the Chenchus are of medium stature, slender and well built, with dark to black-brown complexions, have coarse, wavy hair, a very steep forehead with prominent eyebrows, a flat nose with a depressed root and wide nostrils, a large mouth, and a small, pointed, and receding chin.

Most of the Chenchu settlements are to be found in the midst of thick forest, near a creek or some other source of water. They depend mostly on the forest for their basic diet of edible wild roots, tubers, fruits, leaves, plants, and honey, plus occasional wild game and fish. Nowadays, with the expansion of the State Government's forest department activities, the Chenchu's food-gathering economy is supplemented with wage earning from forest-related labor. Agriculture as an economic mode is also currently making headway with a few Chenchu groups, especially those living on the periphery of the plains areas.

The Chenchus believe that the world is full of mysterious powers with enormous influence over their destiny. These powers are either to be controlled by or subordinated to various esoteric practices, rites, and rituals, or placated with offerings, prayers, and sacrifices for the group's perpetuation. In the midst of stress and strain, the Chenchus try to establish a relationship with the myriad unseen powers, thus generating a spirit of cohesiveness among the group, assuring peaceful living with less tension. Through their tribal experts, the Chenchus therefore practice magic in order to control the spirits they suspect cause them harm (Bhowmick, 1989; Haimendorf, 1943). Influenced by the Hindu religion, the Chenchus also worship certain gods and goddesses in the hope of achieving prosperity, happiness, and release from tensions and anxieties.

Chenchus use white magic for curing diseases and preventing their recurrence. In a state of spirit possession, those who are specialized in white magic diagnose the cause of disease and suggest remedial measures. These magical practices involve incantation, and the use of a talisman for special propitiation (Bhowmick, 1989). Moreover, almost all old Chenchus have knowledge of herbs and their curative properties for various kinds of diseases. However, the modern-day Chenchus are also using the medicines provided by government hospitals and mobile medical unit doctors.

Generally speaking, the Chenchus consider mental disorder or mental depression to be suffering brought about by evil spirits who possess the sick person, and in such a case the services of a spirit doctor or sorcerer are required. A magical rite known as *Datimpu* is performed when a person suffers from chronic sickness or from some other form of major catastrophe (Bhowmick, 1989).

Chenchus believe in the concept of the *evil eye*. Hence the mere glance of certain classes of people is believed to cause ill health, impeded physical growth, loss of economic prosperity for the person on whom the glance is cast, and other disasters. "Evil eye is believed to be born with its possessor," according to Bhowmick (1989). The Chenchus further believe that if a person is thought to have been exposed to the evil eye, a spirit doctor must be called to perform magical rites to cure the person from suffering. In one instance, described by Bhowmick, the spirit doctor was called to attend the patient, and the spirit doctor fixed a day for performing the requisite magical rites.

> The patient was instructed not to take any meals on that day. The spirit doctor himself cooked the food and made the cooked rice into three balls. He uttered some incantations slowly and waved the rice balls thrice around the patient. The patient was asked to walk for some distance without turning back. Thus, the ill effects of the evil eye were believed to have been removed by this rite. (p. 27)

The Chenchus have specific interpretations of the consequences of dreams. Dreaming of particular objects or individuals is expected to cause specific results. For example, if a Chenchu dreams of a Brahmin, it is a good omen, whereas, if he dreams of a goat, it is a bad omen. Similarly, dreaming of illness or death is a sign of good health, but dreaming of a male buffalo attacking a person indicates impending death.

Even though influenced by the traditions of the Hindu religion and by modern rehabilitation and medical programs, the Chenchus continue to believe that many illnesses are due to the anger of some evil spirit or displeased deity. Hence they continue to rely on the curative power of both modern medicine and traditional beliefs.

The Lodhas

The Lodhas are one of the hunting–gathering tribes of Eastern India, living in the rugged terrain bordering West Bengal, Bihar, and Orissa. This terrain is full of dwarf Sal trees and similar types of vegetation. The Lodhas are concentrated in the districts of Midnapur and Jhargram, West Bengal. At present, there are some 26,000 Lodhas in West Bengal, around 4,000 in the Mayurbhanj district of Orissa, and less than 1,000 in the district of Singhbhum, Bihar (*Census of India,* 1991). "For a pretty long time, the Lodhas were treated as one of the ex-criminal tribes, and later as a denotified community" (Bhowmick, 1976, p. 287). The Lodhas are of medium stature, slender build, have a dark-brown complexion, black wavy hair, a wide forehead with prominent eyebrows, a somewhat flat nose slightly depressed at the root, and thick lips. The Lodhas of Jhargram have clung mainly to their traditional forest economy, while the Lodhas of Midnapur have adopted farming or hired out as agricultural laborers. However, they often change their residence in search of better living, and the fear of evil spirits, which they believe are always visiting or hovering over their locality (Bhowmick, 1963).

Living in forests, the Lodhas maintain considerable geographic isolation, and have substantially reduced interaction with other groups. They live on roots, tubers, and other forest products, bartering with neighboring groups to meet their other requirements. However, the Lodhas of the deforested region, particularly in the Midnapur district, are also employed as agricultural laborers by neighboring landowners. As a result, they come in close and frequent contact with various caste groups in the area, and have consequently acquired some local techniques of agricultural practices and minor rituals related to agricultural operations as practiced by local Hindus. Thus, the Lodhas have gradually incorporated some of the local Hindu rituals into their own magicoreligious concepts. The influence of local Hindus' way of living is particularly noticed in the Lodhas' present-day patterns of dress and ornamentation and construction of dwelling huts (Bhowmick, 1976).

The Lodhas have many totems, which are equated with those of clans or gotras of the higher castes. Marriage within the clan is prohibited. Thus, the exogamous clan system brings greater social solidarity and interdependence by bringing one group closer to one or more others. In times of crisis, clan ties provide a cohesiveness that strengthens the entire group. Throughout the Lodhas' life cycle, rites are very important to social and cultural solidarity. During pregnancy, for example, many taboos are available to counteract the evil spirits which, the Lodhas believe, might harm the pregnant woman and her unborn baby. Extensive birth ceremonies, including, for example, the disposal of the placenta, are practiced to ward off the various psychoemotional stresses experienced by the new parents and their family members. For this purpose, the services of the medicineman, sorcerers, and local medical practitioners are sought. In their rituals, the Lodhas, living near the Hindus, are served by such lower-caste members as the barber and the washerman. The scheduled caste midwives are in many cases recruited from the Hadi/Sweeper caste.

At marriage, the two Lodhas become full-fledged members of their society. Before the actual marriage ceremony, formal marriage rites are first performed with trees, with the expectation being that if an accident befalls the couple, the trees will serve as surrogate victims. To this end, many elaborate mortuary rites are practiced to reduce stresses the young couple may experience. Such rituals as calling back of the soul and the purification ceremony are thus meant to buttress some of the shocks of day-to-day life.

The Lodhas believe that mysterious powers influence certain actions in their lives, and that these powers are to be appeased at different phases of their life cycle. Supernatural spirits, according to popular belief, are generally invisible, though, materializing in differing forms, they appear on rare occasions, but only before men. Sometimes the supernatural spirits also appear in dreams. The concept and treatment of diseases so as to avert the evil eye and the effects of *evil mouth* are very important to the Lodhas, as all of these have specific rites and rituals embedded in their social system. They have shamans, men who are possessed by many hovering spirits, and possessed, even, by displeased deities. It is through such forms of spirit possession that typical psychoemotional expressions are channeled. Men who are possessed by spirits utter many verses in a melodious tone and, for preventive purification, warn away the would-be spirit-offenders. Hysterical fits, muscle spasms, and a muttering and foaming mouth suggest immediate solutions to the problems which have so bewildered the onlookers. Thus, rites, rituals, oracles, and many other spirit-type practices are present throughout the Lodha culture, giving its groups a greater capacity for survival and perpetuation.

CONCLUSION

All human individuals and groups owe their very existence to the social relationships and cultural facets they share with yet other individuals and groups. Ironically, it is from this, the individual's and group's greatest source of strength, that some of the greatest threats to human survival originate, namely, the psychological and physical stresses and strains that attend the disruption of long-established ways of life.

Stresses and strains and life-style dislocations are nothing new to mankind, of course. All that is new are some of the contemporary sources of stress and strain. Regardless of how the dislocations may come about, people throughout human history have summoned whatever powers were within their command to reduce the negative effects of radical social and cultural change. Sometimes they have succeeded, sometimes they have not; it was ever so, and is still. In this chapter we have illustrated how, for three tribal populations in present-day India, ancient mystical traditions continue to be relied on, and have even increased in use, for relief from geographic and social dislocations and their attendant strains on the individual's and group's capacity for adjusting to often drastically altered environments.

How effectively these modern-day "primitives" deal with their particular problems in their particular part of the world remains to be examined. Nevertheless, the tribal populations in India appear to have their solutions, just as modern-day populations have their own "sophisticated" solutions. If we look closely enough, we may benefit from seeing that the two sets of solutions have more in common than we may have at first presumed; or that one set of solutions is more beneficial than the other; or that solutions to human problems must necessarily remain historically and culturally relative to time and place. Further cooperative studies of responses to social change can provide answers to such questions.

ACKNOWLEDGMENTS. The authors wish to express their great appreciation to Dr. H. Wayne Hogan for his valued editorial contributions to this chapter.

REFERENCES

Bhowmick, P. K. (1963). *The Lodhas of West Bengal: A socio-economic study.* Calcutta, India: Institute of Social Research and Applied Anthropology.

Bhowmick, P. K. (1976). *Socio-cultural profile of frontier Bengal.* Calcutta, India: Punthi Pustak.

Bhowmick, P. K. (1989). *Chenchus of the forests and plateaux: A hunting-gathering tribe in transition.* Calcutta, India: Institute of Social Research and Applied Anthropology.

Bhowmik, K. L. (1971). *Tribal India: A profile in Indian ethnology.* Calcutta, India: World Press Private Ltd.

Census of India. (1981). Dehli, India: Government of India Publication.

Census of India. (1991). Delhi, India: Government of India Publication.

Ehrenfels, U. R. V. (1952). *The Kadars of Cochin.* Madras, India.

Haimendorf, Furer C. V. (1943). *The Chenchus, jungle-folk of the Deccan.* London: Macmillan.

Tampy, K. P. P. (1959). Religion and worship of Kadar. *Folklore, 2,* 48–50.

Thurston, E. (1909). *Kadir: Castes and tribes of southern India* (Vols. 2–3). Madras, India: Government Press.

4

The Amish Life-Style in an Era of Rapid Social Change

Jerry Savells

The Old Order Amish have been part of American society for three centuries. Although there are variations in the social values and behavioral practices within different Amish church districts, the Old Order Amish have basically resisted the acculturation process that would reinforce and promote a life-style embraced by most of the non-Amish in our contemporary society (Savells, 1988; Kephart & Zellner, 1994; Kraybill, 1989).

The author visited eight Amish communities in six states from 1982 to 1986: Berne and Milroy, Indiana; Ethridge, Tennessee; Intercourse and Bird-in-Hand, Pennsylvania; Kalona, Iowa; Plain City, Ohio; and Montezuma, Georgia. Face-to-face interviews were conducted with a select number of the local Amish population. A structured 12-page

JERRY SAVELLS • Department of Sociology, Wright State University, Dayton, Ohio 45435.

Social Psychiatry across Cultures: Studies from North America, Asia, Europe, and Africa, edited by Rumi Kato Price, Brent Mack Shea, and Harsha N. Mookherjee. Plenum Press, New York, 1995.

questionnaire was used to collect research data using a stratified random sample selected from the *New American Almanac* (Raber, 1983) and the *Ohio Amish Directory* (Gingerich, 1981). A total of 130 questionnaires and/or personal interviews have been completed with select Amish families. Fifty additional interviews have also been completed among "conservative Mennonite" families for future comparisons (Savells, 1990; Savells & Foster, 1987).

OLD NORMS FOR A NEW DAY

Any visit to Amish country will probably leave the outsider with mixed feelings. A casual observer may think about a golden age of the past that is still identified with the simple, yet intriguing, life-style of the Amish. To this observer, the Amish may appear immune to most of the social ills that plague our society.

Visitors to this unique subculture are often impressed with the Amish desire to maintain a simple and devout existence, while the non-Amish population embraces the merits of modern technology. The Amish still go about their daily business as if they were unafraid of nuclear warfare, the acquired immunodeficiency syndrome (AIDS) epidemic, environmental pollution, the escalating national debt, and turmoil in the world. Their life is a stable one, unglamorous by outsider standards, slow-paced, with daily routines, filled with hard work, and devoid of "glitz."

The Old Order Amish have essentially sought to avoid the pitfalls of modern materialism, self-indulgent life-styles, hedonistic behavior, extreme competition, the quest for wealth and status, and careerism as a means of determining one's self-worth. Instead, the Amish have placed a strong emphasis upon serving God, maintaining a simple lifestyle, voluntarily separating from the "ways of the world," respecting the integrity of the family as a sacred institution, and promoting the merits of both hard work and frugality, preferably in close cooperation with the forces of nature (Foster, 1981; Olshan, 1981; Pollack, 1981).

The Amish refusal to adopt modern technology is more than a mere statement about the lessons to be learned from hard work; it is more than just the fear of temptation. Rather, their rejection of modernity is at the very core of their social and religious values about how one *ought* to live in a way that is pleasing to God (Kraybill, 1989). Many of the norms that the Amish continue to embrace are essentially the same as those cherished by Jacob Ammann, their 17th century founder and namesake (Hostetler, 1980; Kephart & Zellner, 1994).

At the same time, the Old Order Amish face the challenges of the 1990s with some of the same values and expectations that have been identified with their subculture from the beginning. It is true that they have been exposed more to the influence of "outsiders," but they do not appear to be hapless victims of seething social change. By practicing voluntary separatism from mainstream society, the Amish have created an effective buffer zone against the unwelcome and unsolicited intrusions from the outside (Bishop, 1993; Kraybill, 1989).

THE AMISH LIFE-STYLE

Stress and the pressure for social change is everywhere today, much of it unavoidable. In a secular society, where both family solidarity and religious conviction may be either lukewarm or nonexistent, men and women discover that they are increasingly alone in their search to cope effectively with social change. They lead lives of "agonizing anonymity," with no guarantee of success.

Standing in sharp contrast to this situation, the Amish life-style appears to offer a cure for many of the ills of social anomie. Any system of social values and beliefs that has served its members well for so long cannot be too deficient or dysfunctional. The Amish have been a separate religious sect for three centuries, and their numbers have consistently grown in recent decades (Hostetler, 1980; Huntington, 1981).

The Amish wish to leave others alone and wish to be left alone. They have a strong sense of family and rarely wonder about "who they are, or what they are." To be Amish is a total life experience. The Amish have a sense of family "roots," life purpose, and a strong belief that their future is in God's hands (Bishop, 1993; Huntington, 1981; Igou, 1993).

In this "Age of Anxiety," where *stress* is the watchword of the day, the Old Order Amish seem to have survived rather well against some stiff odds (Meyers, 1983). They have refused to succumb to the temptation of seeking fame or fortune; indeed, adult members of the Old Order faith would be banished for seeking either of these.

The Amish life-style is characterized by limited uncertainty. Daily routine is fixed and predictable, and there is little tolerance for change.

Outsiders may be prone to characterize the Amish life-style as boring or backward at times, but it is stable and supportive and fully integrated with their religious beliefs. It is obvious that the Amish have gained a great deal of emotional security, but often at the expense of personal freedom. The Amish subculture is literally like a cocoon, providing womb-to-tomb support and security.

However, one is not allowed to deviate from accepted norms while retaining full membership privileges in the Amish community. The demands for conformity are very exacting, and not easily met. The slightest infringement can bring ostracism. There is no emotional outlet for those who oppose the prevailing belief system: "pulling up roots and moving on" seems to be the primary way that the Amish handle dissent (Meyers, 1992).

The natural inclination for adventure and trying new experiences must be quelled in the Amish community. Even the experience of reading "outsider books" is seen as a threat to their youth, so reading material is carefully screened. Amish youth are discouraged from expressing a natural curiosity about their world. They are simply told that some things should not be questioned. To the outsider, it would appear at times that the Amish are fearful of examining their life-style and beliefs too closely, because to do so might raise questions for which there is no easy answer.

The division of labor in the Amish household is rigid and patriarchal. The Amish family may appear to be enslaved to each other, essentially not knowing any other way to live. Wives do not question the authority or decisions of their husbands (especially in public), children do not question the decisions of their parents (at least, not until they are married), and the congregation does not question the decisions of the bishop (Hostetler, 1980; Kraybill, 1989).

The Amish discourage the pursuit of education beyond the eighth or ninth grade, and there is a concerted effort to control their children's exposure to "alien" (outsider) ideas. For those who have a strong desire for learning, such attempts at control often breed resentment and frustration. On some occasions, it may even cause a child to refuse to become Amish (i.e., be baptized into the faith).

Many of the decisions that the Amish live by seem to be an outgrowth of the traditions of their forefathers. For example, although the Amish cannot own automobiles, they are permitted to ride in another's car. While they may not have a phone *inside* their home, they can have one installed near their front porch (which they can hear when it rings). Though they are discouraged from forming business partnerships with outsiders, they can organize "cottage industries" where their primary clientele is the tourist (Kraybill, 1989).

It sometimes baffles the outsider that the Amish are not permitted to use a ballpoint pen because it is considered too modern, yet they can use a pocket calculator. They may often prefer a "folk doctor" when they are sick, but the same person can seek the services of a veterinarian for his livestock. Indeed, although the Amish must not practice modern "birth control," they often use artificial insemination to improve the quality of their breeding stock. Thus, the dividing line between acceptable and unacceptable behavior seems rather arbitrary to those who attempt to logically analyze how and why the Amish live as they do.

To the novice, the Amish appear to live a "dour, introverted, harsh, and plain" life without electricity, phones, television, tractors, insurance, government subsidies, and many of the other necessities of modern life. Although they may appear aloof and withdrawn to the outsider, the Amish are both willing and capable of forming long-lasting friendships, and they often possess a delightful sense of humor.

THE AMISH "PRIVATE SELF" AND "PUBLIC SELF"

The Old Order Amish are in a kind of "Catch-22" when considering how they should best handle the subject of evaluating social change. Although their religious beliefs and family concerns are primarily rooted in a traditional, "folk" society, they are surrounded by all the trappings and temptations of daily contact with a mother culture that has been defined as an urban, mass society.

In a book entitled *The McDonaldization of Society* (1993) George Ritzer suggested that one of the most telling features of the standardization of life experiences in the modern age is the *loss of control of the individual over his or her own fate.* Since economic survival in some Old Order Amish communities necessitates the possibility of nonfarm employment or more conjoint activities with non-Amish neighbors and friends, it becomes increasingly difficult for a young Amish male to find financial security while working in the public sector. The portable lunch pail may be the ultimate symbol of change in the Amish community.

The Old Order Amish have been amazingly successful in preserving their traditions, norms, folkways, mores, etc., because they are reinforced with the conviction that this is the way that God intended for them to live. It does not lessen the sacrifice resulting from their choices, but the knowledge that their sacrifices are both worthwhile and necessary may offer enormous spiritual and emotional comfort. The work lives, play lives, and spiritual lives of non-Amish populations within the mother culture are often separated into autonomous spheres of existence. The Amish not only find this unacceptable, but also believe that it reflects a rather superficial faith.

Turning to the broad issue of mental health, it might be said that one's mental health is better if there is a congruence between the "private self" and the "public self" (Goffman, 1959). Normlessness or anomie is often the result when individuals are bombarded with a mesmerizing array of norms and expectations, many of which may be contradictory to their own personal values and beliefs. The Amish are usually protected from such confusion, because they subscribe to the religious conviction that one is only placed on this earth to serve God—and there is no higher calling. If one, therefore, accepts this observation, there is little desire to alter the public presentation of the self.

Urban development and the growth of tourism and the services have made increasing changes to the character of these Amish communities. Obviously, the Amish population is not uninformed about these forces and their possible consequences, but they cannot control the rapidity or direction of change. Thus, they continue to seek isolation as a basic means of protection.

THE AMISH VIEW OF STRESS

Hostetler (1993) suggested that "the Amish are a church, a community, a spiritual union, a conservative branch of Christianity, a religion, a community whose members practice simple and austere living, a familistic entrepreneuring system, and an adaptive human community" (p. 4). However, very little has been written about the Amish interpretation of stress and how they cope with it (Meyers, 1983).

The author interviewed a board certified psychotherapist who grew up in an Old Order Amish family. Although this psychotherapist was willing to discuss his past and his understanding of stress within the Amish community, he requested anonymity to protect other members of his family who might suffer embarrassment and humiliation by his openness.

This psychotherapist grew up in the Midwest. His family was rather typical in size; there were a total of nine children. By his own admission, he indicated at age 45 that he had only recently been able to discuss his educational and career experiences without strong feelings of guilt for possibly disappointing his parents, relatives, and friends still living in the Amish community where he lived for many years. He left essentially to pursue a high school education. Afterwards, he earned two university degrees.

He suggested that the Amish life-style is often an effective buffer against what outsiders might call sensory overload. However, many of the physiological manifestations of stress, such as ulcers, migraine headaches, hypochondria, and depression, can be found in the Amish community, although it would rarely be discussed with an outsider.

This psychotherapist felt that most Amish who adhere rather rigidly to the teachings of their *Ordnung* (written code of conduct) would experience less stress since they would have no desire for greater assimilation into the mother culture. The Amish have a built-in support system with strong feelings of religious and community solidarity. This typically provides them with strong feelings of emotional security, and insures that they experience little anxiety about being different, or being able to compete effectively. Furthermore, the Amish gain satisfaction about themselves by seeking humility and serving God, not by personal achievement or instant gratification.

In the interview he stated, "The Amish are more at peace with themselves. However, some stress is created by the Amish attempt to *live the perfect Christian life.*" A considerable strain can be produced because of the individual's efforts to constantly seek humility, through the constant scrutiny of his or her behavior within the community, and through the constant threat of banishment.

This psychotherapist mentioned that he had been divorced, and that when he remarried his own parents could not attend his second wedding because this act was forbidden in the Amish community. Hence, the Amish do not tolerate divorce for any of their members, for any reason.

The respondent had left his Amish roots almost three decades ago, and had enjoyed considerable satisfaction in pursuing his professional career. This experience would have been strictly forbidden by the Amish Ordnung. It is obvious that such a departure from one's family and friends can be a cause of great stress. However, in retrospect, it was a decision that he felt was right for him. It must be stated, however, that he was quite complimentary toward his family and his Amish life experiences.

The Old Order Amish the author met in these communities were independent, extremely devout, suspicious of outsiders and their motives, distrustful of Uncle Sam, and very inner-directed. Their social and religious values are centered in the importance of family and faith, and not the pursuit of material goods or success.

The Amish advocate the "therapeutic value of real work" (Foster, 1982). They believe that physical labor is good for the mind, body, and soul in keeping with the biblical teaching regarding the earning of one's bread by the sweat of one's brow. Their daily work is labor intensive, in contrast to the mother culture where the forces of technology and profit margins help establish priorities and patterns of employment (Foster, 1981; Savells, 1990).

Nevertheless, it is reasonable for one to expect that the Amish have shown some vulnerability to the pressures toward modernization (Savells, 1988). For example, many have been asked to sell their land at inflated prices for commercial development. Indeed, the changing economic climate in these eight communities, and the frustration of competing in a money market where agribusiness is a major threat to the small farmer, are having a definite impact upon the Amish way of life (Savells, 1988). The latter source of concern represents values in our society such as the promotion of maximum efficiency, the accumulation of capital or wealth, and the merits of mass production. These are basic trends that are essentially alien to the Amish pursuit of "devotedness, simplicity, and peace" (Savells, 1985).

THE AMISH RESPONSE TO ALIENATION

Alienation is often present whenever personal values and social values are not congruent. Melvin Seeman proposed that alienation has five major components: powerlessness, meaninglessness, normlessness, social isolation, and self-estrangement (Seeman, 1959). The Old Order Amish would not comprehend the term "powerlessness" as used in the sociological literature. The Amish feel that all things are in God's control, and that it is both foolhardy and vain of man to assume that he can control his fate. Since the Amish adhere to beliefs and religious customs that date back to the 17th century, they do not feel vulnerable to the whims and political maneuvers of the elites who present themselves as the movers-and-shakers of our society. The Amish are only powerless to the extent that they are out of favor with God.

The Amish do understand that life is meaningful because it is a genuine expression of love for God and one's family. They assume that God has a definite purpose for them, and this purpose constitutes their reason for being. They do not subscribe to the idea of buying life insurance, since they believe that this is a contradiction of their faith in God to look out for their best interests. The Amish believe that man's search through secular means (yoga, EST, etc.) to discover the true meaning of his existence is extremely vain and doomed to failure.

The concept of *normlessness* can be traced back to Emile Durkheim's explanation of anomie (1947). Toffler referred to this in *Future Shock* (1970) as the option-glut society experiencing overchoice. The Amish have no desire to participate in mainstream society with its glitz and superficiality, where norms change almost daily whenever there are profits and power struggles. Rather than accept the new and untried simply because of novelty, the Amish cling to the time-honored (and tested) folkways of their past. They draw strength from this determination to live a quiet and tranquil existence apart from the helter-skelter pace of our modern society (Bishop, 1993).

The *social isolation* that Seeman (1959) identified, refers to feelings of vulnerability that one has in living as "a number" among the masses. The vagabond or homeless individual in the middle of New York City may feel extreme social isolation. Although there are people everywhere, none of them relate to this person or care seriously about his or her fate. This is a *forced* social isolation, whereas the Amish are *voluntarily* isolated from the outside world, and sustain close ties within the community. There is security that comes from this association: the Amish know they are never alone.

Finally, *self-estrangement* is a psychological dimension of alienation, since the individual feels that he or she is literally cut off from mainstream society. In this situation, one might experience an identity crisis, attempt suicide, use drugs, become violent, accept divorce, etc., all symptoms that are familiar in the world of today. The Amish typically feel a deep and abiding attachment to God and their fellow Amish brethren. Therefore, they are usually immune to feelings of self-estrangement.

RESULTS AND DISCUSSION

The tourist and occasional visitor to Amish country often is left with a very skewed impression of the Amish value system and life-style. Since the Amish typically do not welcome interviews, and rarely solicit conversation with strangers, it is not easy to correct these misperceptions.

If the old cliché that necessity is the mother of invention is true, then there would seem to be only a few social forces at work in the 1990s that would *mandate* change among the Amish. The Amish have never particularly bent to the weight of social pressures or fads anyway. And this is probably the main reason why they have survived so long as a separatist group, quietly practicing their religion and living an austere life.

When assessing social change among the Amish, the researcher becomes immediately sensitized to the idea that change has always been gradual (ever so slow from an outsider's view) and *highly* selective or controlled. The pursuit of technological progress and the good life are often claimed to be the proper social incentives to motivate change. The Amish are almost totally immune to these incentives. Thus, they rarely feel themselves victimized by the forces of social change. Technology is not roaring down upon them forcing an instant adaptation to the forces of the marketplace.

The Amish perceive that much of what is regarded as modern or progressive by today's social standards remains a source of temptation for their young—and potentially could cause conflict and disharmony if not kept at a proper distance. For example, the Amish do not believe that there is anything inherently evil about electricity, telephones, or driving an automobile, but they realize that these modern conveniences, and the side-effects they produce when they are used, would alter the Amish life-style and that of future generations, offering possibly too much temptation to forget the importance of tradition (Savells, 1990). Again, the first concern of the Amish is devotion to God, and technology cannot enhance the attainment of that goal. The Amish do not want to become dependent on these inventions, but prefer to maintain a quiet and simple life unfettered with the complications of the modern world (Savells, 1990).

Historians and sociologists have been aware that in other periods of history, religion has been a powerful motivation for *creating* change. This is evident in the kinship between the growth of Protestantism and industrialism in the Western world. Yet, the Amish have cited their religion as one of the most important reasons why they have essentially avoided most of the social change identified with the Industrial Revolution (Savells, 1990). Most of this resistance has been successful.

Although the Amish honor important traditions regarding their faith and their people, they also recognize that social and economic survival necessitates that some acceptance of change will be both normal and inevitable (Hostetler, 1980; Kraybill, 1989). Acculturation *is* occurring in the majority of the Old Order Amish communities visited by this researcher, but it is neither rampant nor whimsical (Savells, 1990). Rather, where social change has occurred, it has consistently been scrutinized carefully and accepted only gradually when the results could be monitored for possible undesirable side effects.

The Amish have refused to succumb to the commercial, materialistic, and egoistic trappings typified by American television and life in the fast lane. They have remained largely unfettered by the national pursuit of success, careerism, competition, one-upmanship, fame, money, and power seeking. They have a determination to survive that reflects most favorably upon their heritage and ability to be "in the world, but not of the world."

ACKNOWLEDGMENTS. This research has been supported by two grants from the College of Liberal Arts and one grant from the University Research Council at Wright State University, which are gratefully acknowledged.

REFERENCES

Bishop, D. (1993). The enduring Amish: What can they teach contemporary families? *The Family in America, 8,* 1–4.

Durkheim, E. (1947). *The division of labor in society.* (G. Simpson, Trans.). Glencoe, IL: Free Press.

Foster, T. (1980). The Amish and the ethos of ecology. *Ecologist, 10,* 331–335.

Foster, T. (1981). Amish society: A relic from the past could become a model for the future. *The Futurist, 15,* 33–40.

Foster, T. (1982). Learning from the Amish. *New Roots, 21,* 16–21.

Gingerich, E. (1981). *Ohio Amish Directory.* Sugarcreek, PA: Schlabach Publishers.

Goffman, E. (1959). *The presentation of self in everyday life.* Garden City, NY: Doubleday.

Hostetler, J. (1993). *Amish society* (4th ed.). Baltimore: Johns Hopkins University Press.

Huntington, G. (1981). The Amish family. In C. Mindel & R. Habenstein (Eds.), *Ethnic families in America: Patterns and variations.* New York: Elsevier.

Igou, B. (1993). *Traditional family functions and the Amish.* A paper presented at the International Conference on Amish Society, Elizabethtown, PA.

Kephart, W., & W. Zellner. (1994). *Extraordinary groups* (5th ed.). New York: St. Martin's Press.

Kraybill, D. (1989). *The riddle of Amish culture.* Baltimore: Johns Hopkins University Press.

Meyers, T. (1983). *Stress and the Amish community in transition.* (Unpublished doctoral dissertation, Boston University).

Meyers, T. (1992). *The Old Order Amish: To remain in the faith or to leave.* Paper presented at the American Sociological Association Meetings, Pittsburgh, PA.

Olshan, M. (1981). Modernity, the folk society, and the Old Order Amish: An alternative interpretation. *Rural Society, 46,* 297–309.

Pollack, R. (1981). Culture change in an Amish community. *Central Issues in Anthropology, 3,* 51–67.

Raber, B. (1983). *The New American Almanac*. Baltic, OH: Gordonville Print Shop.
Ritzer, G. (1993). *The McDonaldization of Society*. Newbury Park, CA: Pine Forge Press.
Savells, J. (1985). Survival and social change among the Amish in five communities. *Lifestyles, 8*, 85–103.
Savells, J. (1988). Economic and social acculturation among the Old Order Amish in select communities: Surviving in a high tech society. *Journal of Comparative Family Studies, 19*, 123–134.
Savells, J. (1990). Social change among the Amish in eight communities. *Pennsylvania Mennonite Heritage, 13*, 12–16.
Savells, J., & T. Foster. (1987). The challenges and limitations of conducting research among the Old Order Amish. *Explorations in Ethnic Studies, 10*, 25–39.
Seeman, M. (1959). On the meaning of alienation. *American Sociological Review, 24*, 783–791.
Toffler, A. (1970). *Future Shock*. New York: Random House.

5

Reciprocity in Support Networks of Sheltered-Care Residents

STEVEN P. SEGAL AND JANE HOLSCHUH

The socially debilitating effects of long-term hospitalization or institutionalization are well documented (Barton, 1959; Goffman, 1961; Gruenberg, 1967; Shadoan, 1976; Wing, 1962). Rose (1959) and Evans, Bullard, and Solomon (1961) reported that the longer a person was institutionalized, the more his or her social contacts, especially family relationships, became disrupted, disengaged, and disintegrated. However, inequity of support exchanges can lead members of the mentally disordered person's social network to run the risk of excessive burden, exhaustion, and burnout in providing essential care to the disabled

STEVEN P. SEGAL • Mental Health and Social Welfare Research Group, School of Social Welfare, University of California, Berkeley, California 94720. JANE HOLSCHUH • School of Social Work, University of Wisconsin, Madison, Wisconsin 53706.

Social Psychiatry across Cultures: Studies from North America, Asia, Europe, and Africa, edited by Rumi Kato Price, Brent Mack Shea, and Harsha N. Mookherjee. Plenum Press, New York, 1995.

person (Froland, Brodsky, Olson, & Stewart, 1979; Sullivan & Poertner, 1989). This burden has been considered a key element in the abandonment and resulting isolation of persons with serious mental disorders. Thus, mutuality of exchange is considered crucial to the maintenance of effective support systems for this vulnerable population (Froland et al., 1979; Moxley, 1988; Parks & Pilisuk, 1984; Tolsdorf, 1976).

Little work has been done, however, to increase understanding of the factors associated with the development of support exchanges in social networks of the mentally disabled. This chapter examines how sheltered-care housing (i.e., board and care, family care, halfway houses, and psychosocial rehabilitation facilities) contributes to the development of reciprocal support exchange in the social networks of residents with serious mental disabilities.

Mental health professionals often criticize transitional residential programs for supporting "transitions to nowhere"; that is, encouraging unrealistic expectations that emphasize social reintegration goals and opportunities that do not exist within current social, economic, and housing realities. Several authors, on the other hand, have promoted the concept of "normalized" settings, that is, houselike as opposed to institutional environments, which would provide a form of human care or asylum for individuals who are seriously disabled (Bachrach, 1984; Lamb & Peele, 1984). Segal and Kotler (1993) have observed that the amount of time individuals with severe mental disabilities spend in sheltered-care housing arrangements is positively associated with the development of increasing levels of assisted, as opposed to independently initiated, social functioning, such as gaining access to and participating in social, consumer, or economically productive activities with the help and mediation of others. Their findings hold true even when age and level of disability are taken into account.

It is unclear, however, whether or not such assisted functioning is likely to have a long-term positive effect. Is it a reflection of an increasing level of dependency on service providers and home operators? Or have residents found a more compatible social group they can rely on in times of need? Even if the development of such a group is observed, it could endure only in situations fostering mutuality of exchange.

Contrary to expectations, Segal and Holschuh (1991) found that the number of times an individual lived in a sheltered-care setting was related to the resident's development of relationships, which involved receiving and giving emotional support, and receiving instrumental or material supports. The authors offered two possible explanations for this phenomenon: (1) that each episode of sheltered care served as a form of respite care for the family or significant other, which allowed them to continue their provision of care, and (2) that the act of moving in and out of sheltered-care housing focused attention and thus promoted support interactions with these individuals (the squeaky wheel hypothesis).

Neither hypothesis, however, accounts for the finding of significant giving of emotional support associated with the number of episodes in sheltered-care housing. This study proposes that simple placement in such environments allows the individual with a serious mental disability to develop mutually supportive relationships based upon reciprocal support exchanges. We believe that the pattern of increasing assisted social functioning observed by Segal and Kotler is, in part, a reflection of increased mutuality of support, as well as a growing dependency on the material characteristics and supports provided by the sheltered care system. The fact that only 28.6% of sheltered care residents in the Segal and Holschuh study (1991) named formal nonkin as members of their support networks is further evidence supporting this belief. Most of the assistance was not coming from service providers, it was coming from friends and kin.

In order to better understand mutual support in sheltered-care settings, it is necessary to take into account other aspects of this environment and its residents which have in the past been associated with the development of support reciprocity within social relationships. Much has been written about the potentially detrimental effects of transitional housing (Appleby & Desai, 1987; Cometa, Morrison, & Ziskoven, 1979), as well as the need for highly supportive living arrangements (Crystal, Ladner, & Towber, 1986; Drake, Wallach, & Hoffman, 1989). It can be hypothesized that those living in transitional, high-expectation environments would be less likely to develop reciprocal support relationships. On the other hand, residents who had lived in facilities characterized as having supportive environments would be more likely to develop reciprocal relationships.

In addition, regardless of the environment type and the number of sheltered-care episodes, individuals spending more time in such protected settings would have an increased probability of developing at least one reciprocal support relationship in their everyday interactions.

Certain social–psychological disadvantages that sheltered-care residents experience make it more difficult for them to achieve successful independent living (Van Putten & Spar, 1979). In addition to studying the effects of the sheltered-care environment on the development of support reciprocity within social networks, we sought to document how resident levels of psychopathology and institutionalization affected their ability to engage in reciprocal relationships. We hypothesized that higher degrees of psychopathology and institutionalization would negatively affect the residents' ability to form reciprocal relationships.

METHODS

Sample and Data Collection

The data collected were part of a 10-year longitudinal study of a probability sample of 393 adults with serious mental disabilities (excluding developmental disabilities) living in 211 California sheltered-care facilities in 1973. The sample, drawn from 157 census tracts, was designed to be representative of all sheltered-care residents in California between the ages of 18 and 65 with a serious mental disability.

A total of 360 sample members (91.6%) was located at follow-up between 1983 and 1985. No differences were detected between those who were located and those who were not. Of the 360 located, 270 (68.7%) were *alive* and 90 (22.9%) were confirmed dead; 33 (8.4%) were not located. Of the 270 people located alive, 17 (6.3%) refused and 253 agreed to be interviewed. This paper reports on the sample of 234 persons who completed valid interviews both in 1973 and at follow-up. Of these, 178 (76%) had a lifetime diagnosis of a schizophrenic spectrum disorder (Segal & Kotler, 1993).

Structured face-to-face interviews with residents were conducted by trained social workers at baseline in 1973 and at follow-up. Records detailing the lifetime psychiatric hospitalizations of sample members were obtained at follow-up from 119 inpatient facilities in 15 states. The survey methodology used in the 1973 study and at follow-up is described elsewhere (Segal & Kotler, 1993).

Analysis

Using a logit technique (Aldrich & Nelson, 1984), we assessed separately effects on two dichotomous measures of residents' reciprocal support relationships: whether or not residents had at least one relationship that involved the mutual exchange of emotional support, and whether or not they had at least one relationship which involved the mutual exchange of instrumental support. The analyses examined the effects of time in sheltered-care housing and the number of episodes in sheltered care during the 10- to 12-year follow-up period on subjects' probability of having at least one of each type of relationship. Analyses also examined the influence of supportive or high transitional expectations, levels of psychopathology, and institutionalization on support reciprocity outcomes. The analyses controlled for other factors known to be associated with network outcomes, such as physical health, access to family and friends, and sociodemographics.

An approximation of the relative risk of a resident having each of these types of relationships was obtained by calculating the odds ratio through a transformation of the beta coefficient of each independent variable (Hosmer & Lemeshow, 1989). The odds ratio for the predictor variable "length of time in sheltered care" assesses the effect of one year's increase in the duration of stay on the probability of developing a supportive relationship that involved support reciprocity. All scale variables were standardized to make comparisons of odds ratios meaningful.

Outcome Criteria

Information on residents' social networks was gathered at follow-up using the Personal Network Inventory, an adaptation of the Pattison Psychosocial Kinship Inventory (PKI) (Pattison, DeFrancisco, Wood, Frazier, & Crowder, 1975). The PKI elicits information on network size and composition. It characterizes the type of support as emotional or instrumental and assesses reciprocity by documenting whether it is both given and received within each relationship dyad.

The size of the social network was established by asking respondents to list their social relationships during two separate interviews conducted two weeks apart. Specifically, residents were asked to identify "all people who are important to you at this moment, whether you like them or not. . . . Use your own definition of who is important to you." In addition to naming network members, respondents were asked to identify the specific type of relationship they had with each member. Three types of relationship were categorized: relationships with kin, with friends and acquaintances (informal nonkin), and with treatment system professionals or paraprofessionals (formal nonkin).

To measure reciprocity of emotional support, respondents were asked at follow-up to indicate the degree to which each network member helped them and the degree to which they helped that person by "providing emotional support" when needed. The 5-point response categories ranged from "not at all" to "very frequently." We considered only relationships in which the resident indicated that he or she received and gave emotional support "on some occasions," "often," or "very frequently."

We defined the outcome variable of reciprocal emotional support by dichotomizing the residents' responses into those indicating no relationship that involved reciprocal emotional support and those indicating at least one such relationship (Hammer, 1981). The dichotomous measure seemed more consistent with past findings that having any reciprocal relationship was more critical than the quantity of such relationships (Gottlieb, 1981; Lowenthal & Haven, 1968; Miller & Ingham, 1976).

To measure mutual exchange of instrumental support, respondents were asked to indicate the degree to which each network member helped them and they helped that person by "doing things" for them such as assisting on the job, helping with household tasks, providing personal or family care, or even lending money. Response categories ranged from 1 to 5, as for emotional support, and we again considered only relationships in which the resident received and gave instrumental support "on some occasions," "often," or "very frequently." The outcome variable for reciprocity of instrumental support was similarly dichotomized.

Predictor Variables

To measure the general effect of sheltered care, the total number of years spent in the original sheltered-care facility was included as a continuous variable in the analysis. This was obtained by combining two measures, the length of stay prior to 1973, and time between 1973 and follow-up. As a measure of the access to the facility when needed (respite environment), we considered the number of times the resident had been in sheltered-care housing from 1973 through the follow-up interview.

Residents were asked to characterize their sheltered-care environments in 1973 by responding to items from two subscales of the Community-Oriented Programs Environment Scale (Moos, 1974). The total score on each subscale was used as a continuous variable in the analyses.

The support subscale is an 8-item true–false response measure designed to assess the extent to which "residents are encouraged to be helpful and supportive toward other residents, and how supportive the staff is toward residents" (Moos, 1975, p. 41). The transitional, high-expectation subscale consists of 10 true–false items that measure the "extent to which the resident's environment orients him/her toward preparing for release from the program, training for new kinds of jobs, looking to the future, and setting and working toward goals" (Moos, 1975, p. 41).

The severity of psychopathology at the time of the 1973 interview was assessed using the Brief Psychiatric Rating Scale (BPRS) (Overall & Gorham, 1962; Rhoades & Overall, 1988; Segal & Choi, 1991); the score was based on clinicians' ratings of the severity of 17 symptoms. Ratings were based on interaction during the interview and the interviewees' descriptions of their behavior during the week before the interview. The BPRS score was used as a continuous variable in the analyses.

During the 1973 interview, respondents were asked whether they had spent a continuous period of two or more years in a state psychiatric hospital. The response was coded as a dummy variable. This hospital chronicity measure was considered as an indicator of institutionalization (Sommer & Witney, 1961).

Control and Baseline Variables

The literature on social support frequently reports a positive relationship between physical health status and the amount of support received (Berkman & Syme, 1979; Cassel, 1976; Cobb, 1976; Cohen & Syme, 1985), although the mechanisms of the association and the direction of the relationship have yet to be clearly understood (Antonucci & Depner, 1982; Heller, 1979; House, Landis, & Umberson, 1988; Thoits, 1982). The Physical Symptom Scale (Langner, 1962) used to measure health status in 1973 and at follow-up, was included in the analysis to control for the effect (Segal & Choi, 1991). The score on the scale was the sum of reported symptoms. The 1973 score was used in the analysis.

We also needed to control for baseline levels of support and social interaction in 1973. Because the PKI was not administered during the 1973 interview, we used as proxy measures two subscales of the External Social Integration Scale (Segal & Aviram, 1978) that assess residents' access to and participation in family and friendship activities. The family access and participation subscale is a six-item continuous measure that refers to the ease of contact with one's family by phone and visit and the frequency of such contact. Possible responses range from very difficult or never to very easy or very often. The friendship access and participation subscale is a continuous measure of six items that parallel those of the family subscale but pertain to close friends and acquaintances. In addition, demographic characteristics, including age and gender, were controlled for in the analysis.

RESULTS

Characteristics of the Sample

The mean age of the 234 sample respondents in 1973 was 43 years (SD = 12.53), and 53% were male. Most reported few, if any, physical symptoms in 1973; 46% reported between one and three such symptoms. The majority (54.3%) of the respondents in 1973 experienced very mild psychological symptoms as measured by the BPRS. During the 1973 interview, 43.5% reported spending more time in a mental hospital than two continuous years. In 1983, only 22.2% of the follow-up sample remained in the 1973 facility; their mean length of stay in that facility was 4.75 years (SD = 4.01). Over half of the follow-up sample (56.5%) were living in the sheltered-care system at follow-up. In the follow-up sample, the mean number of sheltered care experiences between 1973 and follow-up was 2.2 (SD = 1.83).

Almost two-thirds (62%) of the 234 sample members viewed their 1973 facility environments as supportive. Only one-third (35%) described their facilities as transitional in nature.

Network and Support Characteristics

At follow-up, the mean number of network members named by the 234 respondents was 4.5 (SD = 2.77). As shown in Table 1, only 9.4% named no "important person" or no network members at all. However, further inspection of the data do show that, contrary to popular conceptions, most of these former patients are not totally isolated and have relationships that are important to them.

More than half of the sample (55.1%) named from 1 to 5 network members, and more than a third (35.5%) named from 6 to 10 members. Most networks for people in the general population range from 20 to

Table 1
Social Support Networks Reported at 10-Year Follow-Up[a]
Percentage of Sample (N = 234)

Network composition Number in network	Kin	Informal nonkin	Formal nonkin	Total network
None	20.1	39.3	71.4	9.4
1 to 2	27.4	37.6	26.5	16.2
3 to 5	50.0	21.4	2.1	38.9
6 to 10	2.6	1.7	0.0	35.5
Total	100.0	100.0	100.0	100.0

[a]Columns may not add to total because of rounding

30 members, compared with 4 to 6 persons in psychiatric population samples (Cohen & Sokolovsky, 1978; Froland et al., 1979; Lipton, Cohen, Fischer, & Katz, 1981; Pattison et al., 1975). Two other important features of the composition of the social networks for this sample were the large proportions of residents with no informal nonkin relationships (39.3%) and no formal nonkin relationships (71.4%). Baseline data in 1973 indicated that our sample reported about equal access to and participation in friendship relationships as in family relationships. This finding differs from past studies of the social networks of psychiatric patients, which often reported that psychiatric patients have tightly knit or highly dense networks in which the vast majority of interaction is with the immediate family and other relatives (Hammer, 1963; Lipton et al., 1981; Pattison et al., 1975; Tolsdorf, 1976). For this sample, we found they reported slightly more emotional exchanges than instrumental support exchanges.

Effects of Predictor Variables

As hypothesized, time in sheltered-care housing contributed significantly to the development of relationships characterized by reciprocal emotional support across the follow-up period. Odds ratios shown in Table 2 indicate that for each year in sheltered-care housing, taking all other factors into account, respondents were 11% more likely to have a relationship that involved a mutual exchange of emotional support.

For each additional episode in a sheltered care facility from 1973 to follow-up, residents were 39% more likely to have an emotionally supportive relationship that involved mutual exchanges.

Table 2
Odds Ratios Showing Predictor Effects on the Probability of Reciprocal Relationships[a]

Predictor variable	Emotional support	Instrumental support
Utilization of sheltered-care effect		
One year in sheltered care housing	1.11[c]	1.00
Number of times in sheltered care	1.39[d]	1.14
Environment type		
Support scale	1.34[b]	1.20
Transitional/high expectation scale	.61[d]	.69[d]
Resident disadvantages		
Brief psychiatric rating scale	.69[c]	.66[c]
Two years+ continuous Psych. hospitalization	.35[e]	.51[c]

[a]Analysis controls for physical symptoms, network support characteristics, age, and gender in 1973. (N = 223)
[b]$p<.10$ level, two-tailed test
[c]$p<.05$ level, two-tailed test
[d]$p<.01$ level, two-tailed test
[e]$p<.001$ level, two-tailed test

Specific environmental characteristics of the facility were also significant. For each standard deviation increase in the support subscale score, respondents were 34% more likely to have an emotionally reciprocal relationship. For each standard deviation increase in the transitional/high expectation scale score, residents were 39% less likely to have an emotionally reciprocal relationship.

Both higher levels of psychopathology and 2 years of continuous hospitalization resulted in the expected negative effects. For each standard deviation increase in the score in the Brief Psychiatric Rating Scale, residents were 31% less likely to have a reciprocal emotional relationship and residents with a long-term hospitalization were 65% less likely to have a reciprocal emotional relationship.

In looking at reciprocal relationships involving instrumental exchanges, predictor variables were related only to not having relationships of this type. As expected, for each standard deviation increase in the transitional or high expectation scale score, a resident was 31% less likely to have an instrumentally reciprocal relationship. Similarly, for each standard deviation increase in the score of the BPRS, a resident was 34% less likely to have a relationship in which there was mutual exchange of instrumental support. And finally, residents with a long-term hospitalization were 49% less likely to have a reciprocal relationship that involved instrumental support reciprocity.

DISCUSSION

This study assessed the development of a uniquely important characteristic of social networks, support reciprocity. It considered the probability of developing a reciprocal relationship during a 10-year period as a function of residents' length of time in sheltered care, their number of sheltered-care episodes, the social environment of such settings, and two social–psychological disadvantages, psychopathology and institutionalization. Analyses controlled for physical health status, baseline social network characteristics, age, and gender.

The results may best be interpreted with respect to the opportunity for the development of reciprocal relationships that sheltered-care environments provide. Ewalt and Honeyfield (1981) reported that among residents of a Veterans' Administration domiciliary, the most frequently named "additional opportunity" desired by residents was the opportunity to be helpful to others. Similarly, Brier and Strauss (1984) found that one of the most helpful "functions of social relationships named by patients was reciprocal relating." Becoming "an equal partner" or a person who has something valuable to offer to another contributed to increased patient self-esteem and more satisfying relationships. These studies reveal the importance of reciprocal support relationships to persons with mental disabilities. The results of the current study indicate that given the proper amount of time, the sheltered-care environment promotes an appropriate forum for the development of reciprocal relationships.

Contrary to the notion of the "revolving door," the experience of multiple sheltered-care episodes broadens the opportunity for the development of relationships involving reciprocity for these individuals. The findings also demonstrate that the character of the environment is important since: (1) more supportive environments enhanced the development of mutual exchange involving emotional support; and (2) transitional-high-expectation environments were likely to detract from such mutual exchange relationships.

While residents reported the more frequent mutual exchange of emotional support at follow-up, instrumental exchanges were limited perhaps due to the small amount of resources each individual has in these settings. Even with limited resources, the transitional, high expectation environment clearly inhibits such reciprocal relationships as do psychopathology and institutionalism.

These results are quite consistent with the overall positive effect of sheltered-care housing reported by Segal and Kotler (1993) and enhance understanding of the specific nature of these environments which lead to positive and negative social network outcomes.

ACKNOWLEDGMENTS. This study was supported in party by the National Institute of Mental Health and the Robert Wood Johnson Foundation.

REFERENCES

Antonucci, T. C., & Depner, C. E. (1982). Social support and informal helping relationships. In T. A. Wills (Ed.), *Basic processes in helping relationships*. New York: Academic Press.

Appleby, L., & Desai, P. (1987). Residential instability: A perspective on system imbalance. *American Journal of Orthopsychiatry, 57*, 515–524.

Aldrich, J. H., & Nelson, F. D. (1984). *Linear probability, logit, and probit models*. Newbury Park, CA: Sage.

Bachrach, L. L. (1984). Asylum and chronically ill psychiatric patients. *American Journal of Psychiatry, 141*, 975–978.

Barton, R. (1959). *Institutional neurosis*. Briston, U.K.: Wright.

Berkman, L. F., & Syme, S. L. (1979). Social networks, host resistance, and mortality: A nine-year follow-up study of Alameda County residents. *American Journal of Epidemiology, 109*, 186–204.

Brier, A., & Strauss, J. (1984). The role of social relationships in the recovery from psychotic disorders. *American Journal of Psychiatry, 141*, 949–995.

Cassel, J. (1976). The contribution of the social environment to host resistance. *American Journal of Epidemiology, 104*, 107–123.

Cobb, S. (1976). Social support as a moderator of life stress. *Psychosomatic Medicine, 38*, 300–314.

Cohen, C. I., & Sokolovsky, J. (1978). Schizophrenia and social networks: Expatients in the inner city. *Schizophrenia Bulletin, 4*, 546–560.

Cohen, S., & Syme, S. L. (1985). Issues in the study and application of social support. In S. Cohen (Ed.), *Social support and health*. Orlando, FL: Academic Press.

Cometa, M. S., Morrison, J. D., & Ziskoven, M. (1979). Halfway to where: A critique of research on psychiatric halfway houses. *Journal of Community Psychology, 7*, 23–27.

Crystal, S., Ladner, S., & Towber, R. (1986). Multiple impairment patterns in the mentally ill homeless. *International Journal of Mental Health, 14*, 61–73.

Drake, R. E., Wallach, M. A., & Hoffman, J. S. (1989). Housing instability and homelessness among aftercare patients of an urban state hospital. *Hospital and Community Psychiatry, 40*, 46–51.

Evans, A. S., Bullard, D. M., & Solomon, M. H. (1961). The family as a potential resource in the rehabilitation of the chronic schizophrenic patient: A study of 60 patients and their families. *American Journal of Psychiatry, 117*, 1075–1083.

Ewalt, P., & Honeyfield, R. (1981). Needs of persons in long-term care. *Social Work, 26*, 223–231.

Froland, C., Brodsky, G., Olson, M., & Stewart, L. (1979). Social support and social adjustment: Implications for mental health professionals. *Community Mental Health Journal, 15*, 82–93.

Goffman, E. (1961). *Asylums: Essays on the social situation of mental patients and other inmates*. Garden City, NY: Doubleday.

Gottlieb, B. H. (1981). Preventive interventions involving social networks and social support. In B. H. Gottlieb (Ed.), *Social networks and social support* (pp. 201–232). Beverly Hills, CA: Sage.

Gruenberg, E. M. (1967). The social breakdown syndrome: Some origins. *American Journal of Psychiatry, 123,* 12–20.

Hammer, M. (1963). Influence of small social networks as factors on mental hospital admission. *Human Organization, 22,* 243–251.

Hammer, M. (1981). Social supports, social networks, and schizophrenia. *Schizophrenia Bulletin, 7,* 45–57.

Heller, K. (1979). The effects of social support: Prevention and treatment implications. In A. P. Goldstein, & F. H. Kanfer (Eds.), *Maximizing treatment gains: Transfer enhancement in psychotherapy.* New York: Academic Press.

Hosmer, D. W., & Lemeshow, S. (1989). *Applied logistic regression.* New York: Wiley.

House, J. S., Landis, K. R., & Umberson, D. (1988). Social relationships and health. *Science, 241,* 540–545.

Lamb, H. R., & Peele, R. (1984). The need for continuing asylum and sanctuary. *Hospital and Community Psychiatry, 35,* 798–802.

Langner, T. S. (1962). A 22-item screening score of psychiatric symptoms indicating impairment. *Journal of Health and Human Behavior, 3,* 269–276.

Lipton, F. R., Cohen, C. I., Fischer, E., & Katz, S. (1981). Schizophrenia: A network crisis. *Schizophrenia Bulletin, 7,* 144–151.

Lowenthal, M. F., & Haven, C. (1968). Interaction and adaptation: Intimacy as a critical variable. *American Sociological Review, 33,* 20–30.

Miller, P., & Ingham, J. G. (1976). Friends, confidants, and symptoms. *Social Psychiatry, 11,* 51–58.

Moos, R. H. (1974). *Evaluating treatment environments: An ecological approach.* New York: Wiley.

Moos, R. H. (1975). *Evaluating correctional and community settings.* New York: Wiley.

Moxley, D. P. (1988). Measuring social support networks of persons with psychiatric disabilities. *Psychosocial Rehabilitation Journal, 11,* 19–72.

Overall, J. E., & Gorham, D. R. (1962). The Brief Psychiatric Rating Scale. *Psychological Reports, 10,* 799–812.

Parks, S. H., & Pilisuk, M. (1984). Personal support systems of former mental patients residing in board and care facilities. *Journal of Community Psychology, 12,* 230–244.

Pattison, E. M., DeFrancisco, D., Wood, P., Frazier, H., & Crowder, J. (1975). A psychosocial kinship model for family therapy. *American Journal of Psychiatry, 132,* 1246–1251.

Rhoades, H. M., & Overall, J. E. (1988). The semi-structured Brief Psychiatric Rating Scale interview and rating guide. *Psychopharmacology Bulletin, 24,* 101–104.

Rose, C. (1959). Relatives' attitudes and mental hospitalization. *Mental Hygiene, 43,* 194–203.

Segal, S. P., & Aviram, U. (1978). *The mentally ill in community-based sheltered care: A study of community care and social integration.* New York: Wiley.

Segal, S. P., & Choi, M. G. (1991). Factors affecting SSI support for sheltered care residents with serious mental illness. *Hospital and Community Psychiatry, 42,* 1132–1137.

Segal, S. P., & Holschuh, J. (1991). Effects of sheltered care environments and resident characteristics on the development of social networks. *Hospital and Community Psychiatry, 42,* 1125–1131.

Segal, S. P., & Kotler, P. (1993). Sheltered care residence and personal outcomes. *American Journal of Orthopsychiatry, 68,* 80–91.

Shadoan, R. A. (1976). Making board-and-care homes therapeutic. In H. R. Lamb & Associates (Ed.), *Community survival for long-term patients.* San Francisco: Jossey-Bass.

Sommer, R., & Witney, G. (1961). The chain of chronicity. *American Journal of Psychiatry, 118,* 111–117.

Sullivan, W. P., & Poertner, J. (1989). Social support and life stress: A mental health consumer's perspective. *Community Mental Health Journal, 25,* 21–32.

Thoits, P. A. (1982). Conceptual, methodological and theoretical problems in studying social support as a buffer against life stress. *Journal of Health and Social Behavior, 23,* 145–159.

Tolsdorf, C. C. (1976). Social networks, support, and coping: An exploratory study. *Family Process, 15,* 407–417.

Van Putten, T., & Spar, J. E. (1979). The board-and care home: Does it deserve bad press? *Hospital and Community Psychiatry, 30,* 461–464.

II

Stratification Studies

In Part II, three chapters assess the relationship of stratification variables with mental health and illness. The idea of stratification here differs from the idea of culture presented in Part I by an emphasis on social structure, and the application of epidemiological methods of inquiry. Discussions about culture in Part I tended to consider the values, needs, and unique characteristics of the societies involved. Here, the authors' objective relates more to establishing causation and denoting the ways in which the causal mechanism affecting mental health differs for subpopulations under study. Stratification studies, which typically use survey data, are more typical of research in developed than developing societies. Such is the case here as well: two of the three chapters are written by U.S. researchers, and the third is the result of Swiss research.

In Chapter 6, "Ethnicity, Social Status, and Psychiatric Disorder in the Epidemiologic Catchment Area Survey," Charles Hozler and his colleagues assess the relationship among ethnicity and socioeconomic status (SES) and psychiatric disorder in the United States. That low SES is associated with increased rates of psychopathology has long been noted, particularly for the psychoses.

The relationship of ethnicity to mental disorder has proven more problematic to establish. Generally lower SES among African Americans has appeared to explain apparently higher rates of disorders seen in some studies. Using data from the Epidemiologic Catchment Area (ECA) Program, the authors attempt to distinguish the relative importance of SES and race for the prevalence of psychiatric disorders.

The ECA dataset comprises the results of the most extensive American psychiatric epidemiology survey to date. Approximately 18,000 structured interviews were conducted with community respondents in five areas in the United States between 1981 and 1985. The Diagnostic Interview Schedule (DIS) was used to assess major adult psychiatric disorders based on the *Diagnostic and Statistical Manual*, Third Edition (DSM-III, 1980), the official nomenclature of the American Psychiatric Association. Specific disorders included in the chapter are major depression, alcohol abuse or dependence, cognitive impairment, schizophrenia, and phobias, assessed for the past six months. Socioeconomic status was measured by an index based on the mean of percentiles for education, occupation, and household income assessed at the time of interview.

Consistent with earlier studies, the highest rates of psychiatric disorder generally were observed among the lowest SES groups. The strongest relationships were observed regarding cognitive impairment and schizophrenia. The SES relationship was intermediate for alcohol abuse or dependence and weakest for major depression. Differences were found among the three major ethnic groups—white, African American, and Hispanic—but these differences were quite variable and were strongly influenced by SES, as well as by age and sex.

Many strengths can be attributed to results derived from large-scale epidemiologic studies such as the ECA. Perhaps the most important for psychiatric epidemiology is that it is only with a sample size as large as the ECA that the whole array of psychiatric disorders can be compared. Before the ECA it would have been impossible to compare all major psychiatric disorders at once. Standardized instrumentation also assures relative comparability across study sites, and lends a reasonable assurance of data uniformity. Furthermore, with the ECA being a carefully designed multisite study, it is difficult to refute the robustness of the results. It is unlikely that the *association* of SES and psychiatric disorder could be challenged in the future.

Although the authors are careful not to infer causality from their analyses, their social determinist position is apparent in their language as well as in their descriptive and multivariate analyses. Caution is needed in interpreting the results, since SES is measured by averaging past and current education, current occupation, and current household income. Causality may have been established in a statistical sense, but the temporal sequence has not been established. Because six-month prevalence is not the same as incidence, it is still possible that low SES could result from living with mental disorders, as described by the drift hypothesis. Cognitive impairment and schizophrenia, disorders found to be most strongly correlated with SES, are both among the most chronic disorders. Further, cognitive impairment has been known to strongly correlate with education, which in turn correlates with occupational and income attainment. Onset of schizophrenia typically occurs during adolescence, which is a critical time for obtaining occupational and educational skills. Therefore, strong correlations of these disorders with SES suggest that the prevalence cases for the past six months may include a large proportion of chronic cases.

The authors caution against forgetting the actual heterogeneity of the population considered, citing race as an example. This point leads into a discussion of an important feature of the methods, design, and results frequent in stratification studies. Scientific reductionism is reflected in Holzer's study in order to infer the most general patterns of association. For example, several components of SES, education, occupation and income, race and ethnicity, gender, age, and even psychiatric diagnosis were combined to provide summary pictures.

Multivariate analyses statistically control for confounding effects of demographics on psychiatric disorder, but at the cost of ignoring the specific context in which the association of interest is assessed. The changing situation of women provides an example of how complex it can be to interpret a single numeric SES score. Can a highly educated housewife raising young children be assumed to have the same probability of risk for psychiatric disorder, based on her household income, as her husband who has the same amount of education but *earns* that household income and may not contribute toward the 24-hour childrearing *job*? Such a context of social structure cannot be captured in the ECA dataset.

In stratification studies, specificity of context, of course, can be a focus of their analysis. Gender-specific effects of social support on mental health is the crux of Chapter 7, "Sex Differences in the Relationship between Social Support and Mental Health," by Peter C. Meyer. Numerous investigations have demonstrated the significance of social networks and social support for maintaining and restoring mental health, as well as for coping with social stress. In this chapter Meyer tests the hypothesis that sex differences in social support have an intervening effect on the stress-buffer process.

A random sample of 500 adults residing in an urban community of Switzerland was drawn for the survey. Stressful life events and chronic social stress were the main independent variables. Three outcome variables included seven items of subjective psychological symptoms, 19 items of physical and psychosomatic symptoms, and subjective overall health. Social support was measured as the sum of availability of practical and emotional support in cases of need from six types of relations. Correlational analyses and path analysis models controlling for age and education were employed.

Social support was found to be important in maintaining the health of those who were under a great deal of stress. This result indicates the interactive effect of stress and social support. Under low levels of stressful events, men appeared to feel healthier than did women. The author suggests that men are less sensitive to bad feelings and minor distress than women are. Social support had no influence on the level of psychological symptoms. However, when experiencing a high level of stressful events, women were no more likely to experience psychological symptoms than were men. Instead, gender had a significant effect on social support, which in turn alleviated psychological distress. Women appeared better able to mobilize social support when stressful events were happening to them. At the same time, women were less affected mentally by chronic burdens.

These findings suggest differences in the personal social networks of women and men. Women may have closer, more emotionally supportive relationships, and may be more forthcoming in discussing their personal problems, particularly with women friends. Women also appeared to be more affected by the problems of others than men were. Yet women evidenced greater resilience in coping with significant loss and change. The results here are consistent with other studies that focused on such severe life events as the death of spouse and divorce.

Chapter 8, "Urban/Rural Differences in the Structure and Consequences of Social Support," employs community size, which is another common structural variable. The authors, Ortega and Johnson, note that despite years of research indicating that social support is a major factor in the relationship between economic distress and depression, many questions remained regarding intervening processes. Specifically, it is unclear whether or not informal support systems are equally effective in buffering financial stress in rural and urban areas. This is particularly important where declines in the agricultural economy in many advanced countries have occurred and are occurring.

Ortega and Johnson propose two models. Their structural model postulates additive effects of community size, negative economic events, economic strain, available support on depression and actual support. The second model is considered as a cultural interpretation of community effect on depression and actual support, and assumes that the nature and strength of effects of economic conditions and support vary by community size. The authors translate the differences of these models to mathematically different models and test them using linear structural equation models, which involve sophisticated estimation techniques.

The study was based on data from telephone interviews with a representative sample of 2,500 Nebraskans in the United States. An 18-item depression scale was used as the dependent variable. This scale, while unable to identify clinically significant cases, has been considered to be a good indicator of reactions to acute social stressors. Major independent variables were measures of negative economic events, economic strain, available social support, and actual social support. Negative economic events were measured by a 12-item scale of economically stressful events; the measure of economic strain included six items asking whether or not money for a basic item of necessity was available. Social support indexes measured different types of support from social networks. Because the effect of community context cannot be assumed to be linear, an ordinal measure of community size was used, including five categories of the rural/urban continuum: rural/farm (open country), rural (population less than 2,500), towns (2,500 to 10,000), cities (10,000 to 50,000), and metropolitan areas (larger than 50,000).

The results of the study show that effects of economic strain and social support on depression, and the relationship between economic events and economic strain are conditioned by the community context. The magnitude of these community differences is not trivial, at least in a statistical sense. Thus authors conclude that results are more consistent with a cultural than a structural interpretation of the relationship between community size and depression.

Interpretation of results are not straightforward. When other variables were simultaneously controlled, Ortega and Johnson found that it was only among people living in town-size communities that negative economic events did not affect depression. The poorer economic conditions occurring in small towns did not seem to have led to poorer mental health. Likewise, actual support influenced depression among all groups except farmers, who live in the open countryside. The authors suggest that farmers, by their placing increased value on independence and self-reliance, can be prevented from effectively using the informal supports available to them. Authors state that these findings are inconsitent with any specific cultural theory and speculate on both methodological and theoretical explanations.

The scheme used by Ortega and Johnson resembles that used by Meyer in the previous chapter, although intervening mechanisms involved differ. Both attempt to clarify the stress process and effects of social support to buffer the impact of stress on psychological distress. Gender in Meyer's chapter and community size in Ortega and Johnson's chapter are used as contextual variables that modify the relationship between the source of stress and psychological distress.

The three chapters presented here, by incorporating advanced statistical techniques and elaborate research designs, allow their authors to interpret data with a greater precision than in the descriptive accounts presented in Part I. Contexts, such as race in Holzer and his associates' chapter, gender in Meyer's chapter, and community size in Ortega and Johnson's chapter are approximations of *culture* in the anthropological sense. Because these contexts and their effects are abstracted in stratification studies, the meanings of statistical results are left in the hands of authors. This fact points to certain limits to what structural analysis can accomplish. Nevertheless, their efforts place us closer to a social anthropological approach.

Stratification studies presented here are not only more familiar to American readers, but also are more typical of Western social psychiatry and related fields than of the work being done in developing nations. A major explanation is the need for research training and resources that accompany the often extensive data gathering and analysis required. Such resources often are beyond the capacity of a developing country. In the past, therefore, U.S. or World Health Organization initiatives have been almost prerequisites for conducting epidemiologic studies in developing countries. Some implications of such initiatives will be discussed more fully in the Conclusion. Suffice it to say that a relatively small-scale or inexpensive study can be utilized without sacrificing methodological rigor, as shown in both the Meyer and Ortega and Johnson chapters. Perhaps the popular perception that a good epidemiologic study must be a big study needs to be reexamined.

6

Ethnicity, Social Status, and Psychiatric Disorder in the Epidemiologic Catchment Area Survey

CHARLES E. HOLZER III, JEFFREY W. SWANSON, AND BRENT MACK SHEA

Our previous examinations of the relationship of socioeconomic status (SES) to specific psychiatric disorders using data from the National Institutes of Mental Health (NIMH) Epidemiologic Catchment Area Project (ECA) did not include results regarding race and ethnicity (Holzer, Shea et al., 1986). While at least one paper (Somervell, Leaf,

CHARLES E. HOLZER III • University of Texas Medical Branch, Galveston, Texas 77550. JEFFREY W. SWANSON • Department of Psychiatry, Duke University Medical Center, Durham, North Carolina 27710. BRENT MACK SHEA • Department of Sociology and Anthropology, Sweet Briar College, Sweet Briar, Virginia 24595.

Social Psychiatry across Cultures: Studies from North America, Asia, Europe, and Africa, edited by Rumi Kato Price, Brent Mack Shea, and Harsha N. Mookherjee. Plenum Press, New York, 1995.

Weissman, Blazer, & Bruce, 1989) has presented ECA findings separately for Hispanics and blacks, it did not explicitly address SES per
se in relation to ethnicity or race. The present chapter thus attempts
to systematically examine the joint relationship of ethnicity and SES
to psychiatric disorder.

MENTAL ILLNESS AND SOCIOECONOMIC STATUS

The relationship between mental illness and SES has been repeatedly studied over the last half-century. Since the early study by Faris
and Durham (1939), one of the first American studies to establish this
link, a number of studies have addressed the relationship between
social status and psychiatric disorder. Dohrenwend and Dohrenwend
(1969) in their review asserted that the social class relationship is one
of the best substantiated findings of psychiatric research. In a more
recent review, Neugebauer, Dohrenwend, and Dohrenwend (1980) reported that 17 of 20 studies showed higher overall rates of psychopathology in the lowest social class, with an average ratio of 2.59 between
the lowest and highest classes. Five of the six studies from the United
States showed highest rates in the lowest class, with an average ratio
of 2.4 observed when comparing lowest to highest class. For studies
outside the United States, the ratio was slightly higher at 2.7.

When class distributions were examined by type of disorder, the
psychoses had the strongest class relationship. Six out of eight studies
of psychoses reported the highest rates in the lowest social class, and
only one showed little class effect. For psychoses, the average low-to-
high class ratio was 2.1. In contrast, studies of neuroses showed little
relation to social status, with only 5 of 11 studies showing highest rates
in the lowest class.

In our previous analyses of SES in the ECA data, we confirmed
the overall inverse relationship between social class and psychiatric
disorders (Holzer, Shea et al., 1986). Two major conclusions were
drawn: First, it was evident that the association between SES and
psychiatric disorder was not a simple linear one. The greatest increase
in risk for psychiatric disorder appeared primarily in the lowest SES
category. This was consistent with earlier findings.

Second, the strength and form of the SES relationship to specific
types of disorder varied considerably. We found the highest prevalence
of schizophrenia in the very lowest SES group, with an estimated risk
of 7.9 relative to the highest SES group. For major depression, in con-

trast, the estimated risk in both the lowest and second-lowest SES groups was less than 2.0 relative to the highest SES group.

RACE AND MENTAL ILLNESS

The relationship of race or ethnicity to mental illness also has been of great interest since early treatment statistics in the segregated South. Some studies, based on samples of those treated, found no race difference in mental illness (Pasamanick, 1963; Simon, 1965). However, a number of other studies also based on treatment data concluded that there was more mental illness in blacks.

To explain equivocal findings regarding race differences, contrasting arguments focused on differing concepts of mental illness among whites and blacks, differential amounts of stress in the rural South versus the urbanized North, and biased diagnostic practices influenced either by the race of the examiner or the settings in which diagnosis or commitment proceedings took place (jail versus hospital). Parker and Kleiner (1969) found differences in prevalance among blacks depending on whether they were socialized in the North or the South. Prange and Vitols (1962) predicted that black–white differences in symptomatology would be reduced as a consequence of social and cultural change and greater urbanization.

In spite of these speculations, no solid evidence was available to substantiate ethnic differences in true rates of disorder. Dohrenwend and Dohrenwend (1969) concluded that there was no evidence for differences in disorder between whites and blacks.

A number of community surveys avoided the issue of race by excluding blacks altogether, a practice that has not entirely stopped. The Florida Health Survey was one of the early studies in the South to address the issue of race. Warheit, Holzer, and Schwab (1973) examined racial differences in depressive symptomatology. Initial findings showed blacks reporting significantly higher depressive symptomatology than whites. However, it was shown that, by controlling for SES scores, black–white differences were reduced to an insignificant level.

In further analyses of the Florida Health Survey (Warheit, Holzer, & Arey, 1975), equivalent comparisons were made using alternative symptom indices. Race differences controlling for SES remained significant for a general psychopathology measure and for a phobia measure. On the other hand, blacks reported more symptoms for an anxiety-symptom measure, an anxiety-function measure, and depression scores. Initial race differences disappeared when SES was controlled for. Thus, it appeared as though the joint effect of SES and ethnicity was different, depending on the symptom measure. It is the goal of the present analyses, therefore, to examine the relationship of SES with specific psychiatric disorders, and to determine the extent to which race or ethnic differences remain significant when SES is simultaneously controlled for.

METHODS

The Epidemiologic Catchment Area Program

The data presented here were derived from the first wave of community interviews in the five sites of the Epidemiologic Catchment Area Program (ECA). The goals and scope of this project have been discussed by Regier et al. (1984). Briefly, the ECA used a panel design with coordinated surveys of adult institutional and household resident populations at five sites: New Haven (Yale University), Baltimore (Johns Hopkins University), St. Louis (Washington University), Durham (Duke University), and Los Angeles (UCLA). At each site, 3,000 to 5,000 household residents and 400 to 500 residents of institutions (mental hospitals, nursing homes, and prisons) were interviewed.

All of the five ECA sites employed a nearly uniform interview protocol to gather information about psychiatric disorder, utilization of health and mental health services, and sociodemographic characteristics. The core of the interview used at all five sites is the Diagnostic Interview Schedule (DIS) (Robins, Helzer, Croughan, & Ratcliff, 1981), a fully structured instrument permitting lay interviewers to elicit the elements of a diagnosis, including symptoms and their severity, frequency, and distribution over time.

Diagnoses from the *Diagnostic and Statistical Manual of Mental Disorders* (DMS-III) (American Psychiatric Association, 1980) were generated by computer for various current time intervals or over the respondent's lifetime. The version of the DIS used in the present study covered alcohol abuse/dependence, anorexia, antisocial personality, bipolar disorder, cognitive impairment, drug abuse/dependence, dysthymia, major depression, obsessive–compulsive disorder, panic, phobias, schizophrenia/schizophreniform disorders, and somatization.

In addition, we also utilized a variable indicating the presence of any psychiatric disorder that combines all disorders assessed above, except phobia and cognitive impairment. Phobia was excluded because it varied excessively from site to site (Myers et al., 1984). Cognitive impairment was excluded because it is not a formal diagnosis in DSM-III terms, and because it bears a rather unique and problematic relationship to age and education.

Interviews were conducted by trained interviewers. These lay interviewers received 1 to 2 weeks of classroom training followed by field practice, and were accepted for fieldwork only after passing a test demonstrating competence with the instrument. Typically, interviews were completed in 60 to 90 minutes. The completion rates at each site ranged from 77 to 80%, with refusals accounting for a high proportion of nonresponses.

Data Analysis

Nam and Powers (U.S. Bureau of Census, 1967) developed a procedure for ranking occupations that is based on averages of percentiles for income, education, and occupation. Nam and Powers (1965, 1968, 1983) also have applied their procedure to occupational titles from the 1950, 1960, and 1970 censuses. Ford and Gehret (1984) have similarly analyzed the Public Use Sample (PUS) of the 1980 census and thus provide updated estimates of occupational status. These occupation percentile scores are designated as NAM scores in the analysis.

Percentile scores also were formed for each respondent's education and for household income and personal income when available. These percentiles were calculated from the 1980 U.S. Census *Characteristics of the Population* (U.S. Bureau of Census, 1983). Our socioeconomic status index (SESH) was then formed by averaging education, occupation, and household income percentiles. Where one or two of the three components were missing, SES was calculated as the average of the available scores. For the St. Louis ECA site, only occupation and education were available to compute the index scores.

Procedures for weighting the ECA data are described in Holzer, Spitznagel, Jordan, Timbers, Kessler, and Anthony (1985) and Kessler et al. (1985). The prevalence data in the paper have been weighted to compensate for differing probabilities of selection, and for different completion rates among demographic groups. Weighting the data in such analyses improves overall estimates of population characteristics.

Age, sex, and race are the major variables in the weighting procedures. Therefore, weighting becomes unnecessary, and even masks the true numbers and sampling variance in multivariate analysis where these variables are controlled for. Thus, multivariate models, which included age, sex, and race as control variables, were analyzed using unweighted data.

RESULTS

Sample Description

The total sample size for our analyses was 18,368. When appropriate, missing cases in specific analysis variables were dropped. Table 1 presents basic socioeconomic and demographic characteristics of the persons in the sample stratified by ethnicity. The ethnic groups were composed of persons identifying themselves as whites (67.5%), blacks (20.5%), Hispanics (8.2%), and a residual category (3.8%) containing other ethnic groups and those who did not answer the ethnicity ques-

Table 1
Sociodemographic Characteristics by Ethnicity (Weighted Percentages)

Category		White (N = 12, 053) %	Black (N = 4, 234) %	Hispanic (N = 1, 433) %
Summary SES	0–25	12.4	28.9	33.9
(SESH quartiles)	25.1–50	30.3	41.9	38.5
	50.1–75	36.6	22.4	22.5
	75.1–100	20.7	6.7	5.0
Education (years)	0–8	14.4	19.9	41.9
	9–11	15.9	27.9	19.8
	12 (HS)	30.1	29.3	19.7
	13–15	19.4	15.2	12.8
	16+	20.2	7.7	5.8
Household income[a]	0–9.9	18.7	39.1	27.9
(thousand dollars)	10–19.9	26.8	33.9	41.1
	20–34.9	33.7	19.6	20.2
	35+	20.8	7.4	10.8
NAM quartiles	0–25	16.1	36.6	38.2
	25.1–50	36.3	38.3	38.5
	50.1–75	26.0	17.3	15.4
	75.1–100	21.6	7.8	7.9
SES	Male	47.0	43.1	48.6
	Female	53.0	56.9	51.4
Age (years)	18–24	15.2	23.2	26.5
	25–44	37.3	42.0	42.3
	45–64	30.0	23.7	22.6
	65+	17.6	11.1	8.6

[a]Income data from 4 sites only.

tion. Respondents in the residual category were dropped from the logistic regression analyses because of their small numbers and the difficulty of interpreting a residual category.

The summary variable for socioeconomic status (SESH) shows that whites had a higher SES than did blacks or Hispanics. The index of the summary SES is categorized into four quartiles. Low scores represent low status, while high scores represent high status. Only 12.4% of the white respondents were in the lowest SES category, as compared to 28.9% of the blacks and 33.9% of the Hispanics. This race difference was found not only for the SES summary variable, but also for its components of education, income, and occupation (NAM). Among Hispanics, only 5.8% reported attending college, while 41.9% reported having no more than an eighth-grade education. On the other hand, blacks reported the lowest incomes, with 39.1% reporting incomes of $0 to $9,999 per year between 1980 to 1982.

Sex distributions were similar among the ethnic groups, although a slightly higher proportion of black respondents were female. Age distribution varied among ethnic groups. The white group was considerably older than the black group, and Hispanics were the youngest, having fewer elderly and more respondents in the youngest age group. The elderly were oversampled in three of the study sites with higher proportions of whites and, to a lesser degree, blacks, an effect that should be compensated for by weighting.

SES, Ethnicity, and Psychiatric Disorders

Table 2 presents the distribution of summary SES scores by age and ethnicity. A noteworthy finding is that there were higher proportions of whites than either blacks or Hispanics in the two highest SES quartiles. Not surprisingly, seniors tended to have lower SES scores than did people in the middle age groups. One further analysis showed that the relationship was somewhat stronger for males. Overall, women had lower SES scores than men, with approximately 14% of the women in each of the two youngest age groups having SES scores in the lowest category. The confounding of SES with ethnicity, age, and sex requires that these variables be controlled in subsequent analyses.

Table 3 presents percentages (rates per 100) of persons with a psychiatric disorder in the past six months by SES without additional controls. Persons with lower SES had higher rates of each disorder. This relationship appears strongest for schizophrenia and cognitive impairment. For depression, the highest rates were found in the next

Table 2
Socioeconomic Status by Age and Ethnicity[a]

Age	Race	Number	Summary SES (SESH quartiles)			
			00–25	25.1–50	50.1–75	75.1–100
18–24	White	1,176	5.6	37.3	45.1	12.0
	Black	679	20.9	51.4	24.9	2.8
	Hispanic	297	26.5	37.7	33.2	2.5
25–44	White	3,762	3.9	23.2	42.5	30.4
	Black	1,697	15.5	43.7	29.5	11.3
	Hispanic	712	31.7	37.7	23.2	7.5
45–64	White	2,711	13.2	31.6	35.2	20.0
	Black	934	39.9	40.3	15.0	4.8
	Hispanic	272	35.6	43.8	15.6	5.0
65+	White	4,434	35.3	37.2	18.9	8.6
	Black	938	73.1	18.9	6.2	1.7
	Hispanic	147	64.7	29.0	5.6	0.8
	Other	119	41.5	34.8	21.2	2.5
All	White	12,083	12.5	30.3	36.5	20.6
	Black	4,248	29.0	41.9	22.4	6.7
	Hispanic	1,428	34.1	38.3	22.6	5.0

[a]Ns are unweighted; percentages are weighted.

to lowest SES category. However, the overall inverse relationship is still observed.

Table 4 presents rates per 100 of psychiatric disorder present in the past 6 months by ethnicity. Without additional controls, there was some variation among ethnic groups. Blacks reported a somewhat higher rate of any disorder (11.9%), and substantially higher rates of

Table 3
Weighted Rates of Psychiatric Disorder by Socioeconomic Status (Per 100)[a]

Psychiatric disorder	Socioeconomic status (SESH quartiles)			
	00–25 (N = 4,300)	25.1–50 (N = 6,100)	50.1–75 (N = 5,150)	75.1–100 (N = 2,555)
Any	11.5	12.0	10.9	7.6
Alcohol	5.3	5.2	4.6	3.3
Depression[b]	2.5	3.4	2.9	1.9
Schizophrenia[c]	1.6	1.1	0.9	0.3
Phobias	12.5	10.4	7.7	5.1
Cognitive impairment	5.8	1.1	0.3	0.2

[a]Ns vary among disorders
[b]Major depressive episodes
[c]Includes schizophrenia and schizophreniform disorders

Table 4
Weighted Rates of Psychiatric Disorder by Ethnicity (per 100)[a]

	Ethnicity		
Psychiatric disorder	White (N = 11,900)	Black (N = 4,190)	Hispanic (N = 1,428)
Any	10.4	11.9	11.7
Alcohol	4.5	4.8	6.2
Depression[b]	2.8	2.9	3.1
Schizophrenia[c]	0.9	1.5	0.4
Phobias	7.9	13.7	7.7
Cognitive impairment	0.9	3.2	1.4

[a]Ns vary among disorders
[b]Major depressive episode
[c]Includes schizophrenia and schizophreniform disorders

phobias (13.7%), schizophrenia (1.5%), and cognitive impairment (3.2%). Hispanics scored highest on alcohol abuse or dependence (6.2%) and depression (3.1%).

Our further analysis indicated that uniformly higher prevalence rates of disorder occurred for younger persons and for persons of lower SES. This pattern was strong for whites and all but the oldest group of blacks, but not for Hispanics. The strong trends seen in these analyses were obscured when all age categories were combined.

Two forms of multivariate analysis were subsequently performed, which simultaneously incorporated SES, ethnicity, sex, and age. One treated all variables, including age and SES, as categorical using SAS procedure CATMOD, and a second treated age and SES as intervals through specification of them as "direct" effects in the model. The categorical analysis creates dummy variables for all but the last level of each predictor variable, so that the order of categories is ignored. The direct model uses age and SES as quantitative effects so that both the order and interval of categories are considered.

Table 5 presents regression results for any disorder (except phobia and cognitive impairment). The overall fit of the model is assessed by the significance level of the likelihood ratio on the last line of the table. The nonsignificant interaction term in the categorical model was retained for comparison with the direct model. Other two-way interaction terms were tested and discarded when found to be nonsignificant.

The categorical analysis found significant main effects of age, race, and SES. Race was present in three of the significant interaction terms. The direct-effect model had significant main effects, including race

Table 5
Sociodemographic Predictors of Any Psychiatric Disorder[b] in the Past Six Months

	Categorical			Age and SES direct		
Source	DF	Chi-square	Prob	DF	Chi-square	Prob.
Intercept	1	1,341.37	0.0001	1	0.35	0.5557
Sex	1	48.81	0.0001	1	46.24	0.0001
Age	3	94.25	0.0001	1	81.33	0.0001
Race	2	1.43	0.4884	2	23.27	0.0001
SESH	3	15.55	0.0014	1	19.88	0.0001
Sex[a] race	2	5.12	0.0771	2	6.65	0.0359
Age[a] race	6	14.72	0.0225	2	16.68	0.0002
Age[a] SESH	9	12.78	0.1727	1	5.67	0.0173
RACE4[a] SESH	6	21.70	0.0014	2	9.49	0.0087
Likelihood ratio	62	63.32	0.4295	82	159.58	0.0001

[a]Indicates interaction term
[b]Excludes phobia and cognitive impairment

and has four significant interaction terms. Other potential two-way interaction terms were not significant and were dropped from the model. This model has a significant lack of fit as indicated by the likelihood ratio, but is considerably more parsimonious than the categorical model.

CONCLUSION

In this chapter we have examined the joint relationships of ethnicity (race) and socioeconomic status (SES) with psychiatric disorder, controlling for age and sex. Clearly, while blacks and Hispanics have an increased risk of disorder due to their low status, SES by itself is not sufficient to explain all of the ethnic differences found. Although it is possible to speculate about the sources of the ethnic differences for specific disorders, to do so would go beyond the present data. We leave the present findings as an invitation to explore the extent to which ethnic differences are a consequence of the assessment methodologies, a consequence of particular stressors present differentially in the various subpopulations, or whether the differences lie in factors more closely intertwined within the subcultures of these various groups.

Although we have conducted an analysis using several large ethnic or racial categories, we should be careful not to reify these categorizations, as each is richly heterogeneous, including Northern and Southern blacks, Mexican-American and Puerto Rican Hispanics, and a polyglot of people with European and non-European ancestries.

ACKNOWLEDGMENTS. The present analysis was supported in part by NIMH grant MH44214, the Center for Cross Cultural Research at the University of Texas Medical Branch in Galveston, Texas. The Principal Investigator is Fernando M. Treviño, and Co-Principal Investigators are Charles E. Holzer and Robert E. Roberts. Data compilation for the present analysis was also supported in part by grants MH34224 and MH15783; the Epidemiological Catchment Area Program was supported by U01 MH 34224 (Yale University), U01 MH 33870 (Johns Hopkins University), U01 MH 33883 (Washington University), U01 MH 35386 (Duke University), and U01 MH 35865 (University of California/Los Angeles).

REFERENCES

American Psychiatric Association. (1980). *Diagnostic and statistical manual of mental disorders* (3rd ed.) (DSM-III). Washington, DC: Author.

Dohrenwend, B. P., & Dohrenwend, B. S. (1969). *Social status and psychological disorder: A causal inquiry.* New York: Wiley.

Faris, R. E. L., & Dunham, H. W. (1939). *Mental disorders in urban areas: An ecological study of schizophrenia and other psychoses.* Chicago: University of Chicago Press.

Ford, K., & Gehret, J. (1984). *Occupational status scores from the 1980 Census Public Use Samples.* Unpublished manuscript. Johns Hopkins University, Department of Population Dynamics, Baltimore.

Hozler, C. E., Spitznagel, E., Jordan, K., Timbers, D., Kessler, L., & Anthony, J. (1985). Sampling the household population. In W. W. Eaton & L. L. Kessler (Eds.), *Epidemiologic methods in psychiatry: The NIMH Epidemiologic Catchment Area program.* Orlando, FL: Academic Press.

Holzer, C. E., Shea, B. M., Swanson, J. W., Leaf, P. J., Myers, J. K., George, L. K., Weissman, M. M., & Bednarski, P. (1986). The increased risk for specific psychiatric disorders among persons of low socioeconomic status, evidence from the Epidemiologic Catchment Area Surveys. *American Journal of Social Psychiatry, 6,* 259–271.

Kessler, L. R., Folsom, R., Royall, R., Forsythe, A., McEvoy, L., Holzer, C., Rae, D., & Woodbury, M. (1985). Parameter and variance estimation. In W. W. Eaton & L. L. Kessler (Eds.), *Epidemiologic methods in psychiatry: The NIMH Epidemiologic Catchment Area program.* Orlando, FL: Academic Press.

Myers, J. K., Weissman, M. M., Tischler, G. L., Holzer, C. E. III, Leaf, P. J., Orvaschel, H., Anthony, J., Boyd, J. H., Burke, J. D., Kramer, M., & Stoltzman, R. (1984). Six month prevalence of psychiatric disorders in three communities: 1980–1982. *Archives of General Psychiatry, 41,* 959–967.

Nam, C. B., & Powers, M. G. (1965). Variations in socioeconomic structure by race, residence, and life cycle. *American Sociological Review, 30,* 97–103.

Nam, C. B., & Powers, M. G. (1968). Changes in the relative status level of workers in the United States, 1950–1960. *Social Forces, 47,* 158–170.

Nam, C. B., & Powers, M. G. (1983). *The socioeconomic approach to status measurement.* Houston, TX: Cap and Gown Press.

Neugebauer, D. D., Dohrenwend, B. P., & Dohrenwend, B. S. (1980). The formulation of hypotheses about the true prevalance of functional psychiatric disorders among adults in the United States. In B. P. Dohrenwend, B. S. Dohrenwend, M. S. Goulde, B. Link, R. Neugebauer, & R. Wunsch-Hitzig (Eds.), *Mental illness in the United States.* New York: Praeger.

Parker, S., & Kleiner, R. J. (1969). Social-psychological aspect of migration and mental disorder in a Negro population. *American Behavioral Science, 13,* 104.

Pasamanick, B. (1963). Some misconceptions concerning differences in the racial prevalence of mental disease. *American Journal of Orthopsychiatry, 33,* 72–86.

Prange, A. J. Jr., & Vitols, M. M. (1962). Cultural aspects of the relatively low incidence of depression in Southern Negroes. *International Journal of Social Psychiatry, 8,* 104–112.

Regier, D. A., Myers, J. K., Kramer, M., Robins, L. N., Blazer, D. G., Hough, R. L., Eaton, W. W., & Locke, B. Z. (1984). The NIMH Catchment Area Program. *Archives of General Psychiatry, 41,* 934–948.

Robins, L. N., Helzer, J. E., Croughan, J., & Ratcliff, K. S. (1981). The NIMH Diagnostic Interview Schedule: Its history, characteristics and validity. *Archives of General Psychiatry, 38,* 381–389.

Simon, R. I. (1965). Involutional psychosis in Negroes: A report and discussion of low incidence. *Archives of General Psychiatry, 13,* 48–154.

Somervell, P. D., Leaf, P. J., Weissman, M. M., Blazer, D. G., & Bruce, M. L. (1989). The prevalence of major depression in black and white adults in five United States communities. *American Journal of Epidemiology, 130,* 725–735.

U.S. Bureau of Census. (1967). *Subject reports, socioeconomic status final report* (PC 2-5C). Washington, DC: U.S. Government Printing Office.

U.S. Bureau of the Census. (1983). *Characteristics of the population. U.S. summary* (PC 80-1-A1). Washington, DC: U.S. Government Printing Office.

Warheit, G. J., Holzer, C. E., & Schwab, J. J. (1973). An analysis of social class and racial differences in depression symptomatology: A community study. *Journal of Health and Social Behavior, 14,* 291–299.

Warheit, G. J., Holzer, C. E., & Arey, S. A. (1975). Race and mental illness An epidemiologic update. *Journal of Health and Social Behavior, 16,* 243–255.

7

Sex Differences in the Relationship between Social Support and Mental Health

PETER C. MEYER

Numerous investigations have demonstrated the significance of social networks and social support for the maintenance and restoration of mental health and for coping with social stress (Aneshensel, 1992; Cohen & Syme, 1985; Gottlieb, 1981, 1983; House, Umberson, & Landis, 1988; Lin, Dean, & Ensel, 1986; Meyer & Suter, 1993). To date research has focused predominantly on the positive effects of networks, namely on social support. In many studies preventive, stress-buffering, and rehabilitative effects were demonstrated. According to the "stress-buffer hypothesis," social support is primarily of importance in main-

PETER C. MEYER • University Hospital, Culmannstr. 8 CH-8091 Zürich, Switzerland.

Social Psychiatry across Cultures: Studies from North America, Asia, Europe, and Africa, edited by Rumi Kato Price, Brent Mack Shea, and Harsha N. Mookherjee. Plenum Press, New York, 1995.

taining the health of those who are under a great deal of stress (Lin et al., 1986).

Several studies have demonstrated gender differences in the structure and function of social networks (Belle, 1987). Male participation in social networks is more "extensive" but less "intensive" than for women. While men tend to participate in more activity-focused relationships, women maintain more emotionally intimate relationships. Women benefit from a greater variety of "confiding" relationships than men, who tend to rely on one provider for emotional support exclusively, primarily their wives or girl friends. Women mobilize more social supports in time of stress and provide more frequent and more effective social support to others than men do.

Although women's social network patterns may serve them well in times of stress, a chronic imbalance of "giving and getting" often characterizes women's social roles in contrast with those of men. The wife (or female friend) normally provides a high level of support for her husband, while he often supports her less. In a nine-year follow-up study of mortality in a sample of 7,000 adults, Berkman and Syme (1979) found that marriage was much more protective for men than for women. Women, unlike men, benefited more from contact with friends and relatives and from involvement in formal and informal groups. The overall protective effects of social contact were stronger for women than for men.

We therefore expect the function of social networks for health to be different for men and for women. In this chapter we test the hypothesis that women's social networks are better social resources for coping with stress than men's networks. We assume that the negative effects of social stress for women is more efficiently buffered by the support they receive, and therefore results in fewer psychological disorders than it does for men.

METHODS

The Data

Within the framework of our research project on social networks and health, a random sample (N = 500) of adults residing in an urban community were surveyed through interviews. The sample for the statistical analysis presented here consisted of 325 Swiss citizens aged

20 to 64 years. For a detailed description of the sample and its representativity, see Meyer-Fehr & Bösch (1988).

Measures

Received social support was measured through an adapted version of the "Social Support Questionnaire" (Schaefer, Coyne, & Lazarus, 1981). Our scale of social support was the sum of practical and emotional support, which was provided by six social networks (partner, relatives, adult children, friends, colleagues at work, neighbors) in case of need. This measure of social support correlates highly with the size of the social network that has been surveyed by means of a revised and translated version of the "Social Network Index" (Berkman & Syme, 1979).

Two aspects of social stress have been surveyed: stressful life events and chronic social stress. We used a short and modified version of the German life event scale "Inventar zur Erfassung lebensverändernder Ereignisse" (ILE) (Siegrist & Dittmann, 1983), which measures not only the incidence of such events during the last two years but also their subjective significance. Chronic social stress is measured through eight items on the daily stress scale originating from five social networks (partner, relatives, children, friends, and neighbors) and from three areas of life (home, work, and health).

To evaluate the stress-buffering effects of social support, health and well-being are considered as outcomes of the stress process in our model. Two health indicators are used to measure the amount or intensity of symptoms during the last 12 months. The indicator "psychological symptoms" consists of seven items; for example, "Was it difficult for you to concentrate?" The indicator "physical symptoms" consists of the frequencies of 19 different symptoms, such as cough, headache, lack of appetite, back pain, fever, and stomachache.

Table 1 shows the mean values of the main indicators by sex. Education is an indicator for social status and is measured by the highest level of formal school education reached. Men are significantly better educated than women. As for health, women state more symptoms, but the sex difference is significant only for physical symptoms. There is no difference by sex in stressful life events. The mean chronic social stress is slightly higher for men than for women. Women receive more social support from others than men do. The last two mentioned sex differences, however, are rather weak (Eta = .12 resp. .13).

Table 1
Mean Values of Main Indicators by Sex

	Men (N = 130)	Women (N = 195)	Eta sig.
Age	39.1	42.3	.11
Education	3.38	3.03	.18[b]
Psychological symptoms	1.81	1.90	.07
Physical symptoms	1.60	1.76	.21[c]
Chronic social stress	6.68	5.74	.12[a]
Stressful life events	4.76	5.06	.03
Social support	22.1	24.1	.13[a]

Significance: F-Test Level: [a] = 5%; [b] = 1%; [c] = 0.1%

FINDINGS

We tested for sex differences in the stress-buffer hypothesis of social support. The stress-buffer hypothesis implies an interactive effect of social support on health according to the level of stress. Under high stress, social support is assumed to have an important, positive (buffering) effect, whereas it is assumed that under the condition of low stress, social support has no effect on health since there is nothing to be buffered. We took stressful life events as the main independent variable in our analysis.

To test our hypothesis, correlational analyses and path analytic models were applied separately to two subgroups of the representative general population sample (N = 500, including the elderly). The median value of the stressful life event scale was used to separate the high-stress from the low-stress group. This dichotomization was statistically useful, since the distribution of the stressful life events scale was highly skewed. In the group with low stress, the subjects experienced no or very little stress (scores in the range of 0 to 3), whereas in the group with high stress there was a large range between middle and very high stress (scores between 3 and 25).

Since it is known that high life event stress has a negative impact on health, we assumed that the members of the high-stress group had more symptoms than the ones of the low-stress group. We wondered whether this difference is sex-specific.

The results of Table 2 confirm the well-known negative association of stress with health. All groups with high stress had significantly more symptoms than the groups with low stress. It is interesting that this

Table 2
Mean Scores of Symptoms and Social Support by Level of Life Event Stress, by Sex
(M = Male, F = Female)

		Low stress	High stress	Eta sig.
Psychological symptoms	M	1.51	2.05	.43[c]
	F	1.73	2.04	.24[c]
Physical symptoms	M	1.49	1.69	.29[c]
	F	1.68	1.83	.19[b]
Social support	M	22.0	22.2	.01
	F	23.5	24.6	.07
N	M	58	72	—
	F	89	106	—

Significance, F-Test Level: [a] = 5%; [b] = 1%; [c] = 0.1%

difference is greater for men than for women. Men had significantly more psychological symptoms under high stress than under low stress (Eta = .43). For women this difference was smaller (Eta = .24). Under the condition of low stress, men had less psychological symptoms than women, but under high stress men and women reported the same amount of psychological symptoms. It seems as if stress caused more distress for men than for women, but under low stress women have more symptoms than men.

As for physical symptoms, the same pattern was seen, but sex differences were smaller. It is not surprising to find that social stress had more effects on the psyche than on the body. Generally, stress had less negative effects on women's health than on men's health. Women seem to be comparatively better balanced.

We hypothesize that this finding can be explained in part by the sex-specific function of social support: women's health is less afflicted by stress because their social support more efficiently buffers negative effects of stress than does men's social support.

Table 3 shows correlation coefficients between social support and our two health indicators. Since these health indicators measure symptoms (i.e., "bad health"), a negative correlation means the higher the support the lower the symptoms. In other words, a negative correlation is consistent with the hypothesis of positive effects of social support on health.

Only one significant correlation is found in this table. A negative correlation is evident between psychological symptoms and social support for women under high stress ($r = -.31$). This result confirms the stress-buffering effect of social support for this group. Although there is no other significant correlation, the sign in all groups under high

Table 3
Relationship (Pearson Correlation) between Social Support and Health Indicators
by Level of Life Event Stress, by Sex

		Correlation with social support	
		Low stress	High stress
Psychological symptoms	All	.04	−.20
	Men	.11	−.07
	Women	−.03	−.31^c
Physical symptoms	All	.01	−.08
	Men	.13	−.13
	Women	−.11	−.09
N	All	147	178
	Men	58	72
	Women	89	106

Level of Significance (one-tailed):
^{a} = 5%
^{b} = 1%
^{c} = 0.1%

stress is negative, which means that the direction of the relationship is in all groups consistent with the stress-buffer hypothesis. Given the criterion of high significance and strong relationships, this analysis of correlations shows that social support has a significant stress-buffering effect on the mental health of women, but no such stress-buffering effect occurs on the mental health of men and on physical health for both sexes.

In order to more closely examine the effects of other variables, we performed path analyses. Besides sex, we considered the variables of age and education and we introduced social support and the two indicators of social stress as independent variables. For our present purposes, we have limited our analysis to psychological symptoms as dependent variables. However, the same multivariate model has been applied using two other dependent health variables: physical symptoms and an indicator of the self-estimated overall state of health. The path analysis of the self-estimated health had quite similar results as on psychological symptoms; the stress-buffering effects were even stronger (Meyer-Fehr & Bösch, 1988). There is no such effect on physical symptoms, as we already indicated in the bivariate correlation analysis.

Since it is not possible to show interactive effects in a path analysis, again we make the analysis separately in the two samples with low or high levels of life event stress. Although the variation of stressful life events within these two samples is less than in the total sample, we used it as an independent variable in the path analysis, as well. We must keep in mind the fact that the two samples are defined by the level of life event stress when we evaluate the statistical effects of this variable within these two samples. These effects are much smaller than in the total sample.

Figure 1 shows the results of the path analysis in the sample with low levels of life event stress. The path coefficients shown are the standardized regression coefficients, Beta. Regression and correlation coefficients with a significance level lower than 10% are omitted. Coefficients with a weak significance of 5 to 10% are included so that comparisons between Figure 1 and Figure 2 can be made. The theoretically postulated direction of causality moves from left to right. In our model the three sociodemographic variables do not depend on any other variable but can have effects on all 4 variables standing to their right. Only the path from sex to psychological symptoms is shown because all the other paths departing from the three sociodemographic variables do not reach the significance level of 10%.

Since in the model there is no causality postulated between the three sociodemographic variables and between the two stress variables, the bivariate correlation coefficient is shown next to lines with arrows at both sides if the coefficient reaches the 10% significance level. The variable of sex has the value 1 for men and 2 for women, so that a positive relationship of any variable with sex means that women have more of the relating attribute than men. The positive path from sex to psychological symptoms (Beta = .21) means that, when controlling for all other independent variables, women have more psychological symptoms than men in the sample with low life event stress.

As expected, chronic social stress leads to more psychological symptoms. The path analysis in this sample shows no significant relationship with social support. Neither sex, age, nor education has a significant effect on social support, which itself does not influence social stress or psychological symptoms. The fact that social support has no significant influence on psychological symptoms in this sample of low stress is consistent with the stress-buffering hypothesis.

Figure 2 in comparison shows the path analysis for the sample with high levels of live event stress using the same model as that in Figure 1. Social support is connected here: there is a positive path from sex to social support and a negative path from social support to psychological symptoms. This means that women in the high-stress

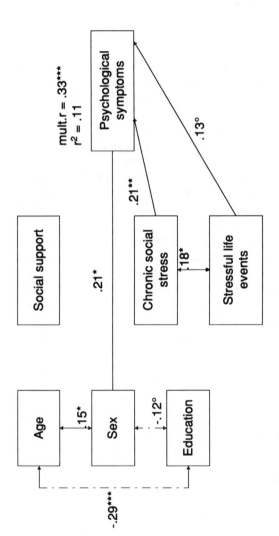

Path coefficients with a significancy under 10% are omitted.

Level of significance: ° = 10%, * = 5%, ** = 1%, *** = 0.1%

－ ‧ － : Negative relationship

⟷ : Correlation

⟶ : Path (beta coefficient)

Figure 1. The effects of sex, social support, and social stress on psychological symptoms: A path analysis. Sample with *low* level of life event stress (N = 147).

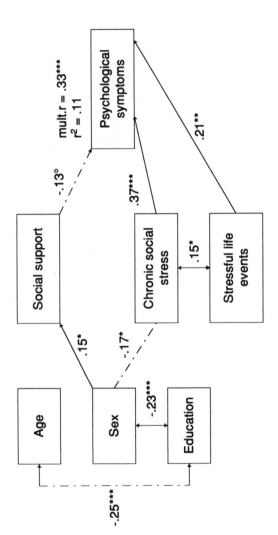

Figure 2. The effects of sex, social support, and social stress on psychological symptoms: A path analysis. Sample with *high* level of life event stress (N = 178).

group can mobilize more social support than men and that social support leads to less psychological symptoms. However, these two paths are quite weak (Beta = .15 resp. −.13).

Chronic social stress has by far the strongest effect on psychological symptoms (Beta = .37) and stressful life events increase symptoms, too (Beta = .21). Women experience less chronic social stress than men do when they are under high life event stress (Beta = −.17). Our variable of chronic social stress measures to a large extent daily stress that originates from social networks. It seems possible that partners, friends, and relatives consider the acute stress occurring for women and withhold some of the demands they usually put on them. We can speculate that this gives women a greater capacity for coping with life event stress, which in turn buffers the increase of psychological symptoms.

To summarize the results of Figure 2, it seems that there are two reasons why women are less afflicted by high life event stress. They benefit from better social support than men experience and they suffer from less chronic social stress than men do when events are stressful.

DISCUSSION

Our empirical findings are consistent with the hypothesis that the stress-buffering function of social support works better for females than for males. However, this does not mean that women are healthier under high life event stress than men. According to our data there is no sex difference in psychological and physical symptoms under conditions of high stress, whereas under conditions of low stress women experience more symptoms than men do (see Table 2).

Men seem to feel healthier than women when they are not afflicted by high social stress. This is especially true for ailments with strong subjective components, such as psychological and psychosomatic symptoms, but it is less true for clearly somatic complaints. This could be explained by sex-specific perceptions of symptoms: men are less sensitive to bad feelings and minor disorders than women are. On the other hand, men are more affected by high life event stress. They experience a much stronger increase in psychological symptoms than women do. This can partially be explained by the fact that under high stress men get less social support and they suffer from more chronic social stress than women. In any event, it seems that men are emotionally much less balanced than women when they experience high stress.

Women have more psychological symptoms than men when they are not under high social stress. It is known that women are more affected by stress, crisis, and the troubles of others. They give more social support to others than men do. This "emotional work" could be one reason for higher psychological symptoms (Wethington, McLeod, & Kessler, 1987). As mentioned above, women are generally more sensitive to psychological problems than men. This means that they have more experience in coping with crises and suffering. This might be one reason why they are less labile and better balanced even when they experience high life event stress.

Another reason could be the fact that they are more involved in emotional, intimate, and confiding relationships than men. In good times this can mean that a woman is more affected by the problems of others. In bad times, however, it means that she can better rely on others than a man can. Our results are consistent with the already mentioned finding of Berkman and Syme (1979) that the protective effects of social contacts are stronger for women than for men.

The evidence of our study is consistent with the research of Wethington and Kessler (1986), who found that the stress-buffering effect of social support is somewhat stronger among women than men. However, our findings seem to be inconsistent with some research on coping with stressors. Pearlin and Schooler (1978) argued that the coping strategies typically used by women tend to be somewhat less effective in buffering the psychological effects of life stress than the strategies used by men. Wethington, McLeod, and Kessler (1987) argue that the image of pervasive female vulnerability to stressors was only established by results from event studies that used a single, aggregated measure of life-event exposure.

Evidence supporting our findings that women have advantages in buffering high life event stress can be found in studies of people who have experienced the same type of life event. Women adjust better than men do to the death of a spouse (Stroebe & Stroebe, 1983) and cope more adequately than men with the long-term aftermath of separation and divorce (Wallerstein & Kelly, 1980). Women seem to cope better than men with serious events that occur to their partner whereas men are less affected by events that occur to more distant relationships. Women have wider fields of concerns than men with respsect to individuals significant to them and they are more likely to be emotionally distressed by the problems of other people and are more likely to provide help (Wethington, McLeod, & Kessler, 1987).

The evidence of sex differences in the stress-buffering effects of social support seem to be influenced by the specific measurement of

life-event exposure. If the measurement stresses grave events that occurred to very close network members, women are probably better
copers than men. If we use a measurement of life events which considers more distant relationships as well, it could be that women are less
effective in buffering the effects of social stress than men. Further
research is needed that considers sex-specific involvement in social
networks and sex differences in the perception, the meaning and the
effects of different types of life events.

ACKNOWLEDGMENT.This research was supported by the Swiss National
Foundation, grants 3.972-0.85 and 3.912-0.88.

REFERENCES

Aneshensel, C. S. (1992). Social stress: Theory and research. *Annual Review of Sociology,*
    18, 15–38.
Belle, D. (1987). Gender differences in the social moderators of stress. In R. C. Barnett,
    L. Biener, & G. K. Baruch (Eds.), *Gender and stress* (pp. 257–277). New York: Free Press.
Berkman, L. F., & Syme, L. (1979). Social networks, host resistance, and mortality: A
    nine-year follow-up study of Alameda county residents. *American Journal of Epidemi-
    ology, 109,* 186–204.
Cohen, S., & Syme, S. L. (Eds.). (1985). *Social support and health.* New York: Academic Press.
Gottlieb, B. H. (Ed.). (1981). *Social networks and social support.* London: Sage.
Gottlieb, B. H. (1983). *Social support strategies: Guidelines for mental health practice.* Beverly
    Hills, CA: Sage.
House, J. S., Umberson, D., & Landis, K. R. (1988). Structures and processes of social
    support. *Annual Review of Sociology, 14,* 293–318.
Lin, N., Dean, A., & Ensel, W. (Eds.). (1986). *Social support, life events, and depression.*
    Orlando, FL: Academic Press.
Meyer, P. C., & Suter, C. (1993). Soziale netze und unterstützung. In: W. Weiss (Ed.),
    Gesundheit in der Schweiz. Zürich: Seismo.
Meyer-Fehr, P., & Bösch, J. (1988). Gesundheitseffekte sozialer unterstützung und sozialer
    belastung bei der einheimischen bevölkerung und bei immigranten. *Medizinsoziolo-
    gie, 2,* 151–167.
Pearlin, L. I., & Schooler, C. (1978). The structure of coping. *Journal of Health and Social
    Behavior, 19,* 2–21.
Schaefer, C., Coyne, J. C., & Lazarus, R. S. (1981). The health-related functions of social
    support. *Journal of Behavioral Medicine, 4,* 381–406.
Siegrist, J., & Dittmann, K. H. (1983). Inventar zur Erfassung lebensverändernder Ereig-
    nisse (ILE). In: J. Allmendinger, P. Schmidt, & B. Wegener. *ZUMA-Handbuch sozial-
    wissenschaftlicher skalen.* Bonn, Germany: Informationszentrum Sozialwissenschaften.
Stroebe, M. S., & Stroebe, W. (1983). Who suffers more? Sex differences in health risks
    of the widowed. *Psychological Bulletin, 93,* 279–301.
Wallerstein, J., & Kelly, J. (1980). *Surviving the breakup.* New York: Basic Books.

Wethington, E., & Kessler, R. C. (1986). Perceived support, received support, and adjustment to stressful life events. *Journal of Health and Social Behavior, 27,* 78–89.
Wethington, E., McLeod, J. D., & Kessler, R. C. (1987). The importance of life events for explaining sex differences in psychological distress. In: R. C. Barnett, L. Biener, & G. K. Baruch (Eds.), *Gender and stress* (pp. 144–156). New York: Free Press.

8

Urban/Rural Differences in the Structure and Consequences of Social Support

SUZANNE T. ORTEGA AND DAVID R. JOHNSON

Perhaps no pattern in psychiatric epidemiology has received as much attention as the inverse relationship between socioeconomic variables such as poverty and unemployment, and mental disorder. Nevertheless, the relationship between economic and psychological distress can scarcely be described as invariant; the extensive literature on social support makes it clear that an individual's coping resources modify the relationship between negative economic events and mental health.

SUZANNE T. ORTEGA and DAVID R. JOHNSON • Department of Sociology, University of Nebraska—Lincoln, Lincoln, Nebraska 68588-0324.

Social Psychiatry across Cultures: Studies from North America, Asia, Europe, and Africa, edited by Rumi Kato Price, Brent Mack Shea, and Harsha N. Mookherjee. Plenum Press, New York, 1995.

Curiously, researchers on coping and support have not made a sustained effort to identify cultural or structural variables that may further impact the association between economic and social resources and psychological well-being.

Research which focuses on rural/urban variation in psychological distress, and which compares the rural and urban toll of economic marginality, may provide one vehicle for understanding the structural and cultural contexts that shape the stress process. In this chapter, we first assess the extent to which there are rural/urban differences in depression. We then test a structural and a cultural interpretation of the relationship between community size and mental health.

THE RURAL/URBAN CONTEXT

Compared with our knowledge of urban problems, relatively little is known about the quality of life and mental health of rural Americans (Keller and Murray, 1982). In fact, it was not until the farm crisis of the mid-1980s that sociologists began to pay serious attention to rural mental health issues. A number of studies of farm families by rural mental health professionals appeared during this period. Most pointed to a pattern of increased depression, alcohol abuse, and domestic violence as concomitants of a declining agricultural economy (Barrett, 1987; Beeson & Johnson, 1987; Garfinkel, Hoberman, Parsons, & Wallker, 1986; Hartig & Ertl, 1986; Heffernan & Heffernan, 1985; Mermelstein & Sundet, 1986; Schulman & Armstrong, 1989). Many of these studies, however, were based on rural-only samples and focused on the challenge that the farm crisis presented to mental health services.

It is not surprising then that few studies have specifically addressed questions regarding the etiological significance of community size. When such questions were raised, community size was seen as a specific indicator of poor economic circumstances. Few studies have investigated the possibility that community size might have effects on mental health independent of those associated with economic conditions. Fewer still have explored the possibility that community size modifies the relationship between economic conditions and psychosocial impairment. As a result, it remains unclear what independent or contextual effects place of residence actually has on psychological well-being.

There are a number of theoretical reasons to expect that community size will influence mental health. Indeed, virtually every factor suggested by the literature as either an explanation or a mediator of the relationship between the economy and mental health is likely to vary across the rural/urban continuum. First, community size may affect depression primarily because it is associated with differing probabilities of experiencing negative economic events, that is, unfavorable economic experiences occurring at a particular point in time. Consistent with the farm crisis literature, this hypothesis would suggest higher rates of depression in rural than in urban communities. On the other hand, given the problems of the urban underclass, it may be that urban residents have higher levels of chronic economic strain or distress.

Although economic events and economic strains are related, they are not coterminous. As Pearlin et al. (1981) point out, both are related to depression. Negative economic events and economic strain may also be related to community size, but not necessarily in the same direction.

In addition, community size may affect depression because it is associated with different levels of social support—both the amount of support perceived to be available and the amount of support actually received. Both types of support appear to influence depression, either directly or by buffering the effects of stressful events (Wethington & Kessler, 1986). Again, both may vary across the rural/urban continuum. For instance, rural areas may provide a more supportive, humane environment than cities, therefore, rural residents may have better mental health than urban residents. On the other hand, negative attitudes toward mental health may make rural residents more hesitant to ask for support when they have stress-related problems (Bachrach, 1981; Wright & Rosenblatt, 1987). For this reason, psychological consequences of negative economic events and of economic strain may actually be exacerbated in farming or other small communities.

As shown in Figure 1, using a modified model of the stress process used by Pearlin et al. (1981), we test two basic explanations for the effect of community size on the economic distress/mental health equation. The first is basically a structural interpretation; it is an additive model which implies that the effects of community size on mental health is a simple function of community differences with respect to negative economic events, economic strain, actual social support, and perceived availability of support. Negative economic events, for example, are hypothesized to have direct effects on economic strain. Additive effects are represented by the black arrows in Figure 1.

Even though a structural interpretation of rural/urban differences is basically additive, such an interpretation does not preclude the possibility that some of the independent variables will interact. Previous

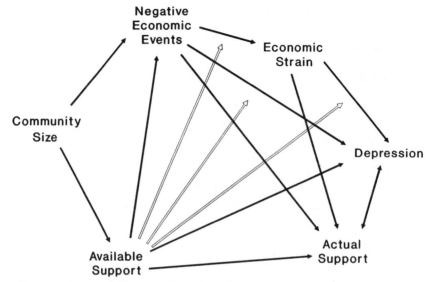

Figure 1. Economic distress model with residence subgroups.

research clearly suggests that social support buffers the effects of economic hardship on depression. Interaction or buffering effects are depicted by the white arrows in our model. Negative economic events, such as the loss of a job, may reduce available support. At the same time, the presence of strong support may actually prevent the occurrence of some other negative events.

Depression and actual support are likely to be correlated (represented by a two-headed arrow), but the causal direction is ambiguous (Ross & Mirowsky, 1989).

In the first stage of our analysis, the basic model outlined in Figure 1 is tested. In the second stage of the analysis, a cultural interpretation of community effects is assessed. Although a structural model may include interaction terms, a cultural model is fundamentally interactive; that is, it is one which posits that the nature and strength of the relationships among independent and dependent variables will vary across the rural/urban continuum. Consequently, analysis focuses on estimating the extent to which the same model parameters fit the data on communities of different sizes.

STUDY DESIGN

The Sample

Data for this study come from a 1989 telephone survey of a representative sample of 2,500 Nebraskans 18 years of age and older living in households. Of them, 1,500 responded to the second wave of a panel originally interviewed in 1986 as part of Nebraska Annual Social Indicators Survey (NASIS). The additional 1,000 respondents were selected in 1989 through random digit dialing including an enriched sample drawn from nonmetropolitan counties.

Measures

The dependent variable for this study is an 18-item depression scale, abridged from the 50-item symptom and impairment scale developed by Warheit (Schwab, Bell, Warheit, & Schwab, 1979). The scale has been used in a number of community surveys, including the 1986 Nebraska survey, and has been validated (Warheit, Bell, Schwab, & Buhl, 1986). Although symptom scales of the type used here do not identify cases of psychiatric disorder, they are generally considered to be good indicators of reactions to acute social stressors (Weissman, Myers, & Rosset, 1986).

Our major independent variables are negative economic events, economic strain, available social support, and actual social support. The index of negative economic events based on the work of Tausig (1982), is a 12-item scale measuring economically stressful events experienced in the past 3 years. It includes items such as being laid off or fired, taking a job that was not commensurate with one's skills, taking a second job to make ends meet, putting off unaffordable medical care, getting behind on bills, and loan foreclosures.

Our measure of economic strain includes 6 of 9 items in Pearlin et al.'s (1981) economic strain index plus one additional question regarding medical insurance. These items ask whether the respondent had enough money for basic necessities such as housing, food, medical care, clothing, and to pay bills.

The two measures of social support used in this study are both derived from the 40-item Interpersonal Support Evaluation List developed by Cohen, Mermelstein, Karmarck, and Hoberman (1985). Items were selected to represent each of the four domains of social support and resources that Cohen and McKay (1984) identified as important: tangible, appraisal, self-esteem, and belonging. The Available Social Support index is a 13-item scale measuring different types of support perceived to be available through existing support networks. The Actual Social Support index is an 8-item scale that tallies the different types of support actually received in the last year.

Community size is a contextual variable in our model. Although most research to date has relied on a simple metropolitan versus non-metropolitan distinction, Wagenfeld and Ozarin (1982) have argued that studies of rural mental health must take into account the heterogeneity of rural life. Consequently, we have used an ordinal measure of community size that reflects five categories of the rural/urban continuum: rural/farm, rural (open country and towns with populations of less than 2,500), towns (populations of 2,500 to 10,000), cities (populations from 10,000 to 50,000), and metropolitan areas (populations larger than 50,000).

The effects of respondent's age, education, and gender were controlled for in all analyses because they were correlated with both depression and community size.

METHODS

General linear structural equation model techniques were used to estimate the parameters in the stress model and test for additive and interactive effects of community size on depression. All variables except community size and gender were treated as interval level measures. Community size was entered into the equations as a set of dummy variables. No significant curvilinear relations were detected for the relationships among the interval level variables. Several variables exhibited skewed distributions (Available Support, Economic Strain, Actual Support). The highly skewed distributions of two variables were corrected by setting high scores to constants. An examination of the distributions of these variables within the five community size groups after the skewness correction found no outliers that would unduly bias the magnitude of their effects.

FINDINGS

The relationship between community size and each of the independent variables is presented in Table 1. In the first column, we present

Table 1
The Relationship of Community Size to Measures of Economic Distress and
Social Support (Unadjusted and Adjusted for Age, Education, and Gender)

| | | Unadjusted (U) and adjusted (A) mean scores | | | | | | | |
| | | Economic events | | Economic strain | | Perceived support | | Actual support | |
	N	U	A	U	A	U	A	U	A
Rural-farm	461	1.20	1.17	.54	.49	12.19	12.22	3.90	3.90
Rural	845	1.40	1.47	.68	.69	11.99	12.05	3.81	3.92
Town	288	1.30	1.33	.69	.70	11.91	11.93	3.92	3.96
City	342	1.31	1.25	.64	.63	12.04	11.98	4.07	3.97
Metro	577	1.15	1.09	.64	.66	12.02	11.92	4.18	4.06
Eta		.06		.05		.06		.07	
Beta			.10^c		.07^a		.08^b		.03

^{a}p<.05
^{b}p<.01
^{c}p<.001

the mean value for each variable before any controls have been introduced. In the second column, we present the mean values for each
community type, controlling for age, education, and gender.

Community size is significantly related to both measures of economic distress. Note, however, that in the late 1980s, individuals living
in rural areas and small towns, not farmers or urban residents, experienced the greatest negative economic events. This finding is consistent
with the view that the ripple effects of the farm crisis are now largely
being felt in small-town America (Hoyt & Redmond, 1989). Even
though the financial position of farmers appeared to be improving,
residents of small rural communities are significantly more likely than
their urban counterparts to have experienced economic distress. The
same general pattern holds for economic strain.

Farmers were experiencing significantly less economic strain than
other rural residents; however, metropolitan residents reported nearly
as much economic strain as individuals living in small rural communities. This pattern of results may suggest that economic hardship is of
a more enduring, long-term nature in metropolitan communities, a
view consistent with the literature on the underclass. Alternatively,
community differences in some other variable, social support being an
example, may lead to differences in the relationship between negative
economic events and economic strain.

The pattern of community differences is less consistent for the
two social support variables than it is for the two economic variables.
Community size is significantly related to the perceived availability of

social support. Although the differences are not large, farmers have significantly higher levels of perceived support than any other group. However, community size is not significantly related to the actual amount of support received.

These findings are consistent with the view that the rural subculture may prevent individuals from actually capitalizing on their support networks. The findings also suggest that rural/urban differences in social support may not be sufficient to insulate rural and small-town residents from the adverse consequences of economic distress.

After controlling for age, education, and gender (see column 2), the relationship between economic hardship and community size became somewhat more pronounced. Farmers and metropolitan residents reported substantially fewer negative economic events than other groups; persons living in rural communities reported substantially more. The rural group and the small-town residents also reported the highest levels of economic strain. Although rural nonfarm residents appeared to have a higher level of perceived social support than individuals living in larger communities, rural advantage was most clear-cut for farmers. On the other hand, farmers and other rural residents reported they received less support than other groups.

Table 2 presents the relationship between community size and depression. The unadjusted correlation (column 1) indicates there are no significant differences in depression across the rural/urban continuum. Furthermore, there are no significant differences when age, education, and gender are controlled for (column 2). There is little support for a simple additive model of the relationship between community size and depression (columns 3 through 5). Indeed, community size does not appear to have any direct effect on depression. This finding stands in marked contrast to results from the 1986 wave of our panel, which showed a pattern of significantly elevated depression among farmers (Beeson & Johnson, 1987). Differences between the findings for farmers in 1986 and 1989 stem, in part, from an improved farm economy. However, increased levels of economic hardship among other rural residents has not been accompanied by increased depression. Social support does not appear to be an intervening variable, at least in any simple additive fashion.

Is there evidence that economic events affect depression differently for residents of different sized communities? First, a model of the stress process was estimated separately for each of the five community size groups. The model used here is the same as the one presented in Figure 1 without community size.

Table 2
The Relationship of Community Size to Depression, Unadjusted, and Adjusted for Age, Education, Gender, Measures of Social Support, and Measures of Economic Distress

			Mean depression scores			
	N	Unadjusted	Adjusted for age, education and gender	Adjusted for social support[a]	Adjusted for economic distress[a]	Adjusted for social support and economic distress[a]
Rural-farm	471	13.16	12.92	13.38	13.28	13.56
Rural	860	13.45	13.18	13.44	12.99	13.27
Town	292	13.62	13.51	13.44	13.37	13.38
City	346	13.53	13.45	13.48	13.49	13.53
Metro	578	13.55	13.75	13.50	13.80	13.62
Eta		.02				
Beta			.04	.01	.04	.02

[a]Also includes adjustment for age, education, and gender.

Next, this basic stress model was fitted to the data from the five residence groups under the assumption that the process works the same within each of the groups. This was accomplished by the use of the multiple group procedure in LISREL VII (Jöreskog & Sörbom, 1988). Age, educational attainment, and gender were also included as controls.

The model estimates were constrained so that the structural coefficients represented by the directional arrows in Figure 1 were invariant across residence groups. Multiplicative terms to test for the interaction effects proposed in the model were included, following a procedure suggested by Smith and Sasaki (1979). Because the mean values differed between the subgroups, we subtracted the grand mean for the variable. This greatly reduced the correlation among the additive and interactive components, but did not eliminate it.

If the stress process is invariant among the groups, then the chi-square test of the fit of the expected and actual covariance matrices should be nonsignificant. The chi-square from this model was statistically significant at the .01 level, however, rejecting the hypothesis that the stress process was invariant between the groups. An examination of the modification indices produced for this model suggested that the Available Support by Economic Strain interaction term had no significant effect in any of the five groups. Therefore, this interaction term was excluded from further analyses.

To identify the groups that were contributing to the lack of fit, alternative models were tested by freeing the constraints on the parame-

128

Suzanne T. Ortega and David R. Johnson

ters in different sets of residence groups. The fit of the model is considered to be significantly improved if the difference of the chi-square values between the previous and alternative models becomes insignificant. The alternative model for the farm and town groups resulted in a significant improvement in the fit when the coefficients in these groups were freed to vary. A model with freed coefficients for these groups provided an acceptable fit (p = .398) and is examined in more detail.

The three sets of structural coefficients from this model are arrayed in Table 3. Coefficients for farm and town samples are presented sepa-

Table 3
Coefficients from Structural Equations Model Fit to Farm, Town, and Other (Metro, City, and Rural Combined) Subgroups

| Independent variables | Dependent variables | | | | | |
| | Economic strain | | Actual support | | Depression | |
	b	beta	b	beta	b	beta
Age						
Other	−.005	−.081[a]	−.026	−.246[a]	.014	−.035
Town	−.006	−.096	−.030	−.241[a]	.001	.003
Farm	−.009	−.122[a]	−.022	−.203[a]	−.006	−.014
Education						
Other	−.039	−.091[a]	.045	.062[a]	−.146	−.053[a]
Town	−.059	−.137[a]	.113	.127[a]	−.064	−.023
Farm	−.079	−.148[a]	.030	.037	.012	.004
Gender						
Other	.171	.072[a]	.566	.142[a]	.847	.056[a]
Town	.100	.051	.634	.157[a]	.207	.017
Farm	.084	.032	.538	.134[a]	.861	.059
Negative economic events						
Other	.348	.485[a]	.070	.058	.491	.108[a]
Farm	.301	.502[a]	.186	.150[a]	.904	.236[a]
Town	.345	.435[a]	.162	.134	.207	.047
Available						
Other	−.167	−.207[a]	.171	.125[a]	−1.407	−.272[a]
Farm	−.089	−.111[a]	.087	.053	− .392	−.273[a]
Town	−.191	−.213[a]	.206	.151	−2.027	−.408[a]
Available support × economic events						
Other	−.060	−.138[a]	.042	.058	−.207	−.074[a]
Farm	−.028	−.061	−.037	−.039	−.106	−.036
Town	−.131	−.283[a]	−.103	−.146[a]	−.099	−.039
Economic strain						
Other			.154	.092[a]	1.561	.245[a]
Farm			.038	.018	.445	.070
Town			.099	.065	1.481	.268[a]

[a]Statistically significant at the .01 level

Table 4
Partial (Residual) Correlation between Actual Support and Depression for the
Five Residence Size Subgroups

Residence subgroup	Partial correlation
Farm	.098
Rural	.176[a]
Town	.183[a]
City	.259[a]
Metro	.180[a]

[a]Statistically significant at the .01 level

rately; a single coefficient is estimated for the combined Metro, City, and Rural subsamples, since the hypothesis of common coefficients for these groups was not rejected. Because relationships were not assumed to be invariant in the models tested, Table 4 presents the correlations between the residuals of Depression and Actual Support for each of the five community types.

How does the economic distress process among farmers differ from the other groups? As shown in Table 3, the major differences were associated with Economic Strain and the buffering effect of Available Support. Among farmers, Economic Strain had no significant effect on Depression, whereas in the other four groups there was a strong and significant effect. For all groups, Available Support significantly reduced Economic Strain, but the magnitude of this effect for farmers was less than half of that found in the other residence samples. Negative Economic Events had the strongest direct effect on depression for farmers. This stronger effect reflected in part the weak intervening role of Economic Strain on Depression among farmers. The total effect of Negative Economic Events on Depression (the direct effect plus the indirect effect through Economic Strain) was similar in all groups.

One final difference is shown in Table 4. The farm sample is the only one in which Actual Support and Depression was not significantly related. Note also that the strongest relationship between Actual Support and Depression was found among respondents living in the city areas.

The Town sample also deviated from the other groups, but the patterns observed here are quite different from those found for farmers. The most apparent difference is that in the towns, the buffering process of Available Support on the effect of Negative Economic Events on Economic Strain was the strongest. The availability of support also had the strongest effect on reducing depression, while the direct effect of

Negative Economic Events on Depression was nonsignificant. Finally, while the relationship is modest, a valuable support also serves to buffer the effects of negative economic events on actual support. This was the only residence group where this interaction was statistically significant. These findings suggest that available support serves a more important role in the stress process among town residents than it does among residents in communities in other categories.

DISCUSSION

Results from this study are more consistent with a cultural than a structural interpretation of rural/urban differences in depression. Although all independent variables in our basic model are related to depression and to each other in a way consistent with previous research, they neither explain nor suppress the relationship between community type and depression. Indeed, in contrast to findings from the mid-1980s, rural residents no longer appear to be any more depressed than individuals living in larger communities. In part, this is a function of an improved agricultural economy. However, the poorer economic conditions in small towns does not seem to have resulted in poorer mental health of their residents. The question, of course, is why. Data do not suggest any simple additive explanation.

Instead, results suggest an interactive model; the stress process appears to operate differently in different types of communities. The effects of economic strain and social support on depression and the relationship between economic events and economic strain are clearly conditioned by the community context, and the magnitude of these community differences is not trivial. For example, the effect of available support on economic strain among farm households is less than half the magnitude found among the towns ($-.12$ versus $-.28$, Table 3).

The most straightforward interpretation for community interaction effects appears to be cultural. However, it is possible that some additional, unmeasured variables are producing the findings reported here.

While we believe that our categorization of community types is a marked improvement over the simple nonmetropolitan versus metropolitan distinction used in much of the literature, refinements in the rural/urban measure are still needed. The rural nonfarm category, for instance, includes rural suburbs and very small rural towns. Our failure to find a significant difference for rural communities may simply reflect the very different economic and social support experiences of suburbanites versus traditional small-town residents. Clearly, future research must take this issue into account.

Further specification of informal social support measures and the addition of formal support indicators may also give a clearer indication of how structural variables can explain community effects on mental health. Nevertheless, our findings suggest that cultural factors will also be involved.

It is possible that failure to find a relationship between economic strain and depression for farmers, in contrast to the relationships found for residents of the other four community types, is methodological. Our measure of economic strain may simply not be valid for farmers. Because negative economic events is related to economic strain in approximately the same fashion for all communities, we do not believe that this is the case. It appears likely, then, that it is the meaning or the social–psychological significance of economic strain that varies across communities rather than its causes. This is consistent with a cultural hypothesis.

The relatively weaker effects of social support on the depression of farm residents may also be indicative of cultural differences. The correlation between the perceived availability of support and actual support is smaller for farmers than for other groups. Farmers are the only group that shows no effects of actual support on depression. These findings are consistent with the view that the value placed on independence and self-reliance can prevent farmers from making effective use of the informal supports potentially available to them.

Cultural differences presumably also account for the finding that available social support has a much stronger effect on depression for people living in the town communities than it does for all other groups. However, this pattern does not fit easily with any conventional theory of rural/urban differences in values or life-styles.

Our findings seem generally consistent with a cultural interpretation of rural/urban differences. At the same time, they are inconsistent with any specific cultural theory. Further inspection of our data indicates that variables such as self-reliance, locus of control, and willingness to ask for social support may provide direct measures of the cultural elements presumed to vary across communities and to impact on the economic distress/depression relationship.

Acknowledgments. This research was supported in part by Grant R01-MH44317-01 from the National Institute of Mental Health.

REFERENCES

Bachrach, L. L. (1981). *Human services in rural areas: An analytic review* (Human Services Monograph Series No. 22). Rockville, MD: Project SHARE.

Barrett, J. (1987). *Mending a broken heartland: Community response to the farm crisis.* Alexandria, VA: Capital Publications.

Beeson, P. G., & Johnson, D. R. (1987). *A panel study of change (1981–1986) in rural mental health status: Effects of the rural crisis.* Paper presented at the National Conference on Mental Health Statistics, Denver, Colorado.

Cohen, S., & McKay, G. (1984). Social support, stress and the buffering hypothesis: A theoretical analysis. In A. Baum, S. E. Taylor, & J. E. Singer (Eds.), *Handbook of psychology and health* (Vol. 4, pp. 253–267). Hillsdale, NJ: Erlbaum.

Cohen, S., Mermelstein, R., Karmarck, T., & Hoberman, H. (1985). Measuring the functional components of social support. In I. Sarason & B. Sarason (Eds.), *Social support: Theory, research and applications.* Dordrecht, The Netherlands: Martinus Nijhoff.

Garfinkel, B. D., Hoberman, H., Parsons, J., & Wallker, J. (1986). The prevalence of depression and suicide attempts in rural Minnesota youth. Preliminary Report. Unpublished manuscript.

Hartig, P., & Ertl, C. (1986). Nebraska's public sector mental health outpatient services: A utilization study. Nebraska Department of Public Institutions, Office of Planning, Lincoln, NE. Unpublished report.

Heffernan, W. D., & Heffernan, J. B. (1985). Testimony prepared for a Hearing of the Joint Economic Committee of the Congress of the United States. Washington, DC, September 17.

Hoyt, D. R., & Redmond, C. (1989). *Depression among the rural elderly.* Paper presented at the Annual Meetings of the Midwest Sociological Society, St. Louis, Missouri.

Jöreskog, K. G., & Sörbom, D. (1988). *LISREL 7: A guide to the program and applications.* Chicago: SPSS.

Keller, P. A., & Murray, J. D. (1982). Rural mental health: An overview of the issues. In P. A. Keller & J. D. Murray (Eds.), *Handbook of rural community mental health.* New York: Human Sciences.

Mermelstein, H., & Sundet, P. A. (1986). Rural community mental health centers' response to the farm crisis. *Human Services in the Rural Environment, 10,* 21–26.

Pearlin, L. I., Menaghan, E. G., Lieberman, M. A., & Mullan, J. T. (1981). The stress process. *The Journal of Health and Social Behavior, 22,* 337–356.

Ross, C. E., & Mirowski, J. (1989). Explaining the social patterns of depression: Control and problem-solving—or support and talking? *Journal of Health and Social Behavior, 30,* 206–219.

Schulman, M. D., & Armstrong, P. S. (1989). The farm crisis: An analysis of social psychological distress among North Carolina farm operators. *American Journal of Community Psychology, 17,* 423–441.

Schwab, J. J., Bell, R. A., Warheit, G. J., & Schwab, R. B. (1979). *Social order and mental health.* New York: Brunner/Mazel.

Smith, K. W., & Sasaki, M. S. (1979). Decreasing multicollinearity: A method for models with multiplicative functions. *Sociological Methods and Research, 8,* 35–56.

Tausig, M. (1982). Measuring life events. *Journal of Health and Social Behavior, 23,* 52–64.

Wagenfeld, M., & Ozarin, L. (1982). Serving the under served through rural mental health programs. In H. C. Schulberg & M. Killea (Eds.), *The modern practice of community mental health.* San Francisco: Jossey-Bass.

Warheit, G. J., Bell, R. A., Schwab, J. J., & Buhl, J. (1986). An epidemiological assessment of mental health problems in the southeastern United States. In M. Weissman, J. K. Myers, & C. Ross (Eds.), *Community surveys of psychiatric disorders.* New Brunswick, NJ: Rutgers University Press.

Weissman, M. M., Myers, J. K., & Ross, C. (1986). Community studies in psychiatric epidemiology: An introduction. In M. Weissman, J. Myers, & C. Ross (Eds.), *Community surveys of psychiatric disorders*. New Brunswick, NJ: Rutgers University Press.

Wethington, E., & Kessler, R. C. (1986). Perceived support, received support, and adjustment to stressful life events. *Journal of Health and Social Behavior, 27*, 78–89.

Wright, S. E., & Rosenblatt, P. C. (1987). Isolation and farm loss: Why neighbors may not be supportive. *Family Relations, 36*, 391–395.

III

Specificity and Universality

Social psychiatry makes a major contribution to the field of mental health and illness by working to derive broad generalizations from local observations in human experience with society. The task of generalization is onerous, whether approached from a cultural or a biological perspective. Certainly efforts extended in developing consistent psychiatric disease classification, such as in the *Diagnostic and Statistical Manual of Mental Disorders* and the *International Classification of Diseases*, reflect both the benefits and difficulties encountered when attempting to approximate universality in mental illness.

A tendency to dichotomize between the Western world as the conveyor of fixed methods on the one hand, and developing countries as moving at various speeds toward incorporating Western paradigms on the other, misses the complexities within which social psychiatry must work. Determining an appropriate research approach is the key to finding meaningful results. It is by asking the right questions that we find the right answers. A research design that discounts cultural specificity is unlikely to yield results informative about it.

At issue is not only the efficacy of establishing rigorous psychiatric and mental health concepts appropriate for all cultures accessing the field. The additional possibility exists that cultural differences in life course, social structures and constraints, world views, resources, and so on, could mask fundamental consistencies in etiology, to the extent that a theoretical universality becomes almost irrelevant for developing effective treatment and prevention strategies. The same etiological rootstock thus may produce diverse fruit.

An integration of the two major research orientations described
in this volume, the anthropologic and epidemiologic/sociologic points
of view, may be brought to bear in social psychiatry. The three chapters
presented in Part III, while not to be considered definitive examples
of the disciplinary synthesis called for, may offer some directions for
alternative approaches in balancing the local with the universal, and
the individual with the social.

Chapter 9, "Afro-Surinamese Ethnopsychiatry: A Transcultural
Approach," introduces an Afro-Surinamese disease classification system developed by Charles Wooding, a Dutch clinician who claims that
a knowledge of disease concepts retained by the indigenous sufferers
is necessary for successful treatment.

Under Dutch rule, Suriname was a heterodox area comprising
groups of African Surinamese Creoles, native Indians, European descendants, and East Indian migrants. Migration of the Surinamese,
especially East Indians, to the Netherlands after independence, during
the mid- to late 1970s, confronted practitioners of orthodox Western
medicine with individuals who firmly attributed selected medical problems to supernatural causes. The author has extensively studied the
culture and religion, *Winti,* of the Surinamese Creoles for over 20 years,
using techniques of participant observation and in-depth interviews
with healers and patients. This chapter analyzes the Afro-Surinamese
cultural perception of disease and illness, and the therapeutic techniques of Surinamese folk healers.

Wooding's goal has been to develop a transcultural model, based
upon an understanding of the Afro-Surinamese ethnopsychiatric
model, which he believes would enable European doctors to treat their
Surinamese patients more effectively. His familiarity with the symptom
terminology and classification scheme of Western psychiatry afforded
him insights into indigenous beliefs about causes of psychiatric symptoms. Through this insight, Wooding developed an etiological classification scheme that he claimed was consistent with that perceived by
Surinamese patients. While he often refers to the appropriateness of
considering some symptoms in Western psychiatric terms, his approach
for treatment diverges in the therapies he has devised to rid Afro-
Surinamese patients of underlying etiological forces they believe are
operating on them.

The chapter, abridged from Wooding's original writing, describes
the case study of a female client (of Indian and Chinese descent) who
experienced strange fits of paralysis and pain, accompanied by ghostly
visions. Neither traditional healers from Suriname, nor Dutch doctors,

had been able to relieve her troubles. The patient and her husband both were convinced a metaphysical source was causing her illness, although the patient admitted such a source was illogical, and hard to believe.

The client's life history was first investigated through in-depth interviews, her dreams and visions were then analyzed. A combination of spoken-word magic and magic concoctions cured her paralysis and visions for several months. When she had a severe relapse, presenting somewhat different symptoms, Wooding employed techniques drawn from Afro-Surinamese ritual magic to exorcise the evil spirit the sufferer believed was the underlying cause of her illness. This approach apparently led to complete remission; she was symptom-free 3 years after her treatment. Unfortunately, his case study approach leaves a lingering doubt about the generalizability of his model or the therapies used.

The belief in evil magic plays a central role in Afro-Surinamese ethnopsychiatry. Evil magic can incapacitate an Afro-Surinamese person, even to the extent that death can result from the destructive physical results of severe anxiety and depression. A strong belief in the neutralizing effect of powerful countermagic can stop the process of physiological disintegration and promote healing in the body of the patient. Wooding agrees with the patient's Dutch psychiatrists that her symptoms were psychosomatic. The patient herself expressed conflicted feelings about the inability of her Western psychiatrists to cure her, and doubted that her problems could arise from a supernatural source. Nevertheless, alleviation of her symptoms required the therapist's convincing her that he was capable of performing the appropriate treatment for her ills. Since she had already consulted with a traditional Afro-Surinamese healer without relief being obtained, Wooding's success is all the more noteworthy.

The cultural and ethnic plurality of Dutch society, similar to that found in many Western nations, demands an awareness of the problems that alternative perceptions of disease and medical practice pose to Western therapies. One response lies in interdisciplinary cooperation in the field of transcultural ethnopsychiatry, and the construction of alternative methods of treatment for each population group of the particular society.

It is of interest to note that Wooding considers that Surinamers' perceptions of their problems as being the effect of magic is part of the process of adaptation to Dutch society. The incorporation of white European and Indian Hindi figures into his patient's visions draws upon the gamut of Surinamese societal hierarchy, extending beyond remnants of African culture into the world the patient faced after emigration to the largely urban Netherlands. Wooding's ethnopsychiatric model perhaps can be understood best within the context of social change and ethnic conflict confronting the patient as she attempted to make sense of the strangeness and familiarity of her adopted surroundings.

In Chapter 10, "Family Composition, Birth Order, and Gender of Mexican Children in Psychological Treatment," Harry Martin and his colleagues begin with hypotheses developed in the 1950s by Mexican researchers. However, they apply the Western idea of gender conflict to their aim of understanding the effect of birth order and household structure on children's psychiatric problems.

The authors describe the traditional Mexican family structure as being strongly founded on paternal authority and male preference. The arrival of a girl as the first-born child is considered unfortunate, impugning the father's masculinity and exacting a long-term emotional and economic burden on the family. Gender themes are further complicated by the presence of a grandmother in the household, with attending tensions produced by conflict between mother and grandmother as generational differences are expressed. While the strain of being a female child can be found elsewhere, the authors noted that the tendency is unusually strong in traditional Mexican culture.

The authors posit that given this background a differential effect on mental health should be observed in Mexican children in terms of gender, birth order, household structure, in particular, presence of grandmother. They hypothesize that girls in treatment would have a greater probability than boys of being from extended family households, of being firstborn, of having a grandmother present in their extended family households, and of being firstborn girls with grandmothers in the household. The chapter, in essence, attempts to test the hypothesis that the mental health of firstborn females is at greater risk than that of firstborn males because traditional Mexican culture emphasizes the value of the first child being male.

A random sample of children and adolescents who received psychological treatment between 1980 and 1984 at a mental health facility in Monterrey, Mexico was drawn for the study. The 154 patients for whom data were analyzed averaged 9.5 years of age.

The results generally supported three of the four hypotheses. Females in treatment were more often from extended households than were males, were more often firstborn children, and were more often from households with live-in grandmothers. However, only the last difference was statistically significant.

These results only partially address the question of the effect family structure has on the Mexican family. Nevertheless, such evidence of a gender-specific negative influence associated with a culture's traditional values underscores how insight into cultural-specific context can serve to refine epidemiologic concerns such as the effect of gender inequality on mental health. The image of a girl entrapped by conflict between mother and grandmother may be somewhat counterintuitive to people accustomed to the daily life of a nuclear family. On the other hand, those raised in an extended family household perhaps would see that such intergenerational tensions may not be unique to Mexican families.

Extended family structures, like tribal kinship structures, allow preservation of traditional values and customs. In the United States, at least, extended families sometimes exist in the vacuum of stable nuclear families, perhaps as a way to consolidate resources, or in some senses, as an option to placing grandchildren in foster care. Such a transformation of the meanings and function of the extended family in some societies indicates our ability to take advantage of traditional ways of living to meet new challenges brought in from structural changes in society at large. If Martin's and his colleagues' finding about the negative effect of a live-in grandmother lends a lesson about the traditional pattern of extended family structures in Mexico, perhaps American society might be able to find ways to alleviate its effect when such a family composition structure becomes prevalent again. Martin's findings suggest that an additional extended family member might prove to be a significant protective factor, if three generations of women, grandmother, mother, and female child, are to live within one household.

In the final chapter of Part III, "Protective Factors for Drug Abuse: A Prospectus for a Japanese–U.S. Epidemiologic Study," Price and her colleagues present a more overtly cross-cultural proposal. Their prospectus begins by contrasting the history of drug abuse patterns in Japan and the United States as a way of demonstrating the impact of sociocultural factors on the prevalence and trend of drug use and abuse between the two societies. Measures of childhood psychopathology are compared across countries, leading into the formulation of a heuristic model that integrates developmental psychopathology and environmental factors. The authors then present hypotheses on culturally unique factors protective against conduct problems and substance abuse. The chapter concludes with a proposal for a five-phase cross-cultural study aimed at explicating risk and protective factors.

Their model, linking early temperament to childhood and adolescent conduct problems to adult antisocial personality, with attendant drug and alcohol abuse, derives largely from American research. The authors state three working hypotheses to identify culturally unique factors protective against conduct problems and their pathway to substance abuse, making the point that it is necessary to study a culture in which problems have not reached at endemic level in order to readily identify protective factors. Prevention measures can be developed by experimentally introducing the identified protective factors into a prevention design suitable for the society experiencing endemic problems.

The authors plan first to reanalyze existing large-scale cross-cultural epidemiological databases from the United States, Canada, Taiwan, Korea, and New Zealand. They then propose to review existing literature on childhood conduct problems among native Japanese, Japanese Hawaiians, and Japanese Americans in California, and to review literature relating to protective factors of substance use and abuse in Japan and America. Finally, after a pilot instrumentation phase, a cross-sectional study of Japanese and U.S. children and adolescents at two sites will be conducted via structured interviews.

The train of thought in this chapter is one in which the existing conceptual model is adapted as a beginning point; however, it is actual working hypotheses that express specificity of sociocultural effects on the manifestation of the disease concepts. Research is designed to be progressive so new findings of cross-cultural difference can be incorporated into the reexamination of the model as well as design of the adjacent phase.

As previously expressed, a concern pertinent to cross-cultural research is the dilemma presented by the need for a study protocol to be well defined before funding can be obtained, while pertinent cross-cultural work must have been performed already in order to design an effective and culturally sensitive protocol. Unfortunately, the kind of design for cross-cultural work presented in this chapter, though it seems reasonable, could often face considerable scrutiny in the atmosphere of financial constraints currently seen in grant funding.

A tendency for Western researchers to take too definitive a lead in designing cross-cultural studies, or a tendency for non-Western researchers to defer too readily to Western colleagues, could have a potentially unwelcome effect on research outcomes. The authors seem to suggest that it is only through researchers familiar with indigenous cultures, working on an equal footing with Western researchers, that valid cross-cultural concepts will be derived. Such collaboration would appear to be needed in order to reformulate working hypotheses specific to the societies under study, to derive appropriate measures, and to interpret results that make sense to the indigenous people. What is prescribed extends well beyond accurate translation and suitable presentation of Western paradigms for application elsewhere. Integral conceptualizations appropriate to the cultures to be considered would appear to be required for meaningful, if not universal, results.

9

Afro-Surinamese Ethnopsychiatry

A Transcultural Approach

Charles J. Wooding

INTRODUCTION TO THE RESEARCH PROBLEM

Shortly before and after the political independence of Suriname in 1975, migration to the Netherlands increased significantly and the practitioners of orthodox medicine were confronted, more than in the past, with individuals who attributed their problems to supernatural causes. These people complained that their disorders were diagnosed from a biomedical viewpoint and treated with biomedicine while this kind of therapy was not always necessary and effective.

Psychic and psychosomatic problems can be treated according to folk or popular healing models that belong to the broad field known

Charles J. Wooding • Postbox 16202, 25000 BE Den Haag, The Netherlands.

Social Psychiatry across Cultures: Studies from North America, Asia, Europe, and Africa, edited by Rumi Kato Price, Brent Mack Shea, and Harsha N. Mookherjee. Plenum Press, New York, 1995.

as ethnomedicine, which can be defined as "the way human groups handle disease and illness in the light of their cultural perspective" (Fabrega, 1982, p. 301). When the Surinamers migrated to the Netherlands, some took with them their perceptions of disease and illness, and their own folk models for treatment. Disorders ascribed to metaphysical entities have always been treated in Suriname by traditional or popular healers. Some of these healers have moved to the Netherlands where they practice a form of psychotherapy or psychiatry that I will call ethnopsychiatry. The belief in metaphysical pathogenic agents, and anxiety about and fear of them, play a key role in this system. This contrasts greatly with biomedical paradigms.

Ethnopsychiatry is a relatively new branch of anthropology, and it constitutes a reality with the same ambiguous contours as medical anthropology (Bibeau, 1982) concerning the perception of functional disorders and their treatment in folk healing models. It demands an inter- or multidisciplinary approach with inputs from anthropology, psychology, psychiatry, psychotherapy, and medicine in order to reach a better understanding of disease and illness and their treatment. These academic disciplines are imperative if we want to make cross-cultural comparisons with the folk perception of disease and the factors involved in the psychotherapeutic relationship between folk healers and their clients.

The paradigms of the metaphysically oriented ethnomedical systems clash with those of orthodox medicine, but their efficacy in solving mental problems "involving sociocultural, ritualistic, and psychological ramifications has been long recognized" (Ademuwagun, 1979, p. 166). People make use of them because they have been sanctioned by the cultural traditions that offered people knowledge of how to deal with sickness.

This knowledge is the combination of three sets of factors, according to Young (1979). He distinguishes between (1) technological factors consisting of interpretative schemes such as language, material apparatus, and the necessary skills to use it; (2) technophenomenological factors consisting of appearances of sickness and efficacy, that is, the results of applying technological factors to aspects of the material world; and (3) social relations that produce distinctive forms of knowledge. The cultural tradition is reflected in these factors, and they are, in fact, the product of the society's level of development. In the Afro-Surinamese ethnomedical systems, the technophenomenological factors supply folk healers with rituals that serve as the technical armament, and they are also applied in the Netherlands where there is access to more sophisticated forms of medical treatment.

The practitioners and consumers of Afro-Surinamese ethnopsychiatry do not consider the psychiatric, psychotherapeutic, or psychological aspects of the so-called supernaturally caused disorders. A vast majority of them do not even know that these disciplines might bring relief. The popular healers often boast that they are able to cure all sorts of functional disorders that are beyond the expertise of specialists of orthodox medicine. However, questions have not been asked about the extent to which Afro-Surinamese ethnopsychiatry contributes to the cure of functional disorders attributed to magic, how much disorders are culture-bound and therefore incompatible with a Western nosological system, and which variables are involved in the therapeutic relationship between the folk healer and his clients.

I shall answer the following questions in this chapter.

1. What is the Afro-Surinamese cultural perception of disease and illness?
2. What are the therapeutic techniques of the folk healers?
3. Can we construct and successfully apply a transcultural model based on profound knowledge of the inner workings of the Afro-Surinamese ethnopsychiatric model?

The point of view presented here is that of a therapeutic anthropologist who applied the ethnomethodological approach to collect the data.

The data have been collected with techniques of participant observation and in-depth interviews with healers and patients. The basic proposition is that health, disease, and illness, as well as therapy, depend on how they are perceived in a specific cultural context which, in the case of the Afro-Surinamese ethnomedical system, is the supernatural world of spirits. The system's inner working has been studied systematically and coded. The basic variables of the therapeutic system and the healing methods have been established in the in-depth interviews.

I have studied *Winti*, the cultural and traditional religion of the Creoles extensively for more than 20 years, and I have treated Surinamese patients in the Netherlands who could not be treated adequately by specialists of orthodox medicine. The patients were of the opinion that their problems were not understood and wrongly diagnosed by the medical doctors. Working with them made me aware of a clash between the Afro-Surinamese perception of disease and illness and that of Western medicine.

Much of my data on the cosmological and ethnomedical aspects of Winti has been published in my books *Winti: Een Afroamericaanse Godsdienst in Suriname* (*Winti: An Afro American Religion in Suriname*) (1972), and in the English version entitled *Evolving Culture: A Cross-Cultural Study of Suriname, West Africa, and the Caribbean* (1981). These books and other works (e.g., Wooding, 1984) represent the first systematic studies of the traditional religion of the Creoles.

AFRO-SURINAMESE ETHNOPSYCHIATRY

In order to facilitate a systematic introduction to Afro-Surinamese ethnopsychiatry and the disease theory that related to the traditional religion of Winti, I shall divide my discussion into two broad aspects: the conceptual and the operational.

The Conceptual Aspect

The world and all things in it are dominated by a magicoreligious force called *srama* or *obeah* that is conceived as omnipotent, omnipenetrable, and omnianimating. It is the essence of all supernatural beings and living things, all of which share in it to varying degrees.

The cosmos and the earth are inhabited by supernatural beings, deities, who live in one of the following four pantheons of sky, water, earth, and forest. Each pantheon is headed by a chief deity, but the Mother Goddess of the Earth is the chief of all the deities, and they are her children. *Srama* or *obeah* is the magical power of the Creator who shared some of it among the deities. Deities are anthropomorphous entities who can materialize themselves by means of their magical power so as to be seen by a human being. If they do not want to be seen, but still be noticed by man, they will create a sensation that can be perceived in an extrasensory way.

This magicoreligion's potency is considered to be the source of life to which all life returns after death and from where reincarnation takes place. In Afro-Surinamese psychology, man is the incarnation of two supernatural beings. These are the supernatural parents, *djodjo*, of the individual, to whom they have given a bisexual soul, *akra*. The gender of the person is the same as that of the supernatural parent who, therefore, possesses and dominates his or her soul. In this way, the individual's soul is integrated into the metaphysical world and equipped with magic. The supernatural parents grant prosperity and sanity to their human child. His or her body is subordinate to magical stimuli and other influences from the supernatural world and these are conceptualized as Good or Evil, Health or Sickness. The soul and the supernatural parents communicate with each other, usually during sleep through the agency of dreams.

All disorders have a metaphysical cause, either magical or spellbound and ethereal. A magical or spellbound disorder is cast on a person by an evil supernatural being who has been asked by someone to do so. An ethereal disease or disorder is cast on a person directly by a supernatural entity of its own free will. Those who may do so are the supernatural parents, the ghosts of ancestors who founded the extended family or clan, and the deities these founding ancestors brought with them to Suriname.

Because of the close relationship between a supernatural parent and his or her human child, the former can take the latter into possession. This is also possible by a deity who is the guardian of a human being. One example is a folk healer, *bonuman*, who is accustomed to being possessed by his or her god(s). The person ceases during the state of possession by a supernatural entity to be a human being and becomes the entity who has entered into his or her body; the soul of the individual and the supernatural being merge and that explains why a person is not aware of what has happened while possession was occurring.

THE OPERATIONAL ASPECT

The operational aspect deals with the application of methods and techniques by a healer. The methods and techniques are the conceptual tools of folk or traditional healers by which means they attempt to heal disorders to which metaphysical causes have been ascribed. They function at the grass-root's level of society as ethnopsychiatrists, that is to say, ethnopsychotherapists who base their therapeutic diagnoses on the metaphysical doctrine that supplies the answer to the question of who caused the illness. In other words, the people who consult the healers already have a supernatural explanation for their problems, and they find it confirmed in the healer's diagnoses. Since both ethnopsychotherapist and clients have internalized the social norms and cultural values of the society in which they grew up, there is no cultural barrier between the two.

The bonuman will usually be possessed by one of his guardian spirits, or obeah, who diagnoses the cause of the client's disorder and prescribes the therapy. His function is socially sanctioned, and his expertise is derived from the supernatural being who uses his body as a vehicle. When we examine the diagnoses of the folk healers, they always indicate one of the following causes: (1) problems between the soul of the patient and a supernatural parent; (2) problems between the patient and an ancestral ghost; (3) problems between the patient and his or her family deities; (4) an evil spirit or deity of a low rank; or (5) evil magic. These five causes guide both the therapist and the patient in their attempts to alleviate the disease. In the diagnosis, the client finds confirmation of suspicions concerning the cause of his or her problems.

The process of turning to a traditional healer would usually be (1) recognition of being sick; (2) the inability of medical doctors, who are specialists of orthodox medicine, to find the cause or causes of the problem; and (3) dreams indicating a metaphysical cause.

Dreams are one of the most important criteria for judging whether the cause of an illness or a social problem is metaphysical or not. Dreams, therefore, can be considered as a means of self-diagnosis since they indicate how the problem started, and in some cases, what kind of therapy should be applied.

Diseases are divided into organic and supernatural or metaphysical according to the cause. Organic diseases have a cause that can be explained rationally and established empirically, as is generally the case with injuries, infirmities of old age, and fractures. They are treated by a Western-trained medical doctor and often, too, with home remedies.

The causes of metaphysical disease and illness have been discussed in this chapter. To this category belong schizophrenia, stress, and phobias when diagnoses have indicated that they have been inflicted on the patient by means of evil magic. The same applies to some organic disorders that cannot be cured when Western medicine is applied, for example the sores of diabetes patients. This may sound strange, but some Creoles who have sores that do not respond to treatment with Western medicine interpret this as the effect of black magic.

THE ETIOLOGY OF DISORDERS: DISEASES WITH A METAPHYSICAL CAUSE

Afro-Surinamese ethnopsychiatry belongs to the category that Tseng and Hsu (1979) have termed the supernaturally oriented healing systems. People believe that a disease has either a natural or a supernatural cause, which makes the disease theory a dualistic one (Conco, 1979.) This dual theory is expressed in two classes of disorders known as *gado-siki* (God's diseases) or *datra-siki* (doctor's diseases), and *doti-skin* (dirty skin) or *siki fu dungru kondre* (diseases of the supernatural world).

Doctor's diseases are all the disorders with natural causes, including the problems of old age. They are perceived as organic disorders and treated with herbal medicine by those who cannot afford the fees of medical doctors or when there is no access to one. This class of diseases includes psychiatric conditions that are treated with biomedicine.

The second class of disorders are functional disorders ascribed to supernatural causes when Western biomedicine is not effective. They are treated by popular healers. Table 1 describes the etiology of disorders based on the supernatural disease theory and shows the disease categories, the agents that cause them, the accompanying symptoms, and the therapeutic techniques.

Although Afro-Surinamese ethnomedicine recognizes two classes of disorders, it is not always possible to make a sharp distinction between organic and functional disorders, both of which can have a supernatural cause. For example, when a disorder with a clearly natural cause cannot be cured, this raises doubts on the part of the sufferer or his relative and social milieu. The organic disorder then is suspected to be of supernatural origin despite its apparently natural cause. The individual may have stepped on a nail and, if the injury lasts for months and a cure by neither home remedies nor biomedicine proves to be effective, it is attributed to malevolent magic, thus carrying the problem into the supernatural sphere.

Table 1
Etiology of Disorders

Categories	Caused by	Symptoms	Therapy
I. Nengre-siki			
1. Kra fjofjo or Doti skin	Individual's soul; supernatural parents	Apathy, weariness, tiny black pimples, barrenness, being unsuccessful in life	Propitiation rites, purification baths, sacrificial feasts and meals, magical concoctions
2. Jorka fjofjo	Ancestral ghosts	Cold shivers, crooked and stiff fingers, sudden death of relatives, nasal speech, rolling of the eyeballs when death is near	Propitiation rites, purification baths, animal sacrifices, ritual meals and dancing, magical concoctions
3. Winti-fjofjo	Hereditary deities of the extended family	Barrenness, asocial behavior, sudden death of relatives, phantom pregnancy, inexplicable pains and leprosy, tuberculosis	Propitiation rites, purification baths, ritual meals and dancing, magical concoctions, sacrifices of animals and jewels
II. Kroi Tai Akra	All forms of evil magic	Apathy, melancholy, depression, unwitting actions, zombification, implicit obedience, being under petticoat government	Propitiation rites, purification baths, ritual meals, magical concoctions, amulets
III. Ogri ai	The magical power of an individual	Restlessness, crying, fever, vomiting, diarrhea, emaciation, rolling eyeballs when death is near	Propitiation rites, purification baths, amulets

Table 1 *(Continued)*

Categories	Caused by	Symptoms	Therapy
IV. Wisi	Magical spells, malevolent magic from ghosts: Bakru, heby-anu	Accidental death and lethal accidents, sudden illness or death, severe pains and spasms, sores, ulcers, psychosomatic complaints, phobia, paralyzed limbs, leprosy, schizophrenia, sudden contraction of the musculature when death is near	Conjuration rites, purification baths, countermagic, magical concoctions; often also ritual meals and drinks, jewels, amulets

The disease categories I to IV in Table 1 are all supernaturally caused. Nevertheless, they differ according to the pathogenic agent and the nature of the stimulus involved. When speaking of the nature of the stimulus, one distinguishes whether the magical potency was executed automatically or by spell. All metaphysical entities, to whom an individual is attached through birth by being descended from ancestors of an extended lineage, as well as the child of supernatural parents, can punish him automatically whenever they decide to do so. They are the only ones who are entitled to do that and the disease can be called ethereal.

Other forms of sickness take place by means of magical spells in which an evil spirit is requested to cast malevolent magic upon an individual, and in this case, the disorder is known as a magical disease. Diseases with a supernatural cause then are divided into two subcategories: ethereal (I and III) and magical (II and IV).

1. Fjofjo: Diseases with a metaphysical cause are called *nengre siki* (negro disease) by the Creoles. The folk healers, however, speak of *fjofjo*, of which there are the following three kinds, depending on the cause. All the categories of fjofjo are related to social norms and cultural values that foster cohesion between individuals and within a social collectivity.

2. *Kroi Tai Akra:* This name means under petticoat government. it is believed that the soul of the partner can be bound magically by

adding magic to his or her food and drink. The person becomes a pawn of the partner but is not aware of the situation.

3. *Ogri-ai:* This is the evil eye, caused by the evil of a person's visual faculty projected at a victim whose personal magic is weaker. The victims are usually babies and young children.

4. *Wisi:* Wisi is evil magic, which is conveyed in different ways but always with the help of evil spirits and gnomes (*bakru*). One particular type of black magic is *heby-anu* (heavy hand), in which a touch from a treated hand will cause death or submission to the will of the aggressor. Wisi is accompanied by many symptoms and illnesses, the majority which are psychosomatic. Anxiety brought about by black magic results in death or paralysis.

ANALYSIS OF THE ETIOLOGY OF DISORDERS

These four categories of disorders with a supernatural cause are coded in terms that do not correspond with the nosology of functional disorders within orthodox medicine. These categories and their corresponding symptoms reveal what Frank (1961) described as "the close interplay of assumptive systems and emotional states and the intimate relation of both health and illness" (p. 36). However, the symptoms presented within the disease categories are known to orthodox medicine.

In the Afro-Surinamese ethnopsychiatric paradigm, there is no sharp distinction between the organic and the functional, which are fused into a single metaphysical category. This lack of duality, considered to be the basic fundamental theory of traditional African medicine, can be clearly seen in the symptoms ascribed to the disorder category Wisi. In other words, a continuum exists between body and mind, and this is established by the metaphysical conception of the all-embracing magicoreligious force, known as srama or obeah.

The combined symptomatic and etiological approaches, shown in Table 1, give a clear understanding of the range of functional disorders known in Afro-Surinamese ethnopsychiatry. The table shows that some symptoms (e.g., somatic complaints) are found in more than one category and have a common source, which is magic. Bibeau (1982) calls the principle leading to the establishment of these links in disease etiology the principle of resemblance. He sees this principle of resemblance as a demonstration of what has been termed iconic thinking, which means that "people are simply establishing links between things belonging to different realms of reality on the basis of one element they have in common" (p. 59).

Among the symptoms, some are related to social norms and cultural values, such as having no success in life, asocial behavior, implicit obedience, and being under petticoat government. They are conceived of as punishments for breaking moral rules set by ancestral spirits and ghosts who are the custodians of the moral order of society. Here, again, we see that the dualist theory cannot be applied absolutely and that it extends via the metaphysical to the social world.

The disease categories and their respective symptoms are the basic variables of the Afro-Surinamese ethnopsychiatric model. They are the conceptual aspects of the model the folk healer will use in diagnosis. The symptoms, however, will influence neither diagnosis nor therapy because the healer will concentrate on the pathogenic agent and name the disease.

THE TRANSCULTURAL APPROACH

Transcultural, in this context, means the application of techniques pertaining to Afro-Surinamese ethnopsychiatry. Such application may be interpreted as ethnopsychotherapy in combination with psychosocial or in-depth interviews, and dream analysis by a therapist who is not a folk healer (ethnotherapist).

The case study described here is an example of such a psychotherapeutic intervention (Wooding, 1983). The case study shows the effects of a strong belief in the supernatural causation of functional disorders. It is an amalgam of psychosomatic Western psychiatry and medical science with Afro-Surinamese metaphysics. The therapeutic intervention demonstrates what may be called therapeutic anthropology.

Case Study: Paralysis and Voodoo Death

The client was a married woman with a Hindustani mother and Chinese father. She had moved to the Netherlands years before, and was familiar with ethnopsychotherapy from having consulted various folk healers who could not treat her adequately and heal her problems. She nevertheless believed in the supernatural cause of her disorders because (1) the diagnosis of one of these ethnotherapists had revealed that her birth was surrounded by mystery (family troubles at the time, a difficult delivery); (2) the mystery had been kept a secret but was told to her by her mother when confronted with the healer's diagnosis; (3) her dreams indicated a magical cause; (4) one folk healer, who was living in a city far away, had noticed during a ritual he was performing that something horrible had taken place in her house; and (5) phantoms were waylaying her and one of them had even whipped her.

Two of the phantoms, an English lady and a pallbearer, had told her that she would die. In Afro-Surinamese culture, the symbols of burial and the pallbearer are interpreted as messages that somebody will die. In this case, that person was the patient herself, but it could have meant someone else. The patient still had hopes of living although the English lady was pressing her to give in. Her will to stay alive offered resistance to the menaces of the phantoms.

Her symptoms had occurred over several years and included paralysis of her arms and legs, fainting spells, severe pain, and extreme fatigue. Her husband said she would sometimes scream and rave. Both described hearing strange noises in their house and seeing door knobs turning with no one there. Once the woman was beaten by a Creole man who suddenly appeared in the room. The husband said that he heard her scream and that upon running into the room he found red welts on her face.

She had consulted a Western psychiatrist, her general practitioner, a neurologist, and a gynecologist. No physical causes for her symptoms were found. The conclusion was that all her symptoms were psychosomatic. Her condition had deteriorated recently, leading to hospitalization.

Shortly before she left the hospital, her husband had called me requesting me to help her. He said he had heard that I had cured a relative of a cousin's wife. He said he feared his wife was going to die. His fears had been aggravated after his wife confirmed that the phantoms would come back once she was at home and that she would finally give in on her birthday.

She came to see me with her husband. She and her husband gave their histories. I gave her a drink that I told her would keep her on her feet. I said the concoction contained strong countermagic, that the phantoms would not come back, and that the pains would gradually disappear.

Two months later the woman returned alone to see me. She said she had not seen the evil spirits any more. There was a slow but steady improvement in her health. On occasions when paralysis returned, application of the concoction I gave her had brought relief.

In this meeting, she described her frustrations about her illness, because her psychiatrist and other medical people had not found out what was troubling her. She also said she had not been as frank with medical personnel in the hospital as she had been with me. Her experience in the hospital left her feeling ignored, discriminated against, and alienated. She said she had not been informed of test results, and generally was not treated well. She wondered if there was a physical cause for her trouble and if the doctors were withholding the information from her. She also said she did not believe in black magic but if it was the cause of her suffering she should educate her children about the possibility of such things.

I told her that the doctors would diagnose and cure any medical-biological condition she had. I noted she had experienced improvements in her condition, and that if any continuing pains were the result of black magic, they would disappear within 2 weeks.

Three weeks later my client came to tell me she was completely cured. However, 2 months later I received an urgent request from the husband to come to their house because his wife was very ill again. This time she had been in a stupor for nearly a week. Administration of a traditional Surinamese mixture from a ritual object produced the effect of awakening her. She presented the aspect of possession by an evil spirit, which said that I would not be able to drive it out and that it intended to kill the woman.

The spirit identified itself as an evil *jorka* (the ghost of a dead man or woman) from a grave in Suriname. It had been sent to kill someone else in Amsterdam but my client happened to be the first person to come to the spot where it was waiting.

I prepared a purification bath according to traditional requirements and, after giving the spirit a drink as it requested, ordered it to return to its sender without harming the woman or her family. It argued with me, saying it could not because the sender had strong countermagic. I showed it a ritual object used by Surinamese ethnotherapists. It then responded with terror and said it would leave if I gave it a *paiman* (payment, expiatory sacrifice), since it could not return without fulfilling its obligation. I gave it a glass of water and ordered it to drink. While it drank I poured some of the concoction I had given the woman to cure her earlier on her head, neck, and shoulders.

The evil spirit smashed the glass to the floor. The woman's body made a brief violent shudder, relaxed, and the woman looked around as in a daze and asked me what I was doing there. She was again cured.

Three years after these experiences the woman was in excellent
health and has not had any further symptoms.

Analysis of the Techniques Used in the Case Study

The medical specialists were right when they said that this client's
illness and ailments were psychosomatic. Their medicine did not help
because they were not able to remove the magical cause that the patient
had ascribed to her problems, whereas the so-called concoction had a
definite healing effect. When I told her that the concoction contained
strong countermagic, I put into practice my assumption that the inhibi-
tion of a magical cause must be removed with a strong kind of magic,
so linking the medicine to the cultural perception of the patient. When,
in January 1980, she was slowly dying through the effects of evil magic,
I again cured her with techniques pertaining to her world view and
her perception of the disorder.

This case study is one of the most interesting concerning those
patients of mine who have ascribed the causes of their disorders to
metaphysical matters. It demonstrates how a treatment based on one
medical paradigm can depend on a treatment based on another paradigm. The missing link in all the treatments given to this patient was
the one that related her problems to her cultural perception. I have
called my approach transcultural, being a combination of Afro-Surinamese ethnopsychiatry, in-depth interviews, and dream interpretation.

What we also see in this case study is that the patient had consulted
various folk healers who were not successful in their therapies. Many
of my other clients have had therapies from several traditional healers
who could not help them, and in some cases, the problems had been
made even worse by them.

The Afro-Surinamese ethnopsychiatric model has similarities with
other non-Western therapeutic models, one of which is the metaphysical cause of disorders. Conco (1979) makes the following remark about
these systems:

> On the whole, we could generalize and say that indigenous tribal
> society has or had an all-embracing, supernatural or metaphysical
> theory of disease. Gelfand, while acknowledging regional differ-
> ences in Africa, records that "running throughout all these re-
> searches, we notice a basic pattern and a basic philosophy. It is
> obvious that the traditional African believes firstly, that disease is
> caused by a spirit or supernatural agency; and secondly, that many

illnesses can be alleviated or even cured by the administration of one of many remedies found in nature. (p. 61)

The most important characteristic of these models is their concentration on the supernatural world of deities and ancestral spirits, which functions as a suprasocial and supra-moral plane to regulate human behavior. In this conception, frictions in social relationships, functional disorders, and all kinds of diseases are ascribed to metaphysical causes. In this respect, orthodox medicine cannot help, and the patients have to consult a folk healer, who is expert in matters concerning the metaphysical world.

The folk healer's diagnosis very often confirms the patient's presumption about the case of his or her problems. The healer typically behaves in an authoritarian and paternalistic way. His pronouncements are accepted without argument.

The folk healer, whom I have called the ethnotherapist, ethnopsychiatrist, or ethnopsychotherapist, has a technical arsenal consisting of the following rituals that he applies separately or in combination: the magic of the spoken word, purifying baths, magical concoctions, ritual or ceremonial meals, dance rituals, jewels, and the use of gemstones to make peace between the ego of the patient and the supernatural world. This peace making with the metaphysical entity who caused the illness results automatically in a cure for the patient and in sound social relationships.

I have applied the Afro-Surinamese model of ethnopsychotherapy myself but stripped it of its most pronounced characteristic, which is the possession of the healer by a supernatural entity who diagnoses the cause of the disorder and gives therapy. Healers do not necessarily have to be possessed by a supernatural power, but should have certain qualities to distinguish them from common people who will as a result believe in their gifts (Johnson, 1962). Critical analyses of the dynamics of the therapeutic relationship between the folk healer and his clients made me aware of the basic variable of suggestion, and it was my opinion that this could be achieved through a combination of techniques. The most important are the following.

1. In-depth interviews yielding life histories of the patients. See, for example, my description of the case study discussed here in Wooding (1984).

2. The interpretation of dreams and analysis of dreams.

3. Possession of the patient by his or her guardian spirit. It is believed that an external supernatural entity can reside in the body of

the person possessed and that this person will not remember anything that takes place during that state. My therapies have shown that a consensus between the therapist and the supernatural entity who has taken possession of the patient always leads to a healing of the patient's disorder.

4. Ritual techniques derived from the arsenal of the Afro-Surinamese folk healer, the bonuman. Some of the techniques I apply are derived from rituals in Afro-Surinamese ethnopsychiatry, because they relate to the patient's belief system concerning the cause of the disorder, and the way its alleviation should be sought (Cannon, 1958). An example is the ritual gifts of gems, a feature shared by other cultures (Wallace, 1959).

5. Maintenance of a counseling relationship with the client for only a few months. This serves to bring the empathic relationship gradually to an end, and gives the opportunity to find out whether the therapy has had a continuous positive effect.

CONCLUSIONS

The case study discussed in this chapter shows the central role that the belief in evil magic plays in Afro-Surinamese ethnopsychiatry. A strong belief in the neutralizing effect of strong countermagic can put an end to the process of physiological disintegration and foster a process of reintegration in the body of the patient. This is the aim of all types of metaphysical-oriented ethnopsychotherapy.

Surinamers who ascribe their disorder and social problems to supernatural causes do not recognize that problems can result from the acculturation process. Anthropologists have noted that culture, social structure, and personality are three interrelated variables. The close interplay between personality and culture gives a psychological dimension to the acculturation process that is taking place among the minority groups in the Netherlands. Frictions between the individual and his culture or "culture shock" in response to the impact of the new culture may result in psychological problems.

Anthropologists study these processes too and, in this respect, Frances Hsu calls the discipline psychological anthropology. I see ethnopsychiatry as a branch of psychological anthropology, and I define it as that branch of anthropology that studies psychosocial and psychosomatic problems from the viewpoint of the people who apply therapeutic techniques related to the metaphysical context in which the problems are perceived. An anthropologist whose discipline also studies the behavior of people should be aware of the role he or she can fulfill as a psychotherapist.

If anthropologists in the Netherlands want to lay claim to the role they can play in psychotherapy, they should not only pay attention to the integration of individuals in society, how they function in primary and secondary groups, and how they perceive the culture of the various social groups, but also to the effects of the acculturation process and, in particular, the consequences of the assimilation and integrating processes in the cultural minorities.

Afro-Surinamese ethnopsychiatry has its own therapeutic principles. If they are understood, the therapeutic techniques can be applied by anyone who masters the model. The anthropologist who gains a thorough knowledge and understanding of the dynamic aspects of an ethnopsychiatric system and has applied its techniques successfully, has entered the field of ethnopsychotherapy, which differs only in degree from Western forms of psychotherapy and from the ethnopsychiatric system from which it was developed.

Since the perception of disorders determines the way in which relief will be sought and the therapy should be given, the therapeutic anthropologist will have to adapt his or her techniques, as much as possible, to those applied in the ethnopsychiatric system in which the patient believes. The cultural barrier with clients is minimized, enabling them to respond culturally to methods and techniques that look familiar to them but include Western techniques (Janzen, 1982; Warren, 1979).

REFERENCES

Ademuwagun, Z. A. (1979). The challenge of the co-existence of orthodox and traditional medicine in Nigeria. In Z. A. Ademuwagun, J. A. A. Ayoade, I. E. Harrison, D. M. Warren (Eds.), *African therapeutic systems* (pp. 165–170). Waltham, MA: Crossroad Press.

Bibeau, G. (1982). A systems approach to Ngbandi medicine. In P. S. Yoder (Ed.), *African health and healing systems: Proceedings of a symposium* (pp. 43–84). Los Angeles: Crossroad Press.

Cannon, W. (1958). Voodoo death. In W. A. Lessa & E. Z. Vogt (Eds.), *Reader in comparative religion: An anthropological approach.* (pp. 270–277). Evanston, Ill: Row, Peterson.

Conco, W. Z. (1979). The African Bantu traditional practice of medicine. In Z. A. Ademuwagun, J. A. A. Ayoade, I. E. Harrison, D. M. Warren (Eds.), *African therapeutic systems* (pp. 58–80). Waltham, MA: Crossroad Press.

Fabrega, H. Jr. (1982). A commentary on African systems of medicine. In P. S. Yoder (Ed.), *African health and healing systems: Proceedings of a symposium* (pp. 237–252). Los Angeles: Crossroad Press.

Frank, J. D. (1961). *Persuasion and healing: A comparative study of psychotherapy.* Baltimore:

Frank, J. D. (1961). *Persuasion and healing: A comparative study of psychotherapy.* Baltimore: The Johns Hopkins Press.
Janzen, I. M. (1982). Lubanzi: The history of a Kongo disease. In P. S. Yoder (Ed.), *African health and healing systems: Proceedings of a symposium* (pp. 107–119). Los Angeles: Crossroad Press.
Johnson, H. M. (1962). *Sociology: A systematic introduction.* London: Routledge & Kegan Paul.
Tseng, W. A., & Hsu, J. (1979). Culture and psychotherapy. In A. J. Marsella, R. G. Tharp, T. J. Ciborowski (Eds.), *Perspectives on Cross-Cultural Psychotherapy.* New York: Academic.
Wallace, F. C. (1959). The institutionalization of cathartic and control strategies in Iroquois religions psychotherapy. In M. K. Opler (Ed.), *Culture and mental health* (pp. 63–96). New York: Macmillan.
Warren, D. M. (1979). Bono traditional healers. In Z. A. Ademuwagun, J. A. A. Ayoade, I. E. Harrison, D. M. Warren (Eds.), *African therapeutic systems* (pp. 120–124). Waltham, MA: Crossroad Press.
Wooding, C. J. (1972). *Winti, Een Afroamerikaanse Godsdienst in Suriname: E en cultureel—historische analyse van de religieube verschijn selen in de Para.* Meppel: Krips.
Wooding, C. J. (1981). *Evolving culture: A cross-cultural study of Suriname, West Africa, and the Caribbean.* Washington, DC: University Press of America.
Wooding, C. J. (1983). An Afro-Surinamese case study on paralysis and voodoo death. In *Curare: Zeitschrift für Ethnomedizin und Trans-kulturelle Psychiatrie* (Vol. 6, pp. 13–24). Wiesbaden, Germany: Braunschweig.
Wooding, C. J. (1984). *Geesten Genezen: Ethnopsychiatrie als nieuwe richting binnen de Nederlandse antropologie.* Groningen: Konstapel.
Young, A. (1979). The practical logic of Amhara traditional medicine. In Z. A. Ademuwagun, J. A. A. Ayoade, I. E. Harrison, D. M. Warren (Eds.), *African therapeutic systems* (pp. 132–137). Waltham, MA: Crossroad Press.

10

Family Composition, Birth Order, and Gender of Mexican Children in Psychological Treatment

HARRY W. MARTIN, MARIA EUGENIA RANGEL, SUE KEIR HOPPE, AND ROBERT L. LEON

This chapter describes the composition of family households of Mexican children and adolescents undergoing psychological treatment, and explores hypotheses relative to the differential selection of Mexican children into treatment. The hypotheses, derived from descriptions of the Mexican family by Diaz-Guerrero (1955) and Ramirez and Parres (1957),

HARRY W. MARTIN, SUE KEIR HOPPE, and ROBERT L. LEON • Department of Psychiatry, University of Texas Health Science Center at San Antonio, San Antonio, Texas 78284. MARIA EUGENIA RANGEL • Instituto de Salud Mental de Neuvo Leon, Monterry, Nuevo Leon, Mexico.

Social Psychiatry across Cultures: Studies from North America, Asia, Europe, and Africa, edited by Rumi Kato Price, Brent Mack Shea, and Harsha N. Mookherjee. Plenum Press, New York, 1995.

focus on three variable characteristics: birth order, gender, and family composition. The hypotheses are explored by using data obtained for other purposes from records of a sample of Mexican children undergoing psychological treatment.

THE MEXICAN FAMILY

Diaz-Guerrero (1955) described the Mexican family as resting on two basic sociocultural premises: the unquestioned authority of fathers, and self-abnegation of mothers. These premises, in turn, are described as stemming from a prior assumption that the male is biologically superior to the female, a value-laden belief leading to a strong preference for male children, especially the firstborn. Although acknowledging that similar preferences exist in other cultures, Diaz-Guerrero maintains that the Mexican emphasis is far greater; that is, a male is not just preferable, but "it ought to be a boy."

The arrival of a girl, unless preceded by one or two sons, is something of an emotional trauma. Though a matter of jest nowadays, a firstborn girl puts the virility of the father into question and amounts to a bad break for the family, according to Diaz-Guerrero. Her honor, equivalent to that of the family, must be compulsively guarded at some physical and emotional cost. Marriage, even a good one, brings an outside male into the family fold. Daughters who fail to marry are at risk of becoming *cotorras*, old female parrots with endless neurotic complaints. Within this family context, the girl must grow up to fulfill her destiny: "superlative femininity, the home, maternity" (Diaz-Guerrero, 1955).

In contrast to Diaz-Guerrero, who proceeded from what he viewed as the dominant value pattern underlying the Mexican family, Ramirez and Parres (1957) focused on the extended family household, which they say favors relatives of the wife. Without elucidation, they maintain that such households reflect the late development of Mexican women. Mothers in these families frequently delegate care of their children to their own mothers who, in turn, appropriate the maternal qualities of their daughters to compete with them in childrearing, rather than in the area of feminine values relative to males. Despite this delegation of responsibility, the two women become contestants in the socialization arena. This feature of these families, though not noted by Ramirez and Parres (1957), entraps children between two "mothers."

Prior to the arrival of the second child, the relationship of mother and child typically has been close and intense. At the arrival of the newcomer, however, the first child experiences almost complete abandonment by the mother. It is this feature of the Mexican family, and its personality consequences for males, on which Ramirez and Parres (1957) focus, rather than the structural and potentially conflictual entrapment of children between mother and grandmother. Although anthropological evidence indicates that children can bond to more than one caretaker (Marvin, VanDevender, Iwanaga, & LeVine, 1977), Freud and Burlingham (1973) maintain that two mothers cannot share one child.

HYPOTHESES

The family scenario jointly provided by Diaz-Guerrero (1955) and Ramirez and Parres (1957) indicates that similar values underlie all Mexican families, which are structurally and affectively differentiated by household composition, birth order, and gender of children; and that females, particularly firstborns, occupy a status vulnerable to conflict and anxiety. Our general supposition is that the psychological interior of the families (Handel, 1967) differs according to these characteristics in labeling (Thompson & Bernal, 1982) and causal attributions of behavior by parents (Compas, Adelman, Freundl, Nelson, & Taylor, 1982) as well as children (Bugental, Whalen, & Henker, 1977).

The scenario also suggests that firstborn girls, in comparison to firstborn boys, enter the world in a one-down position. Most specificially, those firstborn girls born into households with a grandmother in residence face a triple jeopardy by being female, firstborn, and entrapped between two powerful socializing agents, the mother and grandmother. Here, any generational differences arising between these two women from social and value change likely exacerbate tension in the triadic relationship.

Given these assumptions, several hypotheses can be generated with respect to Mexican children in psychological care. We focus on four:

Girls in treatment have a greater probability than boys (1) of representing extended family households (those with nonnuclear kin); (2) of being firstborn; (3) of coming from extended family households with a grandmother in residence; and (4) given their triple jeopardy circumstance, firstborn girls have a greater probability of representing households with a grandmother in residence than laterborn females.

THE DATA

The data are a systematic sample (N = 155) of one-third of the child and adolescent patients of the Instituto de Salud Mental de Nuevo Leon (the Institute), Monterrey, Nuevo Leon, Mexico. The children were evaluated and/or treated by the Institute from its second year of operation in 1980 through September 1984.

Subjects and Families

The 154 patients for whom the data were sufficiently complete for analysis averaged 9.5 years of age. Two-thirds were boys, almost half (45%) were firstborn, and a quarter (27%) came from extended households. Of the 41 extended households, 56% had one or two grandparents as household members. Over three-quarters of these were maternal grandparents, confirming the Ramirez and Parres (1957) observation that the Mexican extended family household tends to favor relatives of the wife. Grandfathers, all members of maternal grandparental couples, were present at a rate of less than one to four grandmothers.

Sixty-eight percent of the families were intact, 16% divorced, and the remainder represented common law marriages (*uniones libres*). The median age of the fathers (39.8 years) was three years greater than that of the mothers, who had an average of 3.5 children.

Fathers worked principally in skilled and semiskilled trades (43%) and professional and technical occupations (36%). Most of the mothers (72%) were not employed outside the home. Mothers who were employed had jobs concentrated within four occupational categories, with the largest proportion (10% of total) being in professional and technical occupations.

RESULTS

Table 1 presents findings by household composition, gender, and birth order. Section A of the table tests the first three hypotheses. The percentages in the first three lines of the column are directionally in accord with the hypotheses; that is, the proportion of females from extended households exceeds that of males, the proportion of firstborn females is greater than that of males, and the proportion of females with a live-in grandmother is over twice that of males.

However, only the last difference was statistically significant. The data provide no support for the fourth hypothesis: 51% of the females

Table 1

Composition of All Households, Extended Family Households, and Firstborn
Households by Gender

Household composition	Male (N = 103)	Female (N = 51)	P
A. All households			
1) Percent extended households	25.2	29.4	0.36[a]
2) Percent with firstborns	41.8	51.0	0.18[a]
3) Number with a grandmother	10.7	23.5	0.03[a]
B. Extended households	(N = 26)	(N = 15)	
4) Percent firstborns	34.6	46.7	0.33[b]
5) Percent with a grandmother and other kin	42.8	80.0	0.02[b]
6) Percent with a grandmother only	19.2	60.0	0.01[a]
7) Percent with other kin only	57.7	20.0	0.03[b]
C. Firstborn households	(N = 43)	(N = 26)	
8) Percent with a grandmother and other kin	7.0	23.1	0.06[a]
9) Percent with a grandmother only	2.3	19.2	0.03[a]
10) Percent with other kin only	14.0	3.9	0.24[b]

Fisher exact p's:
[a]one tail
[b]two tail

were firstborn and 49% other born, and equal proportions (24%) had a grandmother living in the home. Further examination of subsamples reveals the unique role of household composition.

Section B of Table 1 examines gender differences by birth order and family composition in the extended household. Firstborn females outnumbered firstborn males 47 to 35%. In households with grandmothers plus other kin as members, the proportion of females was almost twice that of males (80 and 42%). In households with only a grandmother in residence, counts of females exceeded those for males by a factor of three (60 and 19%). This latter pattern, however, reversed among children from households having only other kin members: males exceeded females 58 to 20%. As the table indicates, all but the first of these differences were statistically significant.

Section C examines the composition of the households among the firstborn children. The proportion of firstborn females from households with a grandmother plus other kin members was three times that of males (23 and 7%) and those with grandmother members only was nine times that of males (19 and 2%). In contrast, the proportion of firstborn males from households with only other kin, though not significant, was over three times that of females (14 and 4%).

It appears thus that a live-in grandmother has strong influence on grandchildren's psychological well-being independent of family composition. However, within the specific context of both extended and firstborn households, the magnitude of the effect of grandmother's presence differs. The association of grandmother's presence with the girl's likelihood of being in treatment is highest when no other kin are present, lower with other kin living in the family, and lowest when other kin but not grandmother are living with girls.

DISCUSSION

The present study is limited in several ways. The sample of children was drawn from a treatment source; therefore, we do not know how generalizable our findings may be. The small sample size made it difficult to disentangle the relationship between gender, birth order, and family composition in a more elaborated fashion. Despite this limitation, however, data analyses lent support for three of the four hypotheses. Proportionately, females were more often from extended households than were males, more often firstborn, and more often from households with a grandmother in residence. However, only the third hypothesis predicting negative effects of live-in grandmothers is statistically substantiated.

Controlling for composition of households and birth order enhanced these differences, and also revealed an unanticipated result. Males, for example, were more often from households with other kin only, while females most often represented those having a live-in grandmother. The effect of a live-in grandmother is established as independent of other family contexts. An additional finding of a seemingly negative effect of other kin on boys, however, can yield different interpretations. A straightforward interpretation is that the effect of the presence of grandmother is buffered when other kin are living with children. Thus, the effect is most severe when there is only a grandmother in the household of an extended family. The effect is lower with the presence of the other kin with the grandmother. Finally, the effect of other kin is protective for girls if there is not a grandmother.

It could be argued also that the dynamics of interaction between children and their nonparental caregivers may have negative impacts, regardless of who the caregivers may be. Gender, itself, may play a role in the family dynamics (e.g., girl and grandmother). The finding of a live-in grandmother effect could merely be a reflection of the fact that grandmothers more frequently live with their grandchildren than other kin members in Mexican extended families. Replication with a larger and more representative sample would yield more definitive findings.

Another potential explanation relates to underlying forces that lead to specific family composition. For example, it is plausible that a live-in grandmother is a manifestation of a family's emphasis on traditional Mexican values. Hence, girls reared in such a family face more challenges when attempting to act independently.

Factors affecting treatment-seeking also need to be taken into account. These boys and girls, averaging 10 years of age, undoubtedly did not seek treatment by and for themselves. A higher proportion of girls in treatment and strong association with the presence of grandmother may reflect dynamics of decision making to bring children to psychological treatment. Given the strong preference for firstborn boys, it could be that problems in girls are magnified in the eyes of other family members, especially by grandmothers.

Our results suggest that the unique descriptions of the Mexican family made by Diaz-Guerrero (1955) and Ramirez and Parres (1957) are still relevant to research on the contemporary Mexican family. Clearly, however, stronger theoretical guidance is needed to integrate the three structural aspects of the Mexican family. The tradition of the extended family in Mexico may not provide the same functional purposes as it did in the past. In today's Mexico, facing rapid social change, it may be that extended families exist as a way of coping with changing social and economic structure of the society at large. Such issues need to be incorporated in the theoretical framework in better understanding the determinants of children's mental health.

REFERENCES

Bugental, D. B., Whalen, C. K., & Henker, B. (1977). Causal attributions of hyperactive children and motivational assumptions of two behavior change approaches: Evidence for an interactionist position. *Child Development, 48*, 874–884.

Compas, B. E., Adelman, H. S., Freundl, P. C., Nelson, P., & Taylor, L. (1982). Parent and child causal attributions during clinical interviews. *Journal of Abnormal Child Psychology, 10*, 77–83.

Diaz-Guerrero, R. (1955). Neurosis and the Mexican family structure. *American Journal of Psychiatry, 112*, 411–417.

Freud, A., & Burlingham, D. (1973). Reactions to evacuation. In C. Zwingman and M. Pfister-Ammende (Eds.), *Uprooting and after*. New York: Springer-Verlag.

Handel, G. (Ed.). (1967). *The psychosocial interior of the family*. Chicago: Aldine.

Marvin, R. S., VanDevender, T. L., Iwanaga, M. I., LeVine, S., & LeVine, R. A. (1977). Infant-caregiver attachment among the Hausa of Nigeria. In H. McGurk (Ed.), *Practice in Human Development*. Amsterdam: North-Holland.

Ramirez, S., & Parres, R. (1957). Some dynamic patterns in the organization of the Mexican family.

Thompson, R. J., & Bernal, M. E. (1982). Factors associated with parent labeling of children for conduct problems. *Journal of Abnormal Child Psychology, 10,* 191–202.

11

Protective Factors for Drug Abuse

A Prospectus for a Japanese–U.S. Epidemiologic Study

RUMI KATO PRICE, KIYOSHI WADA. AND
KEITH S. MURRAY

Popular literature often describes the two faces of Japan. One face presents the country's ability to constantly adapt to and modify what comes from outside, such as technology, fashion, and language. This trait is acknowledged by the Japanese, who know their ancestors produced the Japanese language from a combination of indigenous phonet-

RUMI KATO PRICE and KEITH S. MURRAY • Washington University School of Medicine, Department of Psychiatry, St. Louis, Missouri 63110. KYOSHI WADA • Division of Drug Dependence and Psychotropic Drug Clinical Research, National Institute of Mental Health, Chiba, Japan.

Social Psychiatry across Cultures: Studies from North America, Asia, Europe, and Africa, edited by Rumi Kato Price, Brent Mack Shea, and Harsha N. Mookherjee. Plenum Press, New York, 1995.

ics and Chinese characters. The other face of Japan, however, shows its ability to adhere to traditional and even ancient values and customs in the face of global Westernization. These seemingly contradictory traits can confound non-Japanese observers.

When it comes to deviant behaviors such as drug abuse and crime, the impression Japan presents to U.S. readers is one of a society that has managed to escape the plights of Western ills. For example, recent statistics show that the murder rate in 1989 was 1.1 per 100,000 population in Japan, compared to 8.7 in the United States. The rate for serious assaults was 16.1 versus 383.4 (International Criminal Police Organization, 1991). According to a 1991 survey of five major metropolitan cities in Japan, 0.9% of respondents reported having used stimulants, cocaine, or opioids (Munakata, 1994). The prevalence rate of the total Japanese population, including nonurban areas, would be expected to be even lower. Reported experience of illicit drug use in the United States, on the other hand, was 37.1% of the U.S. population aged 12 or older in 1990 (National Institute on Drug Abuse [NIDA], 1991).

The technical definition and period covered for these statistics differ. Furthermore, systematic underreporting could affect the figures, perhaps more so in Japan. Nevertheless, these statistics undoubtedly reflect some real differences between the two societies. Such differences are remarkable given that Japan is as heavily industrialized and urbanized as the United States, and the import of American and European cultures—not just cultural accessories—is very prevalent in Japan.

These differences in crime and illicit drug use rates lead to several questions. Can the differences be traced to the unique histories of the two societies? Is Japan at a certain stage in a process of global Westernization, so that in time it will catch up with the United States in crime and drug use rates? Or are there discernible, deep-seated factors at work that can explain why deviant behaviors such as drug use and criminal behaviors are much less common in Japan than the United States? If such factors exist, can they be reduced to social control issues, such as strict control of drug trafficking and gun control laws? Or are there some enduring traditional practices, in the family or community, for example, that have helped manage drug use and crime problems from becoming endemic concerns in Japan? If such elements exist, could they be implemented in another society such as in the United States?

Our present prospectus is especially motivated to answer the last two questions. The study as proposed and currently implemented is aimed at identifying protective factors for drug use and abuse from a cross-cultural perspective. We assume that the process leading to drug abuse is developmental, and that social and cultural factors, along with economic and geographic factors such as the availability of substances, play a pivotal role in the initiation and continuation of drug use, and its escalation to abuse.

We first summarize trends of use and misuse of illicit drugs in the United States and Japan. This description is intended to highlight historical differences in the types of drug abused, and differences in social control and response between the two countries. Briefly, differences in drug use and abuse between the two countries do not appear to have resulted solely from geopolitical differences and differences in external regulations and enforcement.

We then introduce our theoretical perspective which places drug abuse at the intersection between developmental psychopathology and social and cultural environments. Such a model is an integration of Western, particularly American, research in drug abuse and related areas. We further speculate about how some social and cultural factors may operate differently in the two societies. We use the term, "protective factors," to connote those factors that help suppress or modify the developmental psychopathology that eventually leads to substance abuse. In time we plan to translate our findings on protective factors into prevention strategies, which are desperately needed in some areas of the United States.

DRUG ABUSE IN THE UNITED STATES AND JAPAN

The U.S. history of illicit drug use and abuse exhibits several rather discrete periods of epidemic spread and containment. Two categories of drug addicts existed through the first decade of the 20th century. The first consisted of opium smokers, who were characterized as underworld whites, such as gamblers and thieves. The other consisted of medical addicts who had become addicted to morphine or opium as a consequence of introduction to these drugs through physicians. This second group constituted an estimated 70% of opiate addicts during the 1890s, about 220,000 people. Most were white females, either married or widowed, middle-aged, and housewives (Courtwright, 1982; Kane, 1982; Lindesmith, 1968).

With the emergence of heroin, a new epoch in drug abuse history began around 1910. The Harrison Narcotic Act followed soon afterwards in 1914. Heroin users at first used the drug orally or by nasal inhalation. By 1920, however, intravenous injection became the dominant method of administration. Initially confined to the New York City area until about 1920, heroin thereafter quickly moved into almost every large city. By 1940, the profile of the drug-addicted population had shifted from medical addicts to lower-class white males living in the cities (Courtwright, 1982). The connection between drugs and crime became more visible to the general American public, as well as the association of drug trafficking with organized crime. A series of antinarcotic laws turned the addicts into law-breakers. Soaring prices of black market heroin led to criminal activities becoming a frequent feature of heroin addiction (Lindesmith, 1968; Musto, 1973).

The supply of opiates in the United States dried up during World War II. By the 1950s, a new population of addicts emerged, represented by young blacks living in urban ghettos (Scarpitti & Dateman, 1980; Tieman, 1981). In the early 1960s, the number of opiate addicts in the country rose to an estimated 61,000. Although the Drug Abuse Control Amendments were passed in 1965, a trend toward increased use continued into the late 1970s. Estimates of numbers of U.S. heroin addicts ranged between 387,000 to 453,000 at the peak of usage (Kaplan, 1983). Males comprised 80% of addicts, and people under 30 years old comprised 70% of new users (Winick, 1965).

Meanwhile, other drugs had spread into the population, and drug problems were becoming more widespread. Over half of young adults (ages 18 to 25) and over one-fifth of adolescents aged 12 to 17 were reported to have tried illicit drugs by 1974 (U.S. Department of Health and Human Services, 1991). However, illicit drug use slowed and began declining after 1979 for most drug types. An exception was illicit cocaine use, which did not reach its peak of usage until the mid-1980s. While the lifetime rate of marijuana use among college students doubled between 1970 and 1984, cocaine use increased tenfold in the period, from 2.7% in 1970 to 30% among students (Rouse, 1991). More currently, statistics for 1990 show that 37.0% (74.4 million) of the U.S. household population reported having ever used an illicit drug, 13.3% (26.8 million) reported having used in the past year, and 6.4% (12.9 million) reported having used in the past month (NIDA, 1991).

While the history of drug use epidemiology encompasses almost a century in the United States, it is believed that experience with illicit drug use was not a significant feature of Japanese life until the end of World War II. Only anecdotal descriptions are available in this regard. For example, Japanese mythology indicates the use of certain plants for psychotropic effects in ancient times (Wada, 1991). In the countryside where hemp has long been cultivated for textile production, contact with the plant during processing has produced a dizziness or lightheadedness known as *asa-yoi* (hemp-high). However, the farmers never associated this effect with a drug high in the way interpreted by drug users (Oda, 1993), but rather as a work-related inconvenience.

Methamphetamine, developed by Japanese chemists and stockpiled by the Japanese military, were used during the war to increase productivity, especially among soldiers. During the immediate postwar period after 1945, the number of methamphetamine abusers increased rapidly to an estimated peak of over 55,000 abusers. In response, strong regulations and controls were formulated and enforced, including the Cannabis Control Law in 1948, the Stimulants Control Law in 1951, the Narcotics and Psychotropic Control Law in 1953, and the Opium Law in 1954.

Beginning in the mid-1950s, as Japan experienced rapid industrialization and an accompanying increase in the standard of living, opiates, and in particular heroin, replaced amphetamines in popularity among the drug-abusing population. Large amounts of opiates entered Japan through international smuggling routes. Meanwhile, barbiturate and tranquilizer abuse also became a problem among adolescents. In 1963, penal regulations were strengthened and a hospitalization system for drug abusers was introduced.

Between the 1960s and mid-1970s, rapid economic growth began stabilizing, accompanied by a shift to a nuclear family structure and to an information society. Paint thinner use became popular among adolescents. Amphetamine abuse began to reemerge rapidly among adults, entering a second epidemic period. Arrestee records indicated that most drug-related arrests were associated with Japanese organized crime. From 1975 to 1983, amphetamine abuse continued to increase, although the number of amphetamine-related arrests remained at about 20,000 per year.

Drug abuse began to increase among ordinary citizens after about 1983. Numbers of female drug abusers and adolescent paint thinner abusers have been increasing. Cocaine and marijuana use also have been spreading (Drug Abuse Prevention Center, 1993; Fukui, Wada, & Iyo, 1990; Ministry of Health and Welfare [MHW], 1991).

Given this description of general trends in drug abuse in Japan and the United States, three comparisons can be made. First, in both countries, the first wave of epidemic was triggered "from above." In the United States, iatrogenic introduction by physicians led to an epidemic of abuse. In Japan, the military started an epidemic by attempting to increase soldiers' productivity through methamphetamines. Nevertheless, differences are apparent in the societies' response to the first large epidemics.

In the United States, medical opiate addiction became a widespread phenomenon. In Japan, methamphetamine abuse was contained in a relatively short period of time. A comparative ineffectiveness in attempts at strict social control in the United States may be attributed partly to a historical misperception about drugs in the country. Cocaine, for example, was promoted without restriction as a simple remedy for hay fever and also as an antidote to melancholia (Grinspoon & Bakelar, 1985). History indicates that the lingering results of the nation's response to the first drug-abuse epidemic can be seen even today.

A second comparison that can be made between the two societies is that both have responded to each epidemic of drug use by attempts at strict law enforcement. In Japan, this approach accompanied rapid containment of the epidemic. In the United States, however, each epidemic appears to have run through its natural course. One explanation may be that when the opiate addiction epidemic in the United States was at its peak around the turn of the century, control of physicians and drugs was assigned to the individual states rather than assumed by the federal government (Musto, 1993). State-level control was uneven and could not contain an epidemic in its early phases.

However, public response to social ills also may differ in Japan and the United States. The rapid containment of the first methamphetamine epidemic in Japan followed the murder of a child by a methamphetamine abuser, which galvanized public opinion and awareness of drug abuse. While lawmaking in the United States has frequently come in reaction to a well-publicized event (one example being building code regulations following the New York Triangle factory fire in 1911), altering the course of an epidemic after one incident has not been seen in the United States.

Third, despite Japan's geographic proximity to the Golden Triangle of southeast Asia, historically a key source of opium, the use of opiates has never been a major problem in Japan. Although heroin abuse spread for several years around 1960 (MHW, 1991), heroin abuse remained mostly restricted among members of Japanese organized crime (Fukui, 1993). In the United States, in contrast, a variety of drugs have become popular, and popularity has shifted from time to time as specific drugs have moved into and out of fashion, at least among more casual users. It has also been suggested that some Japanese cultural patterns are more conducive to the use of stimulants, as expressed by the cultural anthropological view of dopamine- versus endorphine-susceptible cultures (Oda, 1993).

DEVELOPMENTAL PSYCHOPATHOLOGY AND DRUG ABUSE

The foregoing discussion, admittedly somewhat cursory, indicates that drug abuse is not a static phenomenon, and that depending on social conditions across time, its dynamics change. Nevertheless, persistent trends are seen over time across the two societies, which suggest some stable differences between them.

The Japanese literature also has described certain characteristics of drug abusers that are similar to those reported in the United States. Comparisons can be seen most clearly among solvent users and methamphetamine users, which are two of the most common drugs of abuse in Japan. Epidemiologic and clinical studies suggest that solvent users are disproportionately from multiple-problem families, and are associated with paternal alcohol problems (Ishikawa, 1993). Solvent abusers also have a high likelihood of association with juvenile delinquents even before their first solvent use, and have an increased association with criminals after their first use (Wada & Fukui, 1994). Methamphetamine abuse frequently follows solvent abuse (Fukui, Wada, & Iyo, 1990).

In the United States, juvenile delinquency is a strong precursor of drug use (Kandel, Simcha-Fagan, & Davies, 1986; Loeber, 1988); and patterns of progression from legal to illicit drugs have been well documented (Yamaguchi & Kandel, 1984). Although data are not comparable, these features indicate that there are patterns of development into drug abuse across the two cultures, even though the specific drugs of abuse differ.

Extending from these findings, we base our theoretical guide to cross-cultural epidemiology of drug use and abuse on the developmental perspective developed from Western literature. In this approach, etiologic factors of substance abuse are assumed to be developmental in nature (Glants & Pickens, 1992). Across stages, etiologic factors are not necessarily the same, and early factors affect later factors. Further, we assume that social and cultural factors exacerbate, suppress, or modify the development of psychopathology, from early, less noticeable forms to forms that are prevalent in adolescent years and so on into adult forms. It is further assumed, as much as drug abuse is a socially constructed form of deviance, the severe forms of drug abuse constitute an expression of psychopathology. From a developmental perspective, then, the cross-cultural variations result from risk and protective factors that differentially affect the path from earlier to later, more severe forms of psychopathology.

Consequences of Conduct Problems in Western Society

Among the common forms of psychopathology that first appear in childhood, behavioral and conduct problems are most frequent reasons for referral to mental health professionals in the United States. We may assume that frequency of referral reflects the magnitude of these problems in the general population. Also, these problems, including as they do truancy, acts of cruelty, and such serious disturbances as fire setting and robbery (American Psychiatric Association [APA], 1987), are not only detrimental to the child's development but also disrsuptive to the child's family and school, and to society at large. Arguments for the biological etiology of these problems and their close relation to delinquency have long been made (Earls, 1987; Sheldon, 1949). Indeed, a recent study of twins showed strong, apparently heterogeneous, genetic influences as well as environmental influences (Eaves et al., 1993) on behavior and conduct problems. Pharmacological treatment has not been very successful in helping children with conduct problems, and behavioral therapies appear to be only modestly effective for children with subtypes of these problems (Feldman, Caplinger, & Wodarski, 1983).

Childhood behavioral and conduct problems have been an important topic for child psychiatrists and psychiatric epidemiologists in Western psychiatry, not only because these symptoms often lead to referrals, but also because they are developmentally linked to a number of adult malfunctions. Evidence has accumulated that, at least in the United States, children with conduct problems are particularly at risk for developing problems with drug abuse, alcohol abuse, antisocial personality, and criminality (Loeber, 1988; McCord & McCord, 1960; Robins, 1966).

This evidence has been decisively confirmed by reanalyses of data from the Epidemiological Catchment Area (ECA) Project (Robins & Price, 1991). Although the first wave of the ECA project was a cross-sectional study of the U.S. adult population, retrospective information was available for childhood conduct problems because such problems formed part of the criteria for adult antisocial personality disorder. Analysis revealed that a wide range of adult psychopathology was predicted by childhood conduct problems. Antisocial personality, drug abuse, and alcohol abuse were best predicted by conduct problems, and conduct problems had a weaker impact on other disorders. Further analyses found that the severity of conduct problems also predicted the age of onset of substance abuse and depression; the more severe the conduct problems, the earlier the appearance of the disorder (Price & Robins, 1993).

Reports from epidemiologic studies elsewhere suggest that this developmental link is not unique to the United States, and is sustained in other societies that foster Western-style cultures (Rutter, 1967). It has yet to be seen, however, if the association between conduct problems and substance abuse and antisocial personality also holds as strongly in non-Western cultures.

From Secular Trends to Cross-Cultural Variation

Recent large epidemiologic studies of adult populations repeatedly have found increasing rates of several psychiatric disorders among younger cohorts, including depression (Klerman & Weissman, 1989), alcoholism (Reich, Cloninger, Van Eerdewegh, Rice, & Mullaney, 1988), drug abuse (Anthony & Helzer, 1991), and antisocial personality disorder (Robins, Tipp, & Prezybeck, 1991). At the same time, reports from the ECA project found that the number of conduct problems has been increasing in each successive birth cohort (Robins, 1986). Based on others' and our own work, we have thus hypothesized that the rising rates of conduct problems over time are in part responsible for increasing rates of substance abuse, as well as a lowering of the age of onset of substance abuse in the United States (Robins & Price, 1991).

We now extend the above postulate to a cross-cultural framework. It is believed that conduct problems occur less frequently in cultures that emphasize religious and family values as well as closely supervised child rearing. However, to our knowledge, no systematic data exist to test such a hypothesis.

The most comprehensive cross-sectional study of behavioral problems to date was conducted among primary school children in Japan (Matsuura, Okubo, Kato et al., 1989; Matsuura, Okubu, Kojima et al., 1993). In this study, the prevalence of children with deviant scores using Rutter's (1967) teacher rating scale was 3.9%, and the rate according to parent scales was 12.0%. This teacher rating was the lowest reported among eight studies conducted in the United Kingdom, Uganda, Italy, Mauritius, New Zealand, and China, where scores ranged from 7.9 to 23.3%. The Japanese study also reported that the ratio of antisocial types to neurotic types was higher in the Japanese sample than in any other country considered. This ratio suggests that among those with behavioral problems, the rate of antisocials could be higher than in other societies. The teacher and parent ratings in other Asian countries were 8.3 and 7.0% in China and 14.1 and 19.1% in Korea. The larger discrepancy in Japan between teacher and parent ratings is noteworthy, as is a suggestion of a greater prevalence of behavioral problems in Korea than in Japan.

Several other differences were found among the three countries in Asia. The prevalence of deviance was lower at school and at home among older children in Japan. No such difference between older and younger children was found in China or Korea. The prevalence of deviance in one-parent families was higher in China and Korea, but statistically significant differences were not found in Japan. Finally, deviance at school and school achievement was correlated in Japan and China, but not in Korea.

These findings indicate two additional points. First, Korean children appeared to be at a greater risk for behavioral deviance than were children in the other two Asian countries. Second, risk and protective factors for Japanese children may be more distinguishable from those applicable for Korean and Chinese children.

Protective Factors of Drug Use and Abuse

The overall model integrating developmental psychopathology and environmental factors is presented in Figure 1. This model was devised from our review of a number of contemporary findings from Western research, including our own (Glants & Pickens, 1992; Hawkins, Catalano, & Associates, 1992; Kandel et al., 1986; Loeber, 1988; Robins & Price, 1991). The model is intentionally simplified and heuristic for the

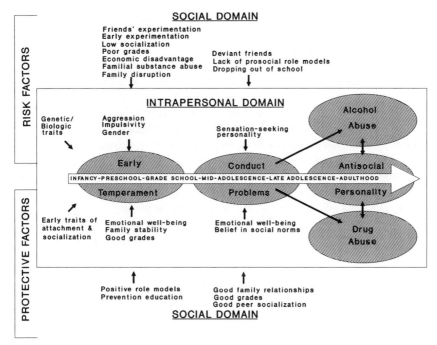

Figure 1. Stage-specific intrapersonal and social factors affecting developmental psychopathology.

purposes of this chapter. We do not necessarily mean this figure to be equivalent to a causal path model.

In this heuristic model, the developmental path in the intrapersonal domain is focused on maladaptive or psychopathological rather than normal development. Based on past literature, some developmental link is assumed from early temperament in infancy and preschool years to conduct problems in mid- to late adolescent years to subsequent antisocial personality. Alcohol abuse, drug abuse, and antisocial personality are strongly correlated (Regier et al., 1990; Robins & Price, 1991), but the causal relationships among the three are inconclusively defined. For example, a substantial proportion of adult antisocials do not have a childhood history of conduct problems. Their symptoms appear largely to have resulted from substance abuse problems (Brooner, Schmidt, Felch, & Biglow, 1992; Cottler, Price, Compton, & Mager, 1995). Risk and protective factors are considered to have differential effects depending on the specific stages of development (Clayton, 1992).

As noted, the model was derived primarily from Western—especially American—research to date. The developmental postulates we have made that link early temperament to conduct problems to subsequent antisocial personality and substance may not hold in some societies. Some risk and protective factors may be different or absent in some societies. It may be that some risk and protective factors are predictors of adult psychopathology and substance abuse; nevertheless, earlier forms of psychopathology such as extreme temperament and conduct disorder have the least impacts on later substance abuse.

In order to identify culturally unique protective factors that inhibit or modify the development of conduct problems and their pathway to substance abuse, we present three competing, working hypotheses that take into account cross-culturally unique factors:

1. Protective factors in infancy through early childhood most effectively inhibit the occurrence of childhood conduct problems. Childhood conduct problems are less prevalent in some societies, even though the association of conduct problems with substance use and abuse in these societies is as strong as their association in societies where these problems are more common.

2. Protective factors exert their influences in infancy through early childhood. Childhood conduct problems are as common in societies with low rates of substance use and abuse as in societies with higher rates. However, manifestations of childhood conduct problems are different in societies with low rates of substance use and abuse. Protective factors modify the developmental course leading to conduct problems so that some forms of childhood conduct problems are less likely to lead to substance use and abuse.

Parenthetically, it is interesting to note that the diagnostic criteria used for conduct disorder in the *Diagnostic and Statistical Manual, Third Edition* (DSM-III), (APA, 1980) had four subtypes: socialized versus undersocialized, and aggressive versus nonaggressive. These criteria, while replaced by one-dimensional symptomatology in the revised DSM-III (DSM-III-R) (APA, 1987), conceivably could capture some of the cross-culturally different manifestations of the underlying childhood behavioral disorder.

3. Protective factors exert their influences most effectively in early to late adolescence. Childhood conduct problems are as common in societies with low rates of substance use and abuse as in those societies with higher rates. Manifestations of these problems also are similar in societies with low and high rates of substance use and abuse. However, influences from protective factors are stronger on children with conduct problems in societies with lower rates of substance use and abuse.

The proposed cross-cultural research has direct relevance for prevention, because our objective is to identify protective factors. As in a case-control study where control is needed to identify risk factors that led to the appearance of cases of a disease, it is necessary to study a culture (or population) in which a disease is not prevalent in order to identify protective factors. Once such factors are identified and their significance is confirmed, a prevention project can be designed by experimentally introducing the identified protective factors (Robins & Earls, 1986).

RESEARCH PROTOCOL

The overall study will identify sociocultural factors that inhibit the development of childhood conduct problems into substance abuse and adult psychopathology. Our proposed research is designed to move from inexpensive reanalyses of existing large epidemiological databases, to reviews of risk and protective factors in Asian societies, where there currently is little information within the drug abuse field. We have chosen to progress in a phased fashion toward the eventual Japanese–U.S. comparative surveys for several reasons.

First, our hypothesis that childhood and early adolescent conduct problems are a major predictor of later drug use and abuse needs to be substantiated for non-Western societies. Second, to the extent that conduct problems are indications of deviance from societal norms, manifestations of deviance in late childhood and early adolescence may differ across societies. Thus, measures of conduct problems currently being used in the United States and other Western societies may require considerable modifications to be applicable to a cross-cultural setting. Lastly, even in the United States, less is known about protective factors than about risk factors for drug use and abuse (Clayton, 1992; Hawkins et al., 1992). Protective factors may not be readily apparent in societies with a low prevalence of drug abuse. Therefore, considerable effort may be needed before valid and reliable cross-cultural measures of protective factors can be constructed. We propose to proceed with the following phases:

Phase I: Reanalysis of existing cross-cultural database.
We plan to analyze five existing general-population epidemiologic databases in which measures of child behavior problems, adult antisocial problems, and drug use and abuse are available. All data are retrospective. The objective is to replicate the associations of conduct

problems with drug abuse and antisocial problems across cultures. The results will provide preliminary information regarding the timing at which protective factors begin to modify the course of developmental psychopathology.

Phase II: Review existing English and Japanese literature and archives to identify different manifestations of childhood conduct problems in three target populations of Asians.

The target populations are the native Japanese, Japanese Hawaiians, and Japanese Americans in California.

Phase III: Review English and Japanese literature and archives relating protective factors of substance use and abuse in the U.S. and Japan.

Our review focuses on child-rearing practices, school and neighborhood socialization, and community integration. We will examine how they deter children at risk from developing conduct problems and deter children *with* conduct problems from becoming adults with substance use and antisocial problems.

These phases will provide information currently unavailable without new survey data collection. The data from these phases will provide sufficient information to propose and design a cross-cultural collaborative study between the U.S. research team and the Japan National Institute of Mental Health. The remaining phases are:

Phase IV: Select two sites, one in the U.S. and one in Japan, and conduct a pilot instrumentation study.

Phase V: Conduct a cross-sectional study of several age groups of children and adolescents across two sites using structured interviews.

Reanalysis of Cross-Cultural Datasets

Cross-cultural epidemiologic studies provide a useful step for identifying risk and protective factors when different prevalence and incidence rates are found. However, different rates could result from differences in assessment methods unless identical procedures are applied. In recent psychiatric epidemiology research, highly structured and highly standardized assessment interviews, such as the Diagnostic Interview Schedule (DIS) (Robins, Helzer, Croughan, Williams, & Spizer, 1981), were developed and were translated into many languages. Use of such an instrument across cultures enables the direct comparison of results, although differences in training, research acceptability, and cultural differences in response patterns can still contribute to the observed differences in symptoms.

Several large databases have been generated by the DIS across several societies. The first phase of the study was modeled after cross-cultural research of alcoholism using the existing DIS-generated database (Helzer et al., 1990; Helzer & Canino, 1992), which compared the prevalence and risk factors of alcoholism from five communities: St. Louis and Puerto Rico (U.S.A), Edmonton (Canada) (Orn, Newman, & Bland, 1988), Taipei and other areas (Taiwan), and Seoul and rural areas (Korea). Rates were found to differ even though all surveys used the DIS (Helzer et al., 1990). The overall background and general methodology of the ECA and DIS studies are described elsewhere (Eaton & Kessler, 1985). Because antisocial personality and drug abuse and dependence were not assessed in the Puerto Rico site, data from this site will not be used for our proposed study. Instead, we will use data from the Christchurh, New Zealand community survey (Wells, Bushnell, Joyce, Hornblow, & Oakley-Browne, 1992).

The target population of these community surveys ranged from 181,000 in Christchurch to 13 million in Korea (see Table 1). The sample from each society was drawn by following procedures similar to those used in the St. Louis ECA. The surveys were conducted in the early- to mid-1980s. Sample size ranged from 1,498 to over 11,000. The interview response rate ranged from 70 to 82%. Respondents were all 18 years of age or older, and women made up between 48% and 66% of the samples. In all societies, the sample respondents were representative of the demographic compositions of the target population, including racial or ethnic minorities. Blacks composed 19% of the sample in the St. Louis ECA. The populations of the two Asian societies are composed of Asians. In New Zealand, 96% people were of European descent and 2% were Maoris.

The prevalence rates of alcohol or drug dependence or abuse, and antisocial personality were similar among residents of the three Western cities of St. Louis (U.S.A.), Edmonton (Canada), and Christchurch (New Zealand). In comparison, prevalence rates were lowest for all alcohol and drug disorders, as well as antisocial personality, among residents in Taipei (Taiwan). Rates of drug dependence were similarly low among residents of the two counties sampled in Korea. However, the rate of antisocial personality was higher (2.1%) in Seoul, and the rate of alcohol dependence or abuse was the highest in Korea than in any of the other countries.

These data indicate that the disorders that are found to highly correlate with conduct problems are higher among Western societies

Table 1
DIS-Generated Studies from Five Societies +

Locale	St. Louis, U.S.A.	Edmonton, Canada	Taipei, townships and rural counties, Taiwan	Seoul and rural locations, Korea	Christchurch, New Zealand
Year data collected	1981	1983	1982	1984	1986
Target population	277,000	394,950	1,570,590	13,520,908	181,000
Number respondents	3,004	3,258	11,004	5,100	1,498
Completion rate (percent)	79	72	70	82	70
Age (percent)[c]					
18–24	16	18	23	18	20
25–44	41	49	45	38	55
45–64	24	22	25	43[a]	24
65+	19	11	7	[b]	[b]
Sex (percent)[c]					
Male	40	41	34	52	48
Female	60	59	66	48	52
Alcohol dependence and/or abuse (percent)	17.0	18.0	7.2	21.7 (Seoul) 22.4 (Rural)	18.9
Drug dependence and/or abuse (percent)	5.6	6.9	0.2	0.9 (Seoul) 0.5 (Rural)	5.7
Antisocial personality (percent)	3.4	3.7	0.2	2.1 (Seoul) 0.9 (Rural)	3.1

[a]Includes 65 years old.
[b]Not included in the sample.
[c]Unweighted percentages.
Sources: Anthony & Helzer, 1991; Compton et al., 1991; Helzer et al., 1990; Helzer & Canino, 1992; Robins, Tipp, & Przybeck, 1991.

than in the two Asian societies. However, Asian societies are not homogeneous in themselves, as exemplified by Korea's high rate of alcoholism and somewhat higher rate of antisocial personality in Seoul. A cross-cultural study of behavioral problems using Rutter's scales (Matsuura et al., 1993) found that behavioral problems are more prevalent in Korea than in China or Japan, which is consistent with the prevalence of the adult disorders found in the DIS-generated studies.

In general, replication of the strong association between conduct problems and adult psychopathology across the five societies would indicate that a search of culturally specific factors needs to focus on infancy to early childhood. On the other hand, a weak association or no association would indicate that either manifestations are different across societies or that protective factors have a strong influence during late childhood to adolescent years.

Identifying Protective Factors in Japan

Comparisons across cultures would still be limited even with the highest level of methodological rigor applied, to the extent to which underlying psychiatric concepts are or are not universal across societies. Close comparability would seem to be rare when two societies have drastically different cultural origins (Kleinman, 1987). While physiological symptoms of drug dependence may be similar, individual perception about and societal reaction to drug abuse would be highly variable. Thus, the reanalyses of the DIS-generated database are intended as a means to provide relatively quick guidance for the focus on th later phases, rather than to make definitive statements about cross-cultural differences.

In the next phase, we will review existing English and Japanese literature and archives to identify differing manifestations of childhood conduct problems in three target populations of native Japanese in Japan, Japanese Hawaiians, and Japanese Americans in California, and identify microenvironmental protective factors of substance use and abuse in Japan and the United States.

Little has been systematized about drug abuse and psychopathology among Asian Americans and Pacific Islanders despite their representing one of America's fastest growing populations. Available information provide only sketchy hint to trace variations in the protective factors. For example, the use of *ice*, which is a pure and smokable form of methamphetamine (Cho, 1990) popular in Japan in the 1950s, became the number one drug problem among Hawaiians around 1990 (Zurer, 1989). This may suggest a similarity of underlying factors between native Japanese and Hawaiians. Perhaps more relevant, though, is the recent finding about the prevalence of psychiatric disorders among Chinese Americans in Los Angeles (Kuo, Lin, Takeuchi, Chung, & Sue, 1994). Using a version of *Composite International Diagnostic Interview* (CIDI) (World Health Organization, 1994), which follows the format of the DIS, the study found that the prevalence rates of some adult psychiatric disorders differed considerably among Chinese Americans depending on the country in which the subjects grew up. For example, disorders moderately associated with substance use, such as major depression and posttraumatic stress disorder, were found to be highest among those who grew up in the United States, in the middle range among those raised in Hong Kong, and lowest among those raised in China or Taiwan. Although reporting bias could explain some of the differences, the resilience of ethnic cultures also may be reflected.

Short of adequate guidance, the choice of three target populations for our study was based on medical literature tracing the migration of the Japanese eastward with accompanying changes in their disease patterns. The most impressive findings relate to cardiovascular disease and mortality rates that are associated with migration patterns and race (Benfante, 1992; Iso et al., 1989). In these findings, diet is one of the most powerful environmental factors responsible for a dose–response relationship to the rate of cardiovascular disease. The rate is lowest among native Japanese and highest among Japanese Americans in California, with Hawaiians falling in the middle. If physical disorders and psychopathology share similar environmental factors, comparisons of the three target populations proposed would yield significantly different results.

There are two reasons for focusing on the areas of child-rearing practice, school, and neighborhood socialization and integration. First, the U.S. literature suggests a positive impact of certain discipline patterns on temperamental children (Earls, 1987; Robins & Earls, 1986) and of school- or neighborhood-based intervention programs on at-risk children (Dolan et al., 1993; Hawkins et al., 1992). The second reason is that microenvironmental protective factors are easier to transfer or apply to a different society when designing a prevention research study than would be the case with macroenvironmental factors such as legal restrictions and global drug trafficking control.

In the face of global Westernization and the time lag involved for risk or protective factors to show their effects, it is possible that indigenous customs and practices that have helped suppress development of conduct problems and substance abuse may not be documented in the contemporary literature. The search for protective factors may need to be extended to archival data from the pre-World War II era.

Epidemiologic Surveys

The data from these phases will provide sufficient information to propose and design a cross-cultural collaborative study between the U.S. research team and the Japanese National Institute of Mental Health. The feasibility of the Japanese–U.S. epidemiologic survey depends on a number of scientific and programmatic factors. Successful completion of the first phases are an essential. If no unique findings suggesting cross-cultural variations are revealed from the reanalyses of existing DIS-generated database, our theoretical framework will require reexamination. Further, if a review of existing literature does not suggest culturally unique protective factors, expensive cross-cultural epidemiologic data collection would not be justifiable merely to confirm the effects of risk and protective factors already known from the Western literature.

Beyond considerations of scientific merit, programmatic feasibility also is a critical issue for cross-national research. Collaborators of selected, specific survey sites need to be located. Cooperation from governmental and nongovernmental institutions in the United States and Japan are needed to facilitate research efforts and to obtain joint funding for data collection. Technical success of a study often depends on such programmatic aspects.

Instrumentation and dissemination require *equal* inputs from researchers of both societies. Although there are currently a number of standardized epidemiologic instruments to assess clinical profile of children and adolescents in English, instrumentation for cross-cultural research on sensitive topics requires more careful attention than technical rigor in translation. For example, in a Japanese instrument used to assess drug use from a general population, questions are phrased in such a way as to assume that the subject is not a drug user until it becomes clear that the subject had an opportunity to use drugs (Fukui et al., 1993; Munakata, 1994). Such an approach might lead to underreporting or could be considered too leading in the United States. However, the researchers decided to give a higher priority to the issue of acceptability of research and the Japanese people's sensitivity to drug abuse. Such decisions should be honored by the Western collaborators.

Sample ascertainment and data collection would also need to take into account unique barriers cross-cultural sites might face. General-population surveys on drug use, although routinely conducted in the United States, may not be an optimal strategy in Japan. Given our theoretical framework, large enough numbers of clinical and subclinical cases of conduct disorder and substance abuse or dependence would be needed. Since a precise estimate of population prevalence is not a primary objective, our study will be more cost-effective with the high-risk sample ascertainment strategy. To avoid selection bias, multiple sources of ascertainment, including psychiatric clinics and the juvenile justice and school systems, should be utilized.

In essence, the study should first and foremost consider what specific questions should be answered by this specific study. Future cross-cultural research should not uncritically adopt study designs devised by Western psychiatric research. While temptation is great for collaborative researchers to apply "big science" techniques, the direction in which psychiatric epidemiodlogy is heading, at least in the United States, such an adaptation would be justifiable only with careful assessment of practical returns.

CONCLUSION

In this chapter we have presented a prospectus for a Japanese–U.S. cross-cultural epidemiologic study on drug use and abuse. We introduced some historical trends of drug abuse epidemiology between the two countries to illustrate some cultural and political differences affecting the drug use and abuse situations between the two societies. The literature also is suggestive of similarities in drug abuse and associated features between the two cultures as well. Based on these observations and the authors' and others' past findings, we presented our theoretical framework integrating developmental psychopathology and environmental risk and protective factors. A research protocol aimed at identifying culturally unique protective factors is described. The study includes multiple phases involving reanalyses of large existing database, archival literature search, and new data collection.

As in any other mental health research, cross-cultural studies ought to address issues relevant for prevention or intervention, because ultimately the goal is to solve the problems that led to the research in the first place. Because protective factors against drug use and abuse at the individual level should be more transportable than macroenvironmental factors such as regulatory mechanism of drug use, we would be able to devise an experimental design that can be conducted on a high-risk sample of American children.

We believe that research that is truly cross-culturally sensitive can be conducted only by carefully utilizing available resources and approaching data collection with equal collaboration between researchers from both societies. We also believe this approach helps ensure the research is cost-effective. At a time when U.S. federal dollars have become increasingly scarce, voices are sometimes heard suggesting that international collaboration is a peripheral diversion of dwindling resources. Cross-cultural research, of course, needs to offer tangible returns for the societies that pay for such research. In order for cross-cultural research to be on a competitive footing, the need for rigor, care, and clarity in study design becomes even more crucial. The return for American research from such studies will be found not only in scientific gains, but also in a broadening of the research scope beyond any habits of Western ethnocentrism. Inevitably, however, the best results will be seen in assisting the people who live in the cultures considered, in particular those who are at risk or are suffering from the problems being studied.

ACKNOWLEDGMENTS. The work for this chapter was supported in part by funds from the U.S. National Institute on Drug Abuse (DA00221, DA07939). The authors also thank Dr. Mark Zoccolillo, who inspired us to extend our earlier findings to cross-cultural replication of DIS-generated datasets. Our appreciation is extended to Dr. Lee Robins and Dr. John Helzer, who provided critical comments to an earlier version of this chapter; and to Dr. Richard Lindblad, National Institute on Drug Abuse, who provided instrumental support for the international collaboration. We also thank David Hilditch and Rosalee Copeland for their editorial assistance.

REFERENCES

American Psychiatric Association. (1980). *Diagnostic and statistical manual of mental disorders* (3rd ed.). Washington, DC: Author.

American Psychiatric Association. (1987). *Diagnostic and statistical manual of mental disorders* (3rd ed., rev ed.). Washington, DC: Author.

Anthony, J. C., & Helzer, J. (1991). Syndromes of drug abuse and dependence. In L. N. Robins & D. A. Regier (Eds.), *Psychiatric disorders in America* (pp. 116–154). New York: Free Press.

Benfante, R. (1992). Studies of cardiovascular disease and cause-specific mortality trends in Japanese-American men living in Hawaii and risk factor comparisons with other Japanese populations in the Pacific Regions: A review. *Human Biology, 64,* 791–805.

Brooner, R. K., Schmidt, C. W., Felch, L. J., & Bigelow, G. E. (1992). Antisocial behavior of intervenors drug abuser: Implications for diagnosis of antisocial personality disorder. *American Journal of Psychiatry, 149,* 482–487.

Cho, A. K. (1990). Ice: A new dosage form of an old drug. *Science, 249,* 631–634.

Clayton, R. R. (1992). Transitions in drug use: Risk and protective factors. In M. Glants & R. Pickens (Eds.), *Vulnerability to drug abuse* (pp. 15–51). Washington, DC: American Psychological Association.

Compton, W. M., Helzer, J. E., Hwu, H., Yeh, E., McEvoy, L., Tipp, J. E., & Spitznagel, E. L. (1991). New methods in cross-cultural psychiatry: Psychiatric illness in Taiwan and the United States. *American Journal of Psychiatry, 148,* 1697–1704.

Cottler, L. B., Price, R. K., Compton, W. M., & Mager, D. (1995). Subtypes of adult antisocial behavior among drug abusers. *Journal of Nervous and Mental Disease, 183,* 154–161.

Courtwright, D. T. (1982). *Dark paradise: Opiate addiction in America before 1940.* Cambridge, MA: Harvard University Press.

Dolan, L. J., Kellam, S. G., Brown, C. H., Werthamer-Larsson, L., Rebok, G. W., Mayer, L. S., Laudolff, J., & Turkkan, J. S. (1993). The short-term impact of two classroom-based preventive interventions on aggressive and shy behaviors and poor achievement. *Journal of Applied Developmental Psychology, 14,* 317–345.

Drug Abuse Prevention Center. (1993). *The basics of drug abuse prevention. Let's live healthy lives* (Part 6). Tokyo: Author.

Eaton, W. W., & Kessler, L. G. (1985). *Epidemiologic field methods in psychiatry: The NIMH Epidemiologic Catchment Area Program.* Orlando, FL: Academic Press.

Earls, F. (1987). Annotation on the familial transmission of child psychiatric disorder. *Journal of Child Psychiatry, 28,* 791–802.

Eaves, L. J., Silberg, J. L., Hewitt, J. K., Rutter, M., Meyer, J. M., Neale, M. C., & Pickles, A. (1993). Analyzing twin resemblance in multisymptom data: Genetic applications of a latent class model for symptoms of conduct disorder in juvenile boys. *Behavior Genetics, 23,* 5–19.

Feldman, R. A., Caplinger, T. E., & Wodarski, J. S. (1983). *The St. Louis conundrum. The effective treatment of antisocial youths.* Englewood Cliffs, NJ: Prentice-Hall.

Fukui, S., Wada, K., & Iyo, M. (1990). History and current use of methamphetamine in Japan. In S. Fukui, K. Wada, & M. Iyo (Eds.), *Cocaine and methamphetamine. Behavioral toxicology, clinical psychiatry and epidemiology* (pp. 219–238). Tokyo: Drug Abuse Prevention Center.

Fukui, S., Wada, K., & Iyo, M. (1993). Yakubutsu izon no *setai* choosa [Surveys on drug dependence]. In S. Fukui (Ed.), *Yakubutsu izon no shakai-igaku teki, seishin-igaku teki tokuchoo ni kansuru kenkyuu* [Sociological and psychiatric characteristics of drug dependence] (pp. 19–23). Tokyo: Kooseishoo.

Fukui, S. (1993). Wagakuni no yakubutsu izon no genjoo [Drug dependence in contemporary Japan]. In H. Sato & S. Fukui (Eds.), *Yakubutsu izon* [Drug dependence] (pp. 50–59). Tokyo: Sekai Hoken Tsushinsha.

Glants, M., & Pickens, R. (Eds.). (1992). *Vulnerability to drug abuse.* Washington, DC: American Psychological Association.

Grinspoon, L., & Bakelar, J. B. (1985). *Cocaine: A drug and its evolution.* (rev. ed.). New York: Basic Books.

Hawkins, J. D., Catalano, R. F. & Associates. (1992). *Communities that care.* San Francisco: Jossey-Bass.

Helzer, J. E., & Canino, G. J. (1992). *Alcoholism in North America, Europe, and Asia.* New York: Oxford University Press.

Helzer, J. E., Canino, G. J., Yeh, E. K., Bland, R. C., Lee, C. K., Hwu, H. G., & Newman, S. (1990). Alcoholismi—North America and Asia. A comparison of population surveys with the Diagnostic Interview Schedule. *Archives of General Psychiatry, 47,* 313–319.

International Criminal Police Organization (Interpol). (1991). *International crime statistics, 1989–1990.* Saint-Cloud, France: Interpol.

Ishikawa, T. (1993). Yuuki-yoozai ranyoo-sha no kazoku-byoori ni kansuru kenkyuu. In S. Fukui (Ed.), *Yakubutsu izon no shakai-igaku teki, seishin-igaku teki tokuchoo ni kansuru kenkyuu* (pp. 107–118). Tokyo: Kooseishoo.

Iso, H., Folsom, A. R., Wu, K. K., Finch, A., Munger, R. G., Sato, S., Shimamoto, T., Terao, A., & Komachi, Y. (1989). Hemostatic variables in Japanese and Caucasian men. Plasma fibrinogen, factor VIIc, factor VIIIc, and von Willebrand factor and their relations to cardiovascular disease risk factors. *American Journal of Epidemiology, 130,* 925–934.

Kandel, D., Simcha-Fagan, O., & Davies, M. (1986). Risk factors for delinquency and illicit drug use from adolescent to young adulthood. *Journal of Drug Issues, 16,* 67–90.

Kane, H. H. (1882). *Opium smoking in America and China: A study of its prevalence and effects, immediate and remote, on the individual and the nation.* New York: Putnam.

Kaplan, J. (1983). *The hardest drug: Heroin and public policy.* Chicago: University of Chicago Press.

Kleinman, A. (1987). Anthropology and psychiatry: The role of culture in cross-cultural research on illness. *British Journal of Psychiatry, 151,* 447–454.

Klerman, G. L., & Weissman, M. M. (1989). Increasing rates of depression. *Journal of American Medical Association, 261,* 2229–2235.

Kuo, W. H., Lin, K. M., Takeuchi, D., Chung, R., & Sue, S. (1994, July). *Prevalence of psychiatric disorders among Chinese-American in Los Angeles.* Paper presented at the XIIIth World Congress of Sociology, Bielefeld, Germany.

Lindesmith, A. R. (1968). *Addiction and opiates.* Chicago: Aldine.

Loeber, R. (1988). Natural histories of conduct problems, delinquency, and associated substance use. Evidence for developmental progressions. In B. B. Lahey & A. Kazdin (Eds.), *Advances in clinical child psychology* (Vol. 2, pp. 73–124). New York: Plenum.

Matsuura, M., Okubo, Y., Kato, M., Kojima, T., Takahashi, R., Asai, K., Asai, T., Endo, T., Yamada, S., Nakane, A., Kimura, K., & Suzuki, M. (1989). An epidemiological investigation of emotional and behavioral problems in primary school children in Japan. The report of the first phase of a WHO collaborative study in Western Pacific Region. *Social Psychiatry and Psychiatric Epidemiology, 24,* 17–22.

Matsuura, M., Okubo, Y., Kojima, T., Takahashi, R., Wang, Y., Shen, Y. C., & Lee, C. K. (1993). A cross-national prevalence study of children with emotional and behavioural problems—A WHO collaborative study in the Western Pacific Region. *Journal of Child Psychology and Psychiatry, 34,* 307–315.

McCord, W., & McCord, J. (1960). *Origins of alcoholism.* Stanford, CA: Stanford University Press.

Ministry of Health & Welfare [MHW], Japan. (1991). *Brief account of drug abuse and countermeasures in Japan.* Tokyo: Author.

Munakata, T. (1994). Drug use and risk of HIV infection. In T. Munakata (Ed.), *AIDS in Japan* (pp. 95–114). Tokyo: Akashi Shoten.

Musto, D. F. (1973). *The American disease: Origins of narcotic control.* New Haven, CT: Yale University Press.

Musto, D. F. (1993). Development of the American drug problems [Summary]. In Workshop Organizing Committee (Ed.), *Proceedings of Japan–U.S.A. Workshop on Drug Abuse Research* (pp. 9–16). Ichigawa, Tokyo: Workshop Organizing Committee.

National Institute on Drug Abuse [NIDA]. (1991). *National household survey on drug abuse:* (DHHS Publication No. ADM-91-1788). Rockville, MD: National Institute on Drug Abuse.

Oda, S. (1993). Nihon ni okeru izonsei yakubutsu shiyoo no jyookyoo to sono bunkateki tokusei ni kansuru kenkyu. In S. Fukui (Ed.), *Yakubutsu izon no shakai-igaku teki, seishin-igaku teki tokuchoo ni kansuru kenkyuu* (pp. 73–79). Tokyo: Kooseishoo.

Orn, H., Newman, S. C., & Bland, R. C. (1988). Design and field methods of the Edmonton survey of psychiatric disorders. *Acta Psychiatrica Scandinavica, 77* (Suppl. 338), 17–23.

Price, R. K., & Robins, L. N. (1993). *Effect of childhood conduct problems on the onset of adult disorders: Epidemiologic evidence.* Unpublished manuscript, Washington University, Department of Psychiatry, St. Louis.

Regier, D. A., Farmer, M. E., Rae, D. S., Keith, S. J., Judd, L. L., Goodwin, F. K. (1990). Comorbidity of mental disorders with alcohol and other drug abuse. Results from the Epidemiologic Catchment Area (ECA) Study. *Journal of American Medical Association, 264,* 2511–2518.

Reich, R., Cloninger, C. R., Van Eerdewegh, P., Rice, J., & Mullaney, J. (1988). Secular trends in the familial transmission of alcoholism. *Alcohol Clinical Experimental Research, 12,* 458–464.

Robins, L. N. (1966). *Deviant children grown up.* Baltimore: Williams & Wilkins.

Robins, L. N. (1986). Changes in conduct disorder over time. In D. C. Farran & J. D. McKinney (Eds.), *Risk in intellectual and psychosocial development.* New York: Academic Press.

Robins, L. N., & Earls, F. (1986). A program for preventing antisocial behavior for high-risk infants and preschoolers: A research prospectus. In R. L. Hough, P. A. Gongla, P. A. Brown, & S. E. Goldston (Eds.), *Psychiatric epidemiology and prevention: The possibilities* (pp. 73–83). Los Angeles: Neuropsychiatric Institute, University of California.

Robins, L. N., Helzer, J. E., Croughan, J. S., Williams, J. B. W., & Spizer, R. L. (1981). *NIMH diagnostic interview schedule* (Version 3). Rockville, MD: National Institute of Mental Health.

Robins, L. N., & Price, R. K. (1991). Adult disorders predicted by childhood conduct problems: Results from the Epidemiologic Catchment Area Program. *Psychiatry, 54,* 116–132.

Robins, L. N., Tipp, J., & Przybeck, T. (1991). Antisocial personality. In L. N. Robins & D. A. Regier (Eds.), *Psychiatric disorders in America* (pp. 258–290). New York: Free Press.

Rouse, B. A. (1991). Trends in cocaine use in the general population. In S. Schober & C. Schade (Eds.), *The epidemiology of cocaine use and abuse,* NIDA Research Monograph 110 (DHHS Publication No. ADM 91-1787) (pp. 5–18). Rockville, MD: U.S. Department of Health and Human Services.

Rutter, M. (1967). A children's behaviour questionnaire for completion by teachers: Preliminary findings. *Journal of Child Psychology and Psychiatry, 8,* 1–11.

Scarpitti, F. R., & Datesman, S. K. (1980). Introduction. In F. R. Scarpitti & S. K. Datesman (Eds.), *Drugs and the youth culture* (pp. 9–29). Beverly Hills, CA: Sage.

Sheldon, W. H. (1949). *Varieties of delinquent youth.* New York: Harper.

Tieman, C. R. (1981). From victims to criminals to victims: A review of the issues. In J. A. Inciardi (Ed.), *The drug–crime connection* (pp. 239–267). Beverly Hills, CA: Sage Publication.

U.S. Department of Health and Human Services. (1991). *Drug abuse and drug abuse research. The third triennial report to Congress from the Secretary, Department of Health and Human Services* (DHHS Publication No. ADM 91-1704). Rockville, MD: U.S. Department of Health and Human Services.

Wada, K. (1991). Kokain to kakusei-zai o meguru rekishiteki urabanashi [Short history of use of cocaine and other stimulants]. *Kokoro No Rinshoo a la Carte* [Mind Clinics A La Carte], *10,* 45–48.

Wada, K., & Fukui, S. (1994). Demographic and social characteristics of solvent abuse patients in Japan. *American Journal on Addictions, 3,* 165–176.

Wells, E. J., Bushnell, J. A., Joyce, R. R., Hornblow, A. R., & Oakley-Browne, M. A. (1992). Alcohol abuse and dependence in New Zealand. In H. E. Helzer & G. J. Canino (Eds.), *Alcoholism in North America, Europe, and Asia* (pp. 199–214). New York: Oxford University Press.

Winick, C. (1965). Epidemiology of narcotic use. In D. M. Wilner & G. G. Kassebaum (Eds.), *Narcotics* (pp. 3–18). New York: McGraw-Hill.

World Health Organization. (1994). *Composite international diagnostic interview. 1.1.* Geneva, Switzerland: World Health Organization.

Yamaguchi, K., & Kandel, D. B. (1984). Patterns of drug use from adolescence to young adulthood: II. Sequences of progression. *American Journal of Public Health, 74,* 668–672.

Zurer, P. (1989). Methamphetamine ice newest drug of abuse. *Chemical and Engineering News, 67,* 6.

Conclusion

Cross-Cultural Perspectives in Social Psychiatry

RUMI KATO PRICE, KEITH S. MURRAY, AND DAVID J. HILDITCH

The main objective of this volume has been to introduce works in social psychiatry across cultures. We believe this objective to be a useful one, both for the field and for the people who may benefit tangibly from cultural research. Pluralism in a discipline is one way for new insights to be born. Furthermore, in the realm of prevention and intervention, where direct returns from research investments can be most clearly seen, protocols must be culturally specific in order for people to understand and accept them. The recent halt in Phase III HIV vaccine clinical trials in the United States (Cohen, 1994) serves to remind us that successful research efforts require community acceptance and support, both in terms of outcome and design.

RUMI KATO PRICE, KEITH S. MURRAY, and DAVID J. HILDITCH • Department of Psychiatry, Washington University School of Medicine, St. Louis, Missouri 63110.

Social Psychiatry across Cultures: Studies from North America, Asia, Europe, and Africa, edited by Rumi Kato Price, Brent M. Shea, and Harsa N. Mookherjee. Plenum Press, New York, 1995.

Building on this main objective, we added a second, which was to contrast culturally focused work with the more quantitative research currently dominant in Western social psychiatry. We were motivated to discuss the comparative merits and disadvantages of these two general approaches to social psychiatry.

Finally, our third objective was to illustrate some directions for synthesis in the field. This concluding chapter extends the efforts presented in Part III. We will first summarize substantive findings, consolidating the three parts of the volume. We will next discuss some pressing questions facing social psychiatry as it attempts to address mental health and illness across cultures. A cross-cultural perspective, we suggest, provides an analytical tool to accomplish sensible and meaningful research in social psychiatry, whether one explicitly attempts to unravel complex etiologic forces of mental illness guided by observations about cross-cultural differences, or to find a remedy for alleviating individuals' psychiatric problems. We will discuss cultural sensitivity issues in American and Western European societies, and then expand our discussion to the dilemmas confronting non-Western researchers in social psychiatry, which has largely been unexplored even among cross-culturally oriented scholars in social psychiatry.

SUMMARY FINDINGS

Across the three divisions of this volume, common findings and interpretations of these findings encompass several topics. Though not exhaustive, they include the issues of acculturation; social support rising within the networks of social relations; gender; socioeconomic status; and social control.

Acculturation

Most cultures today face rapid, far-reaching social change, stimulated largely by extensive contact with other societies. While the specific features of this change vary from place to place, no culture is exempt from the inexorable transformations being wrought by technology, particularly via communications and transportation. Indigenous cultures are popularly seen as undergoing an acculturative process in which traditional characteristics yield to the strengths of a world culture, largely following an American pattern. This world culture is presented as being informed, objective, and attractive, despite its many acknowledged faults and failures. The loss of traditional cultural characteristics—social structures, belief systems, rituals—may be regretted, but is accepted as a natural effect of joining the world culture.

A closer look at works by our colleagues suggests that the acculturation process represents dynamic interaction between people and indigenous cultures confronted by social change. Rather than a wholesale breakdown of the indigenous order or passive acculturation, authors often described traditional culture as being able to perform a mediating or buffering role that protects the individual and preserves integral features of the culture. The most accessible example of a culture's ability to maintain itself and its members despite severe challenges is found among the Jews.

In this volume, the mediating process is described most fully in Savells' chapter on the Amish. The Amish, by controlling exposure to the forces of change, and clearly defining what the group considers to be appropriate responses to the challenges from without, buffer the individual from the need to act singly. The closed circle of the group perpetuates the culture.

Mookherjee and Manna also maintain that active social systems sustain slow acculturation in the midst of social changes in India. While the cultures described have been maintained until recently in relative isolation, they also appear to have responded to recent radical changes in India by reaffirming their ritual practices rather than abandoning them.

The characteristics that permit one culture to maintain itself despite social change and close contact with other cultures, while others quickly yield, are beyond the scope of our speculation. However, we are reminded that the two faces of Japan described by Price and her collagues suggest that a similar acculturation process has long been at work in Japan as well. Future cross-cultural psychiatry should attempt to understand in more detail the coping strategies that are distinctive to cultures, as well as the costs of these strategies.

Social change is not always a haphazard or incidental condition. The example of the former Czechoslovakia shows that political structures can disrupt the social order by the deliberate application of policy and procedures. Worsening problems with alcoholism in the country, according to Bútora, directly resulted from the manipulation of supplies and information, which fed from a traditional socialization of alcohol consumption. He expects subsequent governmental changes after the fall of communism to contribute to a worsening problem with alcoholism in the now-divided Czech and Slovakian republics, because of the lack of effective programs in place to address the effects of social change.

The ability of the cultures described in this volume to endure despite external forces of change, and for the members of these cultures to continue to derive support and meaning from them, of course, gives evidence of the cultures' robustness. That Wooding's patients continued to manifest symptoms and require treatment in ways appropriate to their backgrounds, despite their expressed awareness of the incongruities involved in modern society, is one indication of the impact this robustness can have from a clinical standpoint. Wooding's work shows that the specific diagnostic and therapeutic strategies of folk healers within traditional cultures might be useful tools in the treatment of mental illness. Mookherjee and Manna, likewise, recount the acceptance of Western medicine among the Indian societies they describe. These societies, however, also opt to continue indigenous treatments for those mental disorders that are interpreted as issuing from supernatural sources.

Increased ritualization in a time of rapid social change actually may be part of the mechanism for acculturation, a speculation we can infer from Mookherjee and Manna, as well as Wooding. A process of ritual resistance that incorporates elements of change, such as technological accoutrements, may help comfort the individual, control acculturative forces, and maintain the traditional order, albeit in an altered form.

Such a role served by an indigenous culture suggests something social psychiatry may need to better understand in order to provide optimal service in mental health and illness. Culture, as already stated, does not suggest a mask that covers an underlying universality. Often, when multiple cultural forces collide, there appears to be a dynamic process by which indigenous people maneuver over these forces. Resistance and accommodation both play a part in this process.

Social Relations and Support

Robust systems of social relations that survive change, and the importance of social support to individual mental health, are illuminated in a number of chapters included in this volume. In simple terms, Savells describes the Amish's immunity from feelings of isolation, despite the community's enforced isolation from mainstream America. This cultural security is attributed to a structure of strong family ties and community links with other Amish families. Strong tribal networks of relations are described by Mookherjee and Manna as a prerequisite for survival in isolation among early settlers in India.

Considering culture as an intrinsic, internalized organization of specific features of support and control, social psychiatrists can apply selected principles to what may be considered artificial, or synthetic, societies. Segal notes in his study that a supported housing environment can be important in the development of mutually supportive emotional relationships. Such relationships are perceived as providing a way to bridge patients to society through redefining their social functions.

The comparative lack of such support in Nigeria, as described by Odebiyi and Ogedengbe, isolates the mentally ill, consistent with traditional beliefs about the permanence of such disorders and their potentially dire consequences for the larger family unit. The resilience of such beliefs is evidenced in how Western-trained psychiatric professionals in Nigeria supported occupational restrictions for former patients.

The work of Ortega and Johnson and of Meyer attempts to clarify the buffering effects of social support that mitigate psychological stress process. Ortega and Johnson show how the relationship between economic events and economic strain are conditioned by the community context or community size. The amount of social support available appears to modify the stresses of social change, in this case, in the example of economic downturn. Meyer noted how social support is important in protecting people from the deleterious effects of stress.

Obviously, the existence of potentially supportive social networks and the positive effect of social support are two different matters, as Ortega and Johnson remind us in their presentation of structural equation models. In fact, a negative impact of social support in a traditional culture might be one source of social change as well. For example, we infer from Savells that the protective barrier of tight family and kin networks also applies its own stresses on the individual, by requiring the strict compliance, and accompanying threat of ostracism, needed to maintain the culture. Perhaps a more clear example is shown by Martin and his colleagues. In the cultural context of the traditional Mexican family structure where the birth of a girl, especially a firstborn girl, often is considered unfortunate, they found a negative effect from the extended family and, in particular, of a live-in grandmother, on the mental health of female children.

Gender

The effects of gender can be far-reaching, with differentiation noted throughout the chapters that consider it. Meyer found differences in the personal social networks of women and men. Women appeared to be more readily affected by the problems of others than men were. Nevertheless, women evidenced greater resilience in coping with significant loss and change.

Differing cultural perceptions about the relative worth of one sex over the other obviously can have repercussions for a society's members. Martin's study appears to affirm the hypothesis that the mental health of firstborn females is at greater risk than that of firstborn males because Mexican culture emphasizes the value of the first child being male. It is revelatory to find that an effect of gender inequality is exacerbated by same-gender conflict, in this case between grandmother and female grandchild, and perhaps with the mother's involvement as well.

Although not explicitly theorized in their framework of stigma, Odebiyi and Ogedengbe alluded to the Nigerian situation in which mothers of former psychiatric patients become part of a de facto rehabilitation system, while adequate facilities and legislative measures were lacking and rejection by spouses a common result of mental illness.

Socioeconomic Status

The grand theme of the relationship between socioeconomic status and mental illness was reaffirmed in Holzer and his colleagues' reanalysis of the Epidemiologic Catchment Area (ECA) Project, the largest psychiatric epidemiologic study in the United States. The association was robust in light of the ethnic diversity of American society. Such a relationship would probably hold across most cultures in part because of familial transmission and the devastating effect of psychiatric illness on the patients as well as on family members. For example, Odebiyi and Ogedengbe document downward mobility of former psychiatric patients, in part due to the persistent stigma attached to them.

Bútora documented how governmentally driven alcohol policies in the former Czechoslovakia affected blue-collar workers and the undereducated more severely, in that these low-SES groups were overrepresented in alcoholic populations. He also predicted that in the near future the ranks of alcoholics would be joined by a growing class of new unemployed individuals, victims of the radical political and economic realignment in Czech and Slovakian societies.

Social Control

Bútora also described an aspect of social control in the communist regime of Czechoslovakia about which information was unavailable to the West prior to the 1989 revolution. By suppressing information and controlling supplies, the government of Czechoslovakia is believed to have been responsible for an increased prevalence of alcoholism among its citizens. A similar process was described in the epidemic of methamphetamine abuse in post-World War II Japan, which is believed to have originated with the Japanese military. On the other hand, the tendency for strong social control in the Japanese government was described as being effective in then containing the spread of methamphetamine abuse and, later, solvent abuse in Japan.

Odebiyi and Ogedengbe, on the other hand, described a less overt process of social control in Nigeria, which is filtered down to individuals, including patients themselves. For example, national laws continued to prohibit the former mentally ill from holding public office. Western-trained psychiatric professionals in Nigeria continued to maintain social norms about mental illness leading to permanent disability. An individual's personal belief system about the prospect of his or her recovery from mental illness was affected by such social norms.

In short, while each chapter of the volume described some correlates of mental health and illness and substance abuse unique to that society, a number of common findings are apparent. It appears that societies exert some control mechanisms, which affect the individual's perception and reaction to mental illness and substance abuse. Some indigenous cultures appear capable of more selective acculturation than others. Whether such an acculturation process benefits individuals living in the culture is still questionable.

Classic literature argues that individual autonomy arises from conflicting cultures (Simmel, 1955). The most impressive collection of

longitudinal psychiatric epidemiologic studies spanning several decades altogether shows equivocal results and suggests types and magnitude of social change affect different disorders in different magnitudes
(Strömgren, Nielsen, & Sartorius, 1989). We have not yet had systematic, individual-level information relating to specific conditions under
which individual mental health is positively or negatively affected
by cultural frictions, except in research investigating consequences of
extremely traumatic events occurring in the context of cultural and
political conflict.

In addition, increases in ritualization in times of cultural conflict
might hint at the potential utility of indigenous rituals and beliefs for
treatment; however, this is largely unexplored in scientific terms at
present. In popular terms, certainly, a return to religious practices often
is observed as accompanying times of personal crisis. Whether this
tendency reflects a Western example of increased ritualization in times
of crisis may be debatable.

At the individual level, it appears safe to say that poverty and
low socioeconomic status are strongly correlated with mental health.
Gender is one distinctive feature of human kind that provides contextual differences in causes and consequences of mental health and illness.
As mental health professionals in non-Western societies become more
aware of gender inequality, we would expect more work in gender
and mental health from these societies. Lastly, we have seen in chapter
after chapter a strong indication that networks of relations and their
potentially supportive effects are the linkage between individuals
and social control and change, a major recurring theme of cultural
anthropologists over several decades (Malinowski, 1922; Radcliffe-
Brown, 1940).

OVERCOMING CULTURAL BARRIERS

Observation of the effects of Westernization and the unquestioned
applicability of Western research norms reveals a world view in which
humankind is seen as having greater commonality than differences.
Genetic and biologic makeup is seen as being more important etiologic
factors than the temporal distinctions manifested by separate cultures.

However, a central motif of this volume is to stress the importance
of leaving behind ethnocentric and cultural biases in understanding
mental health issues. Social psychiatry thus far has been dominated

by North American and European research interests, which must be seen as themselves culturally affected, despite attempts to maintain objectivity and pursue a science of universality. The studies collected from several countries in this volume illustrate their cultural and ethnic specificity. They also suggest that prevention and treatment strategies must be suitably flexible and varied to account for the ethnic and cultural pluralism of such problems. Despite its genetic and biologic kinship, the human family occupies many houses.

However, such pronouncements may not be adequate to the task of persuading our American readers. To what end is it necessary for social psychiatry to be culturally sensitive when behavioral genetics have shown the remarkable impact of heredity and its interaction with environment for subject matters ranging from personality to severe psychiatric disorder? Why do we need to pay attention to culturally specific treatment strategies, at a time when pharmacotherapy has become a norm in psychiatric treatment? Are we the last generation of culturalists who resist psychiatry's efforts to become a truly scientific discipline? We shall try to argue the contrary by emphasizing scientific relativism.

Psychiatric epidemiology, having achieved some of its long-dreamed goals with studies of general populations, is turning to studies of special populations. The need for a cross-cultural perspective is increasing because it provides an analytic tool to accomplish sensible and meaningful research in social psychiatry when studying special populations. Such a need is particularly relevant for understanding the phenomenology of psychiatric problems within a specific ethnic or subcultural population, for understanding some of the variations in response to psychiatric problems, and, perhaps most importantly, for devising effective prevention and treatment strategies.

Where a cross-cultural perspective can be most naturally applied, namely, in cross-society studies, a peculiar dilemma confronts working practitioners in non-Western societies because of the historical inequality between the West and non-West. We argue that this dilemma needs to be addressed not just for the sake of philanthropy disguised as science, nor for the sake of simply preserving the cultural diversity of the discipline. Rather we propose that tangible returns may be obtained for the people whose needs and problems we study.

Examples of such returns are readily available for individual treatment. In the prevention area, which would appear to be a more natural focus for social psychiatry, examples are less readily cited. This fact reflects social psychiatry's lack of impetus regarding development of prevention strategies until recently, rather than a failure to find such potentially valuable returns in cross-cultural research.

On Scientific Reductionism

We have already pointed out epidemiology's traditional link with medicine. Thus, while social psychiatry has always been more oriented toward finding social correlates of its subject matter, the influence of a biologic orientation from medicine in comparison to that of social science disciplines such as anthropology was inevitable.

In addition, much of social psychiatry's search for universality went hand in hand with methods that would accomplish that end. One such method is an analytical one, exemplified in psychiatry's almost obsessive efforts at establishing elaborate classification systems. A second is seen in the statistical and methodological advances most definitively applied in general-population psychiatric epidemiology. From a philosophy of science point of view, these advances can be considered as psychiatry's efforts to legitimatize the discipline within medicine.

There was a keen sense in psychiatry that old diagnostic criteria based on a clinician's best judgment or experience had to be replaced by criteria based more on the results of empirical studies (Feighner, Robins, Guze, Woodruff, Winokur, & Munoz, 1972). With the disappearance of the psychoanalytic paradigm, a new diagnostic classification system was called for that would move away from etiologic assumptions, since there was still not yet consensus about the etiology of psychiatric disorder. The process required massive efforts in the compilation of experts' opinions and empirical validation. With the evolution of the *Diagnostic and Statistic Manual*, Third Edition (DSM-III) (American Psychiatric Association [APA], 1980), to DSM-III-R (APA, 1987), and then to DSM-IV (APA, 1994), this process toward empirical classification system appears complete for the time being.

On the practical side, there were real needs for these efforts as well. The Carter Administration first put forward the agenda for expanding federal health programs, including a form of national health insurance, in the late 1970s (Klerman, 1989). Before such plans could be pushed forward, however, it was necessary to assess the magnitude of needs for mental health care in the United States, first by obtaining accurate estimates of the prevalence rates of major psychiatric disorders. Those needs prompted development of the Diagnostic Interview Schedule (DIS) and the ECA project into the early 1980s.

Now the wind may be changing. A Kuhnian paradigm shift (Kuhn, 1970) may be occurring in psychiatry, particularly in psychiatric epidemiology. Social psychiatry must be comfortable with the notion of scientific relativism. DSM-IV is no closer to the *truth* than DSM-III was at the time it was created. With the enormous effort that went into the publication of DSM-IV, there is more faith in its empirical validity of psychiatric disorders, but only as they are understood at this time. In fact, a recognition of relativism is acknowledged by the inclusion of an appendix in DSM-IV that describes culturally specific syndromes.

Efforts have been maintained and even extended in applying psychiatric surveys among general populations, as indicated by the National Institute of Mental Health's present efforts to conduct massive multisite psychiatric epidemiologic surveys on children and adolescents. Having more or less established a range of prevalence rates for major psychiatric disorders in the adult population, and having identified some common demographic risk factors of these disorders, interest has been shifting from general populations of adults to special populations, such as the homeless, women, and minority groups.

In our opinion, it is in these special population studies that a tendency toward scientific reductionism would do more harm than good. Learning cultural contexts that may be unfamiliar to the researchers concerned is a prerequisite when attempting to study problems specific to a special population. As if suggesting such a shift in trends toward culturally sensitive research, ethnographic study is regaining its reputation in studies of phenomena unfamiliar to researchers; for example, crack epidemics among minority groups (Carlson & Siegel, 1990; Holden, 1989). It is no coincidence that the studies that began to reutilize an ethnographic approach are programs aimed at prevention of or intervention in specific problems such as human immunodeficiency virus (HIV) risk reduction among drug abusers, because deliverables had to be addressed.

On Inequity

As in other disciplines, and in wider areas of human activities, social psychiatry maintains an unequal resource distribution between the West and the developing world. This inequity has affected the ability of non-Western researchers to produce the kind of work generally accepted by Western social psychiatry. Resources required for research training and for extensive data gathering and analysis have often been beyond the capacity of researchers in developing countries. In the past, therefore, U.S. or World Health Organization (WHO) initiatives have been necessary for the development of social psychiatry in developing countries. The negative effects of such foreign aid, unwitting and complex, have not been widely discussed. A ready example is the unquestioned expectation that non-Western researchers adopt Western concepts as a condition for successfully completing educational training.

Part of the problem admittedly is historical. Social psychiatry does not have a long history. Furthermore, social psychiatry has only recently begun to develop in non-Western societies. Thus there is a lack of indigenous theories in non-Western societies that are readily accessible to Western social psychiatry. Most major societies do have indigenous metaphysical theories about the world, environment, human body, and psychology, such as seen in *Huangdi Neijin* (The Yellow Emperor's Classic) (Wand-Tetley, 1956). However, their scientific relevance for mental health and mental illness has not been explored in mainstream medicine in the United States, although that trend is changing (Cole, Pomerleau, & Harris, 1992; Friedman, Zuttermeister, & Benson, 1993).

The problem is worsened by barriers to dissemination. The language barrier is one example, the potency of which has been evident throughout the editors' compilation of this volume. A sense of barrier is also caused by ethnocentrism in American and European researchers who, by reflexively concentrating on the scale and sophistication of their own work, may not be open to the value of what may seem the more modest efforts of others.

Newcomers from developing countries still try to acquire the kind of training necessary to conduct methodologically advanced data collection and analyses using sophisticated statistical methods. As already noted, in the process of this acculturation, non-Western researchers often uncritically adapt Western systems for defining the concepts of mental health and illness and for interpreting its causes and consequences.

Remedies

How can we increase cultural sensitivity in Western social psychiatric research? And how can we solve the problems associated with increasing Westernization over non-Western social psychiatric research? Some culturalists appear to suggest a one-step-at-a-time remedy by testing Western schemes and instruments in other societies, correcting them when necessary, and moving toward grounding cross-cultural research in the local ethnographic context (Kleinman, 1987). They also suggest general ongoing sensitization by commitment and devotion with research on culturally unique groups (Rogler, 1989).

Thus, the recent move mentioned toward studying special populations, such as the homeless, women in specific cultures, homosexual populations, and rural populations, in U.S. psychiatric epidemiology is clearly significant in this regard. Increases in the number of practitioners and researchers from diverse cultural backgrounds, minorities, women, and distinctive ethnic groups, can create a context in which cultural sensitization is more readily facilitated. Such changes also may begin to alter the power and resource allocation patterns current within the United States, as well as elsewhere.

Majority researchers need to accept the styles and theoretical pursuits brought in by minority researchers. Western researchers need to accept non-Western researcher's ideas more readily. The other side of the coin is the need for minority researchers to maintain confidence and trust in their own indigenous thinking, ideas and operationalizations. A clinical sociologist, in speaking for Cuban refugees of the last wave, commented that acculturation should involve empowerment (Hoffman, 1985).

Such an issue may not be limited to those oppressed or those who suffer. Non-Western researchers could defer too readily to Western colleagues, given language and cultural barriers. Again, the point is not one of diversity for diversity's sake, but of ensuring that social psychiatry lives up to its potential by allowing diversity within the field to extend its research base and aims.

TANGIBLE RETURNS

Earlier, we contended that the search for generalizability is useful only insofar as its returns are tangible. Normal practice of ignoring cultural differences that are not statistically significant undermines the ability of social psychiatry to make findings available that are substantively relevant for effective prevention and treatment. Furthermore, knowledge of a regularity, even if it is indeed universal, may not do much good to alleviate the patient's psychological pain.

The discovery of a gene responsible for bipolar disorder would be helpful for genetic engineering, but it would not help those suffering from the disorder. Another example would be the WHO's finding that the rate of schizophrenia is similar across several societies. Its eventual utility can be seen in several directions, but from a clinician's or patient's viewpoint, knowing that the probability of an individual experiencing schizophrenia in one society is the same as that in another society would not help the patient manage his or her hallucinations and delusions.

A real test for arguing to preserve cultural diversity in the way we conceptualize problems in social psychiatry may apply to whether such efforts have pragmatic utilities for the people who can afford research. Just as the question of how much biodiversity is necessary to maintain or restore the earth's ecosystem is unanswered among environmentalists (Baskin, 1994a), social psychiatry does not know how much pluralism is needed for social psychiatry or for people. Conservationists, after years of trial and error with indigenous social systems, argue that wildlife that doesn't have direct utility for the people in whose region it lives will disappear (Baskin, 1994b). In a similar vein, we argue that the utility of pluralism in social psychiatry has to be assessed in terms of how its results apply to the mental health and illness of the people.

There is, we believe, a strong chance for the West to gain valuable insights in treatment applications from non-Western regimens. Recent movements in alternative medicine provide clues for what these tangible returns could be for the West, as well as non-Western societies. The areas of alternative medicine currently include diet–nutrition–lifestyle changes, and mind–body control, traditional and ethnomedicine, structural and energetic therapies, and pharmacological and biological treatments (Jacobs, 1993). Direct applications of some treatment regimens to psychiatric problems are evident in some areas.

Perhaps the easiest way to see the potential utility of non-Western treatment practices is by considering herbal medicine, ranging from botanical nomopreparations in the German drug market, including sedatives and antidepressants (De Smet, 1993), to an extract of *kudzu* root (Radix puerariae) long used by the Chinese (Keung & Vallee, 1993), which has antidipsotropic effects against alcohol. Acceptance of herbal medicine is relatively easy without conceptual conversion, since belief in chemicals in herbs is no different from belief in the effect of chemicals from synthetic drugs.

Another example relevant for mental health and illness may be the gradual acceptance of acupuncture in the West and in other areas not traditionally subscribing to it (Colquhoun, 1993; Knottenbelt, 1993). Acupuncture's acceptance in the West in the area of psychiatry requires more readily understanding cultural differences in the conception of the mind–body continuum. Thus, it is of interest to find that the efficacy of electroacupuncture for neurasthenia and depression among the Chinese was explained in terms of its similarity to electroconvulsive treatment (ECT), which is an accepted treatment regimen in the West (Dunner & Dunner, 1983; Chang, 1984). This provides another example that new technology often has been interpreted in the context of an indigenously familiar method to facilitate acculturation, though in this case, the acculturation is occurring in Western medicine.

While these examples of alternative medicine have some applications for psychiatry, they are not the type that social psychiatry can best offer. Both herbal medicine and acupuncture are treatments for individuals, not treatments for social causes, which are to be regarded for all practical purposes as prevention measures. To expect tangible returns from social psychiatry in the area of prevention is logical because social psychiatry studies social correlates of mental health and illness.

Again there are many examples of tangible returns from non-Western ways of life for prevention in many fields of medicine. Non-Western dietary practices are perhaps most quickly adapted by Americans, who have been sensitized by trends for increasing rates of coronary heart disease and knowlewdge about dietary factors apparently protective against coronary heart disease (Willet, 1994) and some forms of cancer (Henderson, Ross, & Pike, 1991) in other cultures. Relaxation techniques (Benson, Beary, & Carol, 1974; Benson, 1993) comprise various methods that can be considered both prevention and intervention measures. Nevertheless, these and other methods in alternative medicine offer some utility for prevention of mental health problems and mental illness, as did the treatment methods already discussed.

Acquiring scientific knowledge linking etiological factors to prevention at the societal level is one of the greater challenges that faces social psychiatry today. When preventive measures are devised on the trial-and-error basis that typically follows a public health crisis, such a research objective is difficult to achieve. How a cross-cultural perspective can best assist has not been well formulated.

One possibility is to start from a theoretical base within the Western paradigm, find the presence and absence of outcome measures that represent exceptions to the theory's predictions, and then identify the protective measures not proposed by the theory. Another strategy could be to learn that Western ethnocentrism disguises how Western society maintains patterns that are relatively anomalous, and then to adapt preventive measures from other societies in which regularity does not cause abnormal outcomes.

A suggestion of this approach can be discerned in a bold thesis proposed by a cultural anthropologist about the nature of marriage as an institution (Fisher, 1994). The thesis, derived from examining over 800 societies, proposes that *serial* monogamy might be the most optimal human reproductive strategy, and that patterns of marriage and divorce in more than 60 industrial and agricultural societies over the past 50 years confirm this hypothesis.

If her thesis is true, why is it that divorce is believed to have devatating adverse psychological effects on children in our society (Cherlin et al., 1991; Barber & Eccles, 1992)? Do other societies sustain a pattern of serial marriage without evidence of a generally negative impact on children? Perhaps Western society is constructed so as to produce the negative psychological effects of divorce so often noted, such as its economic impact on women and children. Our point is that an unexpected cross-cultural finding could offer an opportunity to find a fresh perspective on the ways in which we conceptualize the causes of mental health problems.

CONCLUDING REMARKS

In this chapter, we first summarized major substantive findings of empirical works reprsented from several countries in this volume. Several common themes were apparent, including findings concerning acculturation, social relations and support, gender, socioeconomic status, and social control. Subsequently, we have attempted to summarize several issues specifically on a cross-cultural perspective, which were mentioned throughout the volume. We stressed the importance of cultural pluralism on the basis of our claim that social psychiatry must operate within scientific relativism. We discussed some of the barriers that exist in the pursuit of cross-cultural perspectives, and offered potential remedial measures.

In conclusion, we stress the importance of tangible returns from cross-cultural research. We, however, are reminded that cross-cultural social psychiatry has not yet achieved the objective of offering strategies of social prevention of mental health and illness from our cross-cultural knowledge about social and cultural dimensions of mental health and illness. This, in our mind, needs to be pressed forward, if cross-cultural social psychiatry is to thrive, and assist society at large in thriving.

REFERENCES

American Psychiatric Association. (1980). *Diagnostic and statistical manual of mental disorders* (3rd ed.). Washington, DC: American Psychiatric Association.

American Psychiatric Association. (1987). *Diagnostic and statistical manual of mental disorders* (3rd ed.). Washington, DC: American Psychiatric Association.

American Psychiatric Association. (1994). *Diagnostic and statistical manual of mental disorders* (4th ed.). Washington, DC: American Psychiatric Association.

Barber, B. L., & Eccles, J. S. (1992). Long-term influence of divorce and single parenting on adolescent family- and work-related values, behaviors, and aspirations. *Psychological Bulletin, 111,* 108–126.

Baskin, Y. (1994a). Ecologists dare to ask: How much does diversity matter? *Science, 264,* 202–203.

Baskin, Y. (1994b). There's a new wildlife policy in Kenya: Use it or lose it. *Science, 265,* 733–734.

Benson, H. (1993). *Relaxation response.* New York: Outlook Books.

Benson, H., Beary, J. F., & Carol, M. P. (1974). Relaxation response. *Psychiatry, 37,* 37–46.

Carlson, R. G., & Siegal, H. A. (1990). *The crack life: An ethographic overview of crack use and sexual behavior among African Americans in a Midwest metropolitan city.* Manuscript submitted for publication.

Chang, W. (1984). Electroacupuncture and ECT. *Biological Psychiatry, 19,* 1271–1272.

Cherlin, A. J., Furstenberg, F. F., Jr., Chase-Lansdale, P. L., Kiernan, K. E., Robins, P. K., Morrison, D. R., & Teitler, J. O. (1991). Longitudinal studies of effects of divorce on children in Great Britain and the United States. *Science, 252,* 1386–1389.

Cohen, J. (1994). U.S. Panel votes to delay real-world vaccine trials. *Science, 264,* 1839.

Cole, P. A., Pomerleau, C. S., & Harris, J. K. (1992). The effects of nonconcurrent and concurrent relaxation training on cardiovascular reactivity to a psychological stressor. *Journal of Behavioral Medicine, 15,* 407–414.

Colquhoun, D. M. (1993). Electrical neurostimulation for angina pectoris. Acupuncture and TENS —Where East meets West. *Medical Journal of Australia, 158,* 440–442.

De Smet, P. A. G. M. (1993). An introduction to herbal pharmacoepidemiology. *Journal of Ethnopharmacology, 38,* 197–208.

Dunner, D. L., & Dunner, P. Z. (1983). Psychiatry in China: Some personal observations. *Biological Psychiatry, 18,* 799–801.

Feighner, J. P., Robins, E., Guze, S. B., Woodruff, R. A., Winokur, G., & Munoz, R. (1972). Diagnostic criteria for use in psychiatric research. *Archives of General Psychiatry, 26,* 57–63.

Fisher, H. (1994). The nature of romantic love. *The Journal of NIH Research, 6,* 59–64.

Friedman, R., Zuttermeister, P., & Benson, H. (1993). Unconventional medicine [Letter to the editor]. *New England Journal of Medicine, 326,* 1201.

Henderson, B. E., Ross, R. K., & Pike, M. C. (1991). Toward the primary prevention of cancer. *Science, 254,* 1131–1138.

Hoffman, F. (1985). Clinical sociology and the acculturation specialty. *Clinical Sociology Review, 3,* 50–59.

Holden, C. (1989). Street-wise crack research. *Science, 246,* 1376–1381.

Jacobs, J. J. (1993). Alternative medicine. *Annals of the New York Academy of Sciences, 703,* 304–308.

Keung, W., & Vallee, B. L. (1993). Daidzin and daidzein suppress free-choice ethanol intake by Syrian Golden hamsters. *Proceedings of National Academy of Science, USA, 90,* 10008–100012.

Kleinman, A. (1987). Anthropology and psychiatry. The role of culture in cross-cultural research on illness. *British Journal of Psychiatry, 151,* 447–454.

Klerman, G. (1989). Psychiatric diagnostic categories: Issues of validity and measurement. An invited comment on Mirowsky and Ross. *Journal of Heawlth and Social Behavior, 30,* 26–32.

Knottenbelt, J. D. (1993). Perspectives in acupuncture. *South African Medical Journal, 83,* 241–242.

Kuhn, T. (1970). *The structure of scientific revolutions* (2nd ed.). *International encyclopedia of unified science* (Vol. 2). Chicago: University of Chicago Press.

Malinowski, B. (1922). *Argonauts of the western Pacific.* New York: Dutton.

Radcliffe-Brown, A. R. (1940). On social structure. *Journal of the Royal Anthropological Society of Great Britain and Ireland, 70,* 1–12.

Rogler, L. H. (1989). The meaning of culturally sensitive research in mental health. *American Journal of Psychiatry, 146,* 296–303.

Simmel, G. (1955). *Conflict and the web of group-affiliations.* (K. H. Wolff & R. Bendix, Trans.). New York: Free Press.

Strömgren, E., Nielsen, J. A., & Sartorius, N. (1989). Discussion. In N. Sartorius, J. A. Nielsen, & E. Strömgren (Eds.), Changes in frequency of mental disorder over time: Results of repeated surveys of mental disorders in the general population. *Acta Psychiatrica Scandinavica, 79* (Suppl. 348), 167–178.

Wand-Tetley, J. I. (1956). Historic methods of counter-irritation. *Annals of Physiological Medicine, 3,* 90–98.

Willett, W. C. (1994). Diet and health: What should we eat? *Science, 264,* 532–537.

Index